You Don't Have to Change to Change Everything

SIX WAYS TO SHIFT YOUR VANTAGE POINT, STOP
STRIVING FOR HAPPY, AND FIND TRUE WELL-BEING

Beth Kurland, PhD

Health Communications, Inc.
Boca Raton, Florida
www.hcibooks.com

Disclaimer: This publication is designed as a source of educational information only and is not intended as a substitute for psychological treatment of psychological intervention of any kind. The author and the publisher expressly disclaim responsibility for any adverse effects arising from the use or application of the information contained herein. If mental health treatment is required, readers should seek individual help and services from a licensed mental health professional.

Author's Note: The people in this book were drawn from a composite of people I have known over the years, as well as from my own personal experiences. Resemblance to any one person is purely coincidental. All identities have been disguised, and real names and identifying information are not used.

Library of Congress Cataloging-in-Publication Data
is available through the Library of Congress

©2024 Beth Kurland, PhD

ISBN-13: 978-07573-2502-1 (Paperback)
ISBN-10: 07573-2502-5 (Paperback)
ISBN-13: 978-07573-2503-8 (ePub)
ISBN-10: 07573-2503-3 (ePub)

Publisher: Health Communications, Inc.
          301 Crawford Boulevard, Suite 200
          Boca Raton, FL 33432-3762

Cover art by Kathleen Lynch/Black Kat Design
Interior design and formatting by Larissa Hise Henoch.

To my readers, may you find ease,
well-being and wholeness.

For Alan —my North Star—and to
Rachel and Noah, who bring such light into the world.

Praise for *You Don't Have to Change to Change Everything*

"Beth Kurland's reassuring title says it all and yet offers clear, concise, compassionate instructions for powerful personal transformation."
—**Chris Willard, PsyD,** faculty, part-time, Harvard Medical School, and author of *Alphabreaths* and *How We Go Through What We Grow Through*

"In her true signature form, Dr. Beth Kurland offers a rich tapestry of practical, accessible strategies that help us rethink change and live with greater presence and compassion."
—**Kristen Lee, EdD, LICSW,** bestselling author of *Mentalligence: A New Psychology of Thinking* and *Worth the Risk*

"In a sea of self-help hacks, *You Don't Have to Change to Change Everything* stands apart in its ability to blend the latest research with the wisdom of the ages to give you insights you can actually use. Beth Kurland's voice rings true and clear—a brilliant, empathetic voice reminding us that we aren't flawed beings to be fixed but whole beings whose minds and hearts are on the verge of flourishing. Kurland has given us all a new vantage point from which to see our lives and each other."
—**Terri Trespicio,** author of *Unfollow Your Passion: How to Create a Life that Matters to You*

"In an age when striving for an elusive, perfect kind of happiness infiltrates every domain of life, *You Don't Have to Change to Change Everything* offers us an antidote. Part clinical wisdom, part memoir, and part poetic vignette, Beth Kurland presents six vantage points for living a meaningful life. Drawing on contemporary psychology, neuroscience, and Eastern wisdom traditions, this book offers rich recipes for practical mindfulness and self-care."
—**Tara Cousineau, PhD,** author of *The Kindness Cure*

"With kind eyes and a warm heart, Beth skillfully helps readers navigate the challenging landscape of negative emotional patterns. Having walked this walk and experienced its life-changing benefits, she speaks with clear and passionate conviction. Weaving neuroscience, psychology, and mindfulness seamlessly together, she leaves for us an elegant and detailed trail of breadcrumbs filled with practical handholds and rich personal epiphanies. Her voice is gentle and clear, her invitations useful, her encouragement straightforward and inspiring."
—**Susan Morgan, MSN, RN, CS, and Bill Morgan, PsyD,** author of *The Meditator's Dilemma*

"As a mental health clinician and executive in the field of wellness, I find this book to be a treasure trove of insights. It beautifully bridges the gap between scientific understanding and everyday experiences to offer readers a compelling roadmap to emotional resilience and personal fulfillment. This book shares a refreshing perspective on self-growth and mindfulness and is a must-read for those on a path to deeper self-awareness and well-being."

—**Aimee Gindin, MSCP,** chief marketing officer at LifeSpeak Inc.

"In her thoughtful approach combining leading-edge science from a variety of disciplines, Beth helps us to shift away from chasing a fleeting emotion such as happiness and toward meeting ourselves where we are without shame, blame, or criticism. She reminds us that there's nothing wrong with us, and we don't need to fix anything. Instead, she teaches us how to relate to what's happening inside of our mind, body, and nervous system to realign with our intentions, values, and well-being. Through her six vantage points, she provides us with clever strategies, resources, and perspectives that are easily integrated into our daily lives and, importantly, are incredibly helpful in the face of challenge! Even more, Beth has a gift of playfully sharing her own stories, struggles, and vulnerabilities that are so real, relatable, and meaningful!"

—**Michael Allison,** educational partner with Stephen W. Porges, PhD, and The Polyvagal Institute; developer of The Play Zone—A Neuropsychological Approach to Optimize Wellness, Resilience, and Performance

"I embarked upon *You Don't Have to Change to Change Everything* with a physician's eye and concluded it with deeper breath and stirring hope, realizing that it was exactly what my own nervous system needed. Both wise and disarmingly relatable, Dr. Kurland is an anchor herself as she seamlessly weaves anecdote, theory, and spirituality into a tangible guidebook on how to ease the suffering we all hold tightly inside. This book will remain by my side as I practice medicine, as its profoundly simple tools reveal how true well-being can be cultivated—by any of us—amidst the inevitable messiness of life."

—**Sarah Byrne, MD,** family physician and owner of Root Family Medicine, PC

Contents

Acknowledgments

As much as a book may appear from the outside as a solo endeavor, it is very much part of an often-invisible connection of people who have supported and influenced its birth into the world, sometimes starting well before the first page was even written. At least this has been my experience.

First, I would like to acknowledge the patients with whom I have worked, who have bravely and courageously chosen to walk through the therapy door and entrust their deepest experiences and struggles and heart's longings with me. It has truly been an honor to sit with so many wonderful people through the years and learn about the tremendous resilience of the human spirit, of the ability of the mind-body to heal, and of the strengths we can access when we are given a safe environment for discovery and growth. As much as I hope and believe I have helped my patients, I know that I have learned so much from each person who has come through my door. It has truly been a privilege to hold such sacred space and help others through this human journey.

There are so many individuals along the way who have taught me about the power of resilience, well-being, mindfulness, and mind-body practices. A deep gratitude goes out to Robert Brooks, my mentor during my internship, who forever changed the way that I approach therapy and work with patients, by finding "islands of competence" and working from strength. I have so appreciated our keeping in touch over all these years. A strong foundation for this book grew out of my mindfulness practice. I am so grateful to have come upon Ron Siegel's Mindfulness and Psychotherapy course many years ago, the MBSR program started by Jon Kabat-Zinn, the wonderful guidance of Tara Brach and Jack Kornfield, the teachings of Loch Kelly, and the many wonderful courses taught by Rick Hanson. Thanks also to Richard Schwartz, for his remarkable work bringing IFS into the world. I am immensely grateful for the certificate training offered through the Institute for Meditation and Psychotherapy and all the wonderful teachers who made this such a rich learning experience. This training was transformative for me. A deep bow of gratitude goes out to Bill and Susan Morgan, meditation teachers who I have been so very fortunate to get to know and work with over the years, and whose teachings have been so influential to me. Their teaching became a steady ground through which I turned to especially during the difficult years of the global pandemic (when I wrote much of this book), and their teaching continues to sustain me and help me deepen my meditation practice.

A more recent gift for me has been meeting Michael Allison and learning from his certificate class. He has brilliantly synthesized so much of what we know about polyvagal theory and put it together in such depth but also has made it so accessible and applicable to all aspects of life. Michael is someone who embodies what he teaches, and while much of this book was written prior to my taking his courses, his teachings have profoundly affected how I work with patients and clients, and how I see the world. I also want to acknowledge Stephen Porges and Deb Dana, who have brought the work of polyvagal theory into the world and into the therapy room.

This book would not have evolved without meeting and working with Terri Trespicio over the years. She is a gifted Gateless Writing teacher (among other things!) and it is through her writing workshops that most of the vignettes for this book were written (without having any idea that they would land in this book). Terri is a writing whisperer, and the safe environment she creates allows for creativity to emerge in unexpected ways. Also, my deepest gratitude goes out to Suzanne Kingsbury, who founded Gateless Writing and whom I had the privilege of working with as well, and who read my earliest beginnings of this book and encouraged me to let the work all come out on the page. I am forever grateful to both of their guidance and support.

There have been so many people who have supported me on my personal journey and who have become part of my deep well of well-being over the years. I want to thank the many therapists whom I have worked with over the years who have been a profound part of my healing journey. Likewise, a deep thanks goes out to all the holistic and mind-body practitioners who have supported me through the years, among them Barbara Strassman who I have been fortunate to work with for over three decades. I am deeply grateful to my women's group—thank you Shari Engelbourg, Cheryl Opper, Nadine Vantine-Kelly, and Sara Dolinsky—for the love, support and personal growth journey we have been on together for the past thirty years. A special thanks to Shari for our friendship, for reading my manuscript, and for all our professional collaboration over the years. I am so grateful for the two more recent meditation sanghas of which I am a part, both outgrowths of the IMP certificate program, and I deeply value my connections there. I also want to acknowledge how grateful I am for all the wonderful friends in my life. I cherish our connections and all your support! A special deep expression of gratitude goes out to Elise Siegel, for our weekly conversations and long friendship, which has been so supportive to me through the decades.

I am so incredibly grateful for this book publishing journey and all who have made this book possible. First, a big shout out to Mitch Abblett. I have so enjoyed our collegial connection and your support; and thank you for introducing me to Dani. A tremendous thanks to Dani Segelbaum, my agent at Carol Mann Agency, who has been such a delight to work with, and who believed in this book right from the start and supported me every step of the way. I am forever grateful to Christine Belleris at HCI, who saw the merits in this book, provided this amazing opportunity for me to put my writing out into the world, and created the perfect publishing experience from start to finish beyond what I could have possibly imagined! Thanks to Lindsey Triebel at HCI for your efforts and support in launching the marketing for this book, and thank you, Lindsey, for bringing Lissa Warren on board. I am so grateful Lissa, to have you by my side to help with publicity and getting this book out into the world. I am also so appreciative to Mary Ellen Hettinger and Larissa Henoch at HCI who did a wonderful job editing and formatting this book. Additionally, a huge acknowledgment of thanks to Kathleen Lynch, whose beautiful cover design is such a welcoming invitation for this book. Thanks also to Christian Blonshine at HCI for making a deal with Recorded Books to produce an audio version of this book. One additional big thanks goes out to Amy Sosa, who helps me with all things social media and has been an important part of my team.

I want to send out a big thank you to all of those who took the time out of their very busy lives to review my book and write an endorsement. Thank you Bill and Susan Morgan, Michael Allison, Kris Lee, Christopher Willard, Tara Cousineau, Aimee Gindin, Sarah Byrne, and Terri Trespicio!

Last, but for sure not least, I would like to acknowledge my amazing family. Thank you to my dad and Eve, and my siblings Mike and Cindy for the foundation of well-being and love that supports me always. Thank you to my in-laws, Sue and Ray, for your love and support, and to all my extended family to whom I am so grateful to have in my life. Alan, you are a husband extraordinaire. Your enthusiastic support of all my creative endeavors has given me a foundation upon which to leap forward. I am so grateful for your encouragement every step of the way, for your patience and love, and for meticulously pouring through this manuscript when I was at a most critical point. Thank you to my children, Rachel and Noah, for giving me permission to use little stories about you in the book, and for enriching my life in ways that are beyond words. Please know that you inspire me in how you live your lives, and it is truly the privilege of a lifetime to be your mom. Finally, I would like to acknowledge my mom, whose spirit is with me always.

Introduction

The Happiness Conundrum

An Invitation

What if you were living alone on an island but you didn't even know it. You were so used to living there by yourself that it just became the way things were. On this island you struggle with all the normal human emotional experiences and challenges, such as stress, overwhelm, frustration, anxiety, worry, sadness, loss, and anger . . . but you do so alone. Some days these emotions are like a slow drip in the background of your day; other days you are swallowed up by these emotions, or you may expend effort trying to push them away, muster on, or wondering what's wrong with you that you are feeling this way. Just another day in the life. What you don't realize is that there is a whole vast land not far from where you reside, and it's connected to your island by bridges that you can't see. One day you discover a map, and it guides you to not one, but six possible bridges that show you how your island is connected to this vast, expansive, and beautiful land. Stopping to stand in the middle of each of the bridges, you gain a different vantage point of the island that allows you to see things in a new way. When you follow each bridge, you discover resources that you didn't realize you had access to, and they bring greater ease to your struggles and richness to your life. Once you cross any of the bridges you realize that you are no longer alone, left to struggle by yourself in your emotional distress. There is a greater sense of wholeness as you recognize the interconnectedness of your island with the land that surrounds it. You feel more connected to others around you, to the common humanity we all share. And perhaps most importantly, you feel more connected with the one you were most separated from— your Self, the true essence of who you are.

The first time I met "Miss Fuck You" I was in my early thirties. She wore baggy sweatpants and a hooded sweatshirt that she hid behind; she had unkempt hair and piercing eyes, and she was very angry. She was angry for thinking that she had to be perfect and successful in order to be loved and accepted—even though by all outside appearances she was quite successful. She was angry that, no matter how much she achieved, some deep part of her didn't feel like she was enough. She was angry that she felt such shame about her body because her curves and shape didn't match the bombardment of cultural images she received on how she needed to look in order to attract a man (even though she had a wonderful man in her life). She was angry that for so many years she pushed away her grief and sadness about her mom's death when she was a teen—at the high price of anxiety that masked the sadness. She was rebellious and full of rage, feeling emotions that she had never allowed herself to express. She was everything that I couldn't be. And yet, she was a part of me that I had ignored for many years of my life.

When I was four years old, I remember sitting on my blue embroidered bedspread in our little suburban split-level house in Michigan, anxiously asking the babysitter every time she tucked me in, "Was I good, bad, or rambunctious?" I desperately wanted my parents' approval, and I mistakenly came to believe, from my limited four-year-old perspective, that my parents' love was dependent on me being a happy, never angry, perfectly well-behaved little girl. Later, at fifteen, shortly after my mom died, I wrote in a letter to my then-boyfriend: "I don't know why I'm feeling so depressed. I don't know what's wrong with me—I have so much to be happy about." I never missed a day of school. I never got less than an A. I put away my sadness and grief, and I mustered on.

But I don't think I'm alone. Messages from our culture, from well-meaning authority figures, and from the media tell us that certain feelings are unacceptable; they tell us to be strong, stop fussing, don't get angry, come on—don't be sad! Surely you need to be happy like the people in the ads— here, have some ice cream or buy this product to feel better.

So, we put these feelings away in the service of our well-being, or we become hijacked by our feelings because we don't know how to meet and greet and hold them, and without a safe container, they have nowhere to go and spill over. We may run and hide from ourselves, from the very parts of ourselves that need our deepest attention. We do this because we think it will help us feel better, because we think we are not good enough, or that we need to bury what we perceive as broken. We push our feelings away because we think we need to look or be a certain way to gain approval or even love, or because we think it isn't safe to allow ourselves to feel what is there. *But, when we do this, somewhere along the way, we are abandoned by the very person that we need most: our Self.*

The Happiness Problem

We have a happiness problem in our culture, and it is making many of us—well, unhappy. There is an unspoken myth that somehow, we "should" be happy, at least much of the time, as if happiness is the holy grail or gold standard upon which we determine the value of our life. The problem is that when we don't feel happy, we often feel like we are falling short in some way, or that there is something wrong, or even that there is something wrong with *us*! It is common for me to hear people of all ages talk about their experiences with the social-media comparison trap and how they see all their (online) connections posting pictures that make it appear that they are so happy, that their lives are picture perfect. In contrast, many people feel that their lives don't match up or that something must be missing. What they don't see, of course, is the whole range of human experiences behind the snapshot photos and brief taglines: the heartbreaks and grief and losses and challenges that we all experience.

In this happiness culture, we have come to judge our "other" emotions, our more difficult emotions, as "bad," unwanted, undesirable, or a sign of weakness. Repeatedly, I have sat with patients going through deep grief and loss of all kinds and equating being "strong" with holding it all together, not crying, or not feeling their sadness. The implicit messages that we are taught somehow tell us that feeling difficult emotions intensely is a sign of weakness, and that happiness is what we should strive for.

Additionally, as much as we are taught all manner of skills in our families, schools, and workplaces over the course of our childhood and our adult lives, we are not taught what to do in the face of life's difficulties and with the uncomfortable emotions that may arise. We are taught, directly and indirectly, to value happiness ("Cheer up, look on the bright side, wipe away those tears, and let's see that smile"), but other less pleasant emotions are often sorely neglected, not given airtime, and deemed undesirable.

Being happy is not a problem. In fact, it is a wonderful feeling and I wish that all of us can experience it often. But when we strive for happiness at the expense of all else, we can suffer greatly. Part of the reason for this is because the common notion of "happy" in our culture (at least in the American culture I grew up in with its emphasis on "hedonic" happiness or pleasure) has several limitations:

Happiness is dependent upon mood, upon feeling a certain way. When happiness is the gold standard, there is little room for feeling sadness, disappointment, fear, anger, etc. The implicit message is: When I am not feeling happy there is something wrong with me. I need to change how I am feeling.

Happiness is often dependent upon external circumstances. When certain things happen in life, we feel happy. Those things may look different for each of us, but they are all positive experiences of one kind or another. So, what happens when we encounter difficult experiences? And what about the fact that we can't control many of the more unpleasant experiences that occur in our lives? The implicit message we may internalize is: I need my life circumstances to change in order to be happy. But unfortunately, many times we wait, and wait, and wait for that time to come.

Happiness is often dependent upon doing. We often base our happiness upon things that we do and achieve. We are happy when we get that good job, when we achieve a goal, when we do something that brings recognition. There is nothing wrong with that. Those are moments to be celebrated! The problem is that we can come to value doing and achieving over being. The implicit message is: I need to be doing more or doing different or doing better in order to be happy. I'm not doing enough.

Happiness can often pull us to go after the quick fix. Happiness can offer us a quick hit of dopamine, making us feel good in the moment, but the feeling can often be fleeting, leaving us looking for more. I feel happy when I get a high number of likes on my blogs, when my book sales go up, or when someone compliments me on something that I have done. But that happiness is only momentary, not lasting. If I were to focus only on this, the implicit message becomes: When those things are not happening, something is wrong, something is missing. Something needs to change—I need to get that quick fix to feel okay again. *I am not enough.*

Stop Striving for Happy, Try Well-Being Instead

It was March of 2020. Need I say more? Anyone reading this book who lived through the early stages of the global pandemic will likely have a visceral feeling, a flashback, to some dark and very scary times: of uncertainties, lockdowns, fear of a virus that was killing people and that we knew little about, loss of a sense of safety, and of our lives as we knew them to be. A happy time? Hardly. And yet, something curious emerged in my own life that was unexpected given the horrendous circumstances that were unfolding. Amidst my own strong fear, worry, anxiety, amidst the social distancing and social isolation, amidst the sleepless nights when my mind would race through worst-case scenarios given that my husband was a frontline worker in a hospital, something curious emerged that had nothing to do with happiness and everything to do with well-being.

In a note to my then cohorts in a Meditation and Psychotherapy class I was taking, I wrote on March 22, 2020:

> *Just a word for now to say that my meditation practice has been immensely helpful. I find that my anxiety comes and goes at different points and with different intensities but holding it in a vast space of spacious awareness and loving-kindness has helped to bring ease. Instead of following the initial inclination to push the fear away, I allow it to be there and also invite in something else to sit side by side with it (spacious awareness, self-compassion, stillness at my core, etc.). I have been acutely aware of how much of my suffering is from my mind going into future "what ifs," and I have found some refuge in presence, whether my breath, a run through the woods, or folding my laundry. I have been able to be more present than I ever would have been in the past—and this has surprised me, actually. When my stress (fight-or-flight/fear) response kicks in, I try to thank it for trying to protect me but remind myself that I have more newly evolved ways to find some safety (and that meeting the current circumstances from a place of calm presence is actually more protective than my habitual fear response). (Of course, I have had my moments of neural hijacking too). I have thought a lot about Rick Hanson's teachings[1]—and the challenges for all of us more now than ever—to meet our needs for safety, satisfaction,*

and connection. That being said, I have tried to help myself and my patients find ways to do this nonetheless, even if for short moments. It has been difficult and somewhat exhausting to sit with patients for so many hours talking about COVID-19-related fears and issues—and yet I am so grateful that I can do my work remotely and help to support others.

And from a journal entry in early January of 2022, amidst the height of the Omicron wave here in the Northeast US, when I found myself in a funk, I wrote:

This morning, I got this sinking feeling again—some of that depressive energy from being in now two years of this pandemic . . . missing my old feeling of happiness and excitement each day. What was helpful was to recognize I don't have to be happy right now in this moment, but I can cultivate well-being. And I have been doing that throughout this pandemic. When I can let the sadness and angst and confusion rest in a vast space of compassionate awareness, of just being—not needing to achieve anything in this moment, not needing to change anything in this moment—something in me relaxes, softens; there is ease. From that place of ease, of meeting myself right where I am, often emotions start to shift on their own. When I'm in a funk I may not feel happy, but I can remember to dip into my well-being "well" to do things that nourish me: going for walks in the woods, calling friends and family, going for runs, eating healthy foods, meditating . . . doing things that I care about—that align with my deepest values, with what is most important to me.

Looking back, what was glaringly absent in these writings was a feeling of happiness. But even when happiness was not present, well-being was there to support me. It was like a deep well from which I could draw nourishment. Well-being is something we can cultivate, no matter our life circumstances or situations, no matter how we are feeling, or what is happening around us.

It has everything to do with where we rest our minds, how we regulate our nervous system, what narratives we feed ourselves, how we meet our own suffering.

Here are some qualities of well-being that contrast with those of our traditional (hedonic) version of happiness:

Well-being is not dependent upon mood. It allows us to hold our sadness, frustration, fears, and grief as it sits alongside these and becomes the large container in which these emotions can be held. It does not insist that we feel any certain way but gives us permission to be with whatever is here. Implicit message: It is okay to feel however I am feeling. All my feelings are welcome, and I can take care of all of them.

Well-being is not dependent upon circumstances. It has everything to do with how we are relating to our inner experiences, and our outer ones, but it is the relationship to those things that sets the tone for well-being, not those things themselves. When I am spending time with family and friends, I am happy, but I feel a deep sense of well-being when I draw upon that feeling of love, connection, and support as an inner experience, even when I am not with anyone. Implicit message: no matter my life circumstances, there are ways I can care for myself and cultivate well-being each day.

Well-being is not dependent upon doing, but upon being. I am happy when I am doing activities I enjoy. I feel a sense of well-being when I am connected to the things that most deeply matter to me. When I am living my life in alignment with what is important to me—in my case, creating, connecting, teaching, inspiring, helping—there is a sense of well-being present. Even when I am not actively doing those things, when I am connected to that energy, purpose, and meaning, it nourishes me. When we experience a state of well-being, we don't need to be achieving or striving or accomplishing. There is a deep sense of inner peace and acceptance of things as they are. Implicit message: who I am is enough.

Well-being is not a quick fix. It is like a deep well from which we can draw nourishment. While I am happy when I get likes on my blogs and when my book sales increase, deeper well-being for me comes from the process of contributing or sharing something authentic and putting it out in the world because I believe it matters, regardless of the outcome. Additionally, well-being is there for us to draw from, even when happiness fades away as it inevitably will. Implicit message: even if this moment may be difficult, there is deep comfort in knowing I can handle what is here and I am okay just as I am.

This book will help you cultivate well-being—discover that deep well within you from which you can draw lasting nourishment—and it will help you learn how to work with difficult life experiences and difficult emotions and mind states in a new way.

Part of this new way has to do with changing your relationship to your internal experiences by shifting where you are standing, i.e., your viewing point. When you shift your vantage point, you see things in a new way.

This book will offer you six vantage points that can become foundations of well-being for you. Each of the vantage points shows you how you can develop well-being without needing to change your emotions, your thoughts, your imperfections, your life circumstances; without needing to *do* more or *be* more to become better or more improved. Each vantage point offers you a way to access this well-being, by connecting with what is already here, already whole.

PART ONE

Essential Foundations

CHAPTER 1

What You Weren't Taught in School

You Don't Need to Change (at Least Not in the Way You Think)

The spring that my daughter was learning to drive was one of the rainiest springs that I can remember. The silver Honda was parked on the dirt, grass, and gravel alongside our driveway, and its resting spot often turned into a bit of a muddy mess. On this particular day, "mud pit" was more like it. My daughter had been trying to back the car up, as she always did, but the car had another thought or two in mind. It would have nothing of backing up, and its wheels started to spin in the mud. And spin, and spin some more. The harder she tried to back out, the more stuck she got, sinking deeper and deeper into a rut of muddy muck from which she could not budge. Finally, my husband caught a glimpse of the scene from the window and went out to offer assistance. He showed my daughter how she needed to do something counterintuitive. Rather than continuing to exert effort over and over trying to back up, she needed to move in an entirely different direction: pulling forward toward the house.

Only then could the tires gain some traction and become un-stuck, allowing her to create a new pathway from which she could find her way out.

What if you were misguided in how you were going about things when you come up against emotional challenges and the accompanying discomfort that comes with them (all those human emotions we know and *don't* love, such as frustration, anger, sadness, disappointment, anxiety, worry, grief, despair, etc.)? Maybe you (like I for so many years) have been expending large amounts of energy trying to fix, improve, or change yourself, thinking something is wrong or broken or not enough. Maybe you have told yourself that things will improve once your life circumstances change, and you keep waiting for "someday" to arrive and announce itself in bold colors. Maybe you have subscribed to every kind of self-help you can get your hands on, only to be left feeling like you are missing something, or perhaps even that you are not doing it right or are deficient in some way.

What if, when you encounter emotional challenges, instead of trying to fix yourself, get rid of what you are feeling, or wait for your life circumstances to change, you could move in a different direction, shift your vantage point, the place from which you are standing? From this new place, your relationship to your emotional distress transforms. No longer swallowed up by it or trying to avoid it, you start to see things in a new way and gain access to a whole set of inner resources that were not so easily accessible before. No longer stuck in old brain circuitry focused on helping you survive (but also keeping you more limited in your response repertoire), you can access heartfelt emotions that allow you to experience greater ease and well-being, that uplift and comfort you, that enable you to see a bigger picture, that offer you possibilities you did not see before, and that remind you that you are not alone. In fact, what if the emotional distress that you are feeling, the very thing that is making you feel unease, could be the very thing that, when you relate to it in this new way, allows you to experience a wholeness that brings a deeper sense of peace through life's inevitable storms. There is a plethora of self-help books about change: how to change yourself, how to improve yourself, how to change your life circumstances, etc., in order to find greater happiness. This is not one of them. Not that those books aren't useful; I'm not knocking that kind of change or saying there isn't a place for it. But this book offers something new. It is about moving in a different direction. Instead of trying to "fix" yourself, you reconnect with inner resources that were there all along. Instead of feeling broken or less than, you realize that you were whole all along. From this place, profound change is possible.

Instead of putting effort into trying to change yourself or your circumstances, this book shows you how, when you accept your inner experiences as they are, but view them from different vantage points (which you will learn), you shift the very nature of those experiences in a way that becomes easier to bear. Instead of trying to "fix" yourself, you reconnect with inner resources that were there all along. Instead of feeling broken or less than, you realize that you were whole all along. From this place, profound change is possible.

When Nothing Changes and Everything Changes

Sometimes there are moments when nothing changes at all and yet everything changes. I have had many of these over the years and what stands out most about them is that I go from feeling contracted, tense, anxious inside, as if I am fighting to keep something at bay that, if I let it, will overwhelm me and take me down, to suddenly something relaxing in me, as if naming my fear, grief, or underlying emotions, really coming face-to-face with them, allows the energy of them to transform into something that can be held tenderly, with care.

One of those moments came in my kitchen on a very ordinary day many years ago, as I was caught in mental rumination and worry about deciding whether to put my then-high school son

*on potentially toxic medication for the next six months to ad-
dress a non-life-threatening condition. Being someone who has
tried to do things as naturally and organically as possible, I ag-
onized over this decision and the fear of uncertainty and risk
that weighed heavily on my mind, unsure of what would be best
for my son's well-being. Internally, I fought against this situation
and my own fears, desperately wanting it to be different than
it was. Outwardly, I had long and anxious conversations with
my husband, frantically looking for any other alternative (all of
which we had already exhausted).*

*In this moment standing in the kitchen, gripped with fear and
indecision, I did something that felt counterintuitive. I turned
toward my fear to take a curious and closer look at what was
actually there. I stopped resisting. I let go of the struggle to make
this fear go away. What I discovered from this vantage point was
that underneath the emotional turmoil was deep sadness and
grief at the acknowledgment that no matter how much I love my
son and no matter how much I try to control things and do all
the "right" things, I cannot fully protect him in this life. Coming
face-to-face with this raw vulnerability, I put my hand on my
heart and cried deep heaving tears.*

*In those moments to follow, nothing changed about the situa-
tion, but something released in me. That intense fear that had
been knocking at my door and taking so much of my energy dissipated when I opened the door to my fear. Surprisingly, when I
peered at what was there, what came in alongside the fear was
acceptance—a profound acceptance of life as it is, and of this
fear being only a part of that, held in a vast expanse of love and
care, for my son and for my own human struggles. In the willingness to look at and be with fear, I also discovered courage to help
me move forward, which had not been present in my resistance*

and struggle. I was able to go forward with greater ease and trust in my capacity to be with what was here.

Yes, the first noble truth in action: there is suffering. This is what the Buddha taught some 2,500 years ago, as he observed human suffering and began an inquiry into the different kinds of suffering we humans experience, and eventually discovered a path out of that suffering. The fact that we experience emotional distress is a fundamental truth of this human life. Sitting across from patients for over thirty years in my therapy office, I have seen a good deal of suffering. People come to me because they are experiencing emotional distress of one kind or another, often in the form of high physiological stress, overwhelm, anxiety, low self-esteem, worry, sadness, depression, grief, health challenges, and immense life challenges that feel too hard to navigate alone. No different from you or I, they are looking for a way to manage their day-to-day distress to experience greater ease.

If you are reading this, no doubt as a breathing human being you come up against difficult life experiences on a regular basis that bring with them emotional unease. These might range from the small annoyances—traffic jams, work deadlines, canceled plans, minor illnesses, stress of not enough time—to the bigger difficulties such as relationship challenges, health problems, feelings of unworthiness, and loss. These experiences bring with them accompanying emotions of all kinds and intensities: frustration, anger, sadness, fear, grief, anxiety, disappointment, despair. While it is difficult enough that we as humans experience emotional distress, what is equally problematic is that we are not taught how to relate to these uncomfortable emotions or what to do in the face of them.

But how we relate to our emotional distress can make all the difference between mental wellness and mental un-wellness and where we fall on that continuum. This book is not a treatment for clinical anxiety or depression or any particular condition (and it is not intended to treat trauma), but it does address the human condition and offers a way through difficulties for people who experience emotional suffering of all kinds, to find a way to greater ease.

What We Aren't Taught

It is a curious thing that most of us aren't taught how to deal with challenging emotional situations and the emotional discomfort that accompanies them. As much as we learn copious things in schools, from teachers and mentors and others (much of which we forget or don't end up needing to know to function in life), this is one aspect of learning that is sorely missing. If anything, as we will see further, we learn indirect messages about how it's not okay to feel or show certain emotions. In the absence of knowing what else to do with this uncomfortable internal energy, and driven by our biological wiring, we tend to push our emotions away, think something is wrong with us for having these feelings, avoid what's there, ignore it, or get swallowed up by it to the point where it can overtake us. Often, we disconnect from ourselves in the process.

What if we could learn how to be in relationship with ourselves and our inner experiences in a new way? Instead of trying to change your emotions, what if you could widen the container in which you are holding them? In doing so, something begins to shift. Instead of getting stuck in stress, anger, anxiety, worry, overwhelm, depression, numbing out, or unhelpful habitual behaviors, this book explores what possibilities open when we can greet our day-to-day emotional visitors in a new way.

What if, instead of trying to change yourself, you could learn how to reconnect with yourself—with the whole of who you are? Instead of trying to change your inner experiences, you could learn how to shift the vantage point from which you look at your internal experiences. From this new place, the landscape and your inner experiences begin to shift on their own. Our external experiences may still be difficult, and we may still feel painful emotions, but we can handle them with greater ease, and sometimes we can see new solutions or possibilities that we didn't see before. From this place, genuine heartfelt emotions become available—more expansive emotions that can hold our suffering and soften and soothe what is there.

Many people suffer silently. Unlike physical illness, when we feel emotional distress, we often hide it from others, believe there is something wrong with us, think we shouldn't feel this way, or tell ourselves if we were stronger or smarter or better, we wouldn't be experiencing this. We think everyone else has it all together, that there is something wrong with us.

One of the privileges of my profession is being able to see how very common our common humanity is. From my view from the therapy chair, privy to the intimate details and courageous sharing from my patients, I have learned more than anything that this human condition connects us in ways we don't realize. While my patients often feel alone in what they are experiencing and may worry "What's wrong with me?" what they don't often realize at first is that they are not alone in their struggles, and they are in very good company. You are too.

A New Way to Think About Change

I've sat with hundreds of patients and witnessed some profound changes that have occurred. When I see people make changes, most often it is not that they change their life circumstances or themselves (as in becoming some new, improved version of themselves). It's that they learn to relate to themselves and their internal experiences in a new way and gain access to inner resources they didn't realize they had. This shift in vantage point allows them to see themselves and their circumstances and experiences through fresh eyes. As they learn to shift their relationship to emotional unease, things begin to change. Sometimes they learn to recognize their own strengths and resilience whereas before they had only seen their shortcomings. Sometimes they learn to accept their own imperfections and relax into the possibility that they don't have to be perfect to be okay. Sometimes they learn to relate to their thoughts and emotions from a place where they can see what is there without getting swept away by it. Sometimes they learn to hold the most vulnerable parts of themselves with deep self-compassion—often seeing these parts through kind eyes for the very first time. Sometimes change comes from recognizing all the ways they have coped in the past and rediscovering

inner strengths they didn't realize that they had. Most always, it is about un-
covering what is already there, under the layers, behind the walls, to realize
that they don't have to change, that they are enough just as they are. It is a
process of coming home to themselves and finding refuge there.

The Two Arrows of Suffering

As much as we suffer because of the inevitable challenges we encounter
in life (sickness, aging, loss, death, transitions, and all the obstacles that life
throws at us, large and small), we suffer doubly because of our reactions to
our own suffering.

There is a Buddhist parable commonly shared that captures this notion of
the ways that we can suffer twice. In this parable, the Buddha is said to have
asked a student why, when we experience the pain of being shot by a first
arrow (our natural human suffering beyond our control), do we go ahead
and shoot a second arrow into ourselves.

The Buddha goes on to explain that "In life, we can't always control the
first arrow; however, the second arrow is our reaction to the first. The second
arrow is optional."[2] This second arrow of suffering is what I address in this
book. We often can't change the first arrow; the challenges that life throws at
us are at times painful and difficult. But how we relate to our own suffering
(both the day-to-day bumps and the bigger ones) is within our control. And
that relationship has everything to do with where we are standing.

Our tendency is to stand right in the middle of our muck, to be caught
in the middle of our suffering and pain and irritation and stress the way we
might be caught and stranded within a storm. When we are in the middle of
a storm, with the rain pounding down on us and the wind whipping us off
our feet, it takes everything just to remain standing. Many of the habitual
ways that we react when we come up against emotional discomfort have to
do with the ways our brain and nervous system evolved to help us survive

as a species. These habitual reactions and mental habits contribute to this second arrow of suffering that we feel. We have difficult and inevitable life experiences we must face, but on top of this, we have a brain and nervous system that spend a lot of time scanning for threats and danger, often getting triggered by perceived threats (including our own negative thoughts) that are not true emergencies. Because of this, we often over-perceive everyday challenges as threats, and walk around in heightened states of stress, anxiety, and frustration. In addition, our mind is very good at creating narratives about everything we are experiencing; often these narratives can be rather distorted, inaccurate, catastrophic, or self-critical. We fight against our own emotions, rather than viewing them as helpful information and energy passing through us. We spend excessive amounts of time in mental activity worrying about the future and ruminating about the past, when we can change neither. We blame ourselves in unnecessary ways and see all the ways that we are falling short, while easily overlooking our own strengths.

Caught in our own mental habits, and in our own inner storms, we often react to life's challenges in habitual ways without realizing that we have access to different ways to respond, both to the situation and to ourselves struggling through it.

When we are in the grip of these mental habits, it is as if we are stranded in that storm, without access to inner resources that can help us to calm our nervous system, bring our focus back to the present moment, see a bigger picture and recognize the distortions of our own thinking, meet our unease with self-compassion and kindness, and recognize the strengths and resources we have to cope with whatever is occurring. We are, in essence, cut off from, or have lost access to, our own inner toolbox that can help us experience greater ease and well-being.

This book is not about stopping the storms. But it is about learning where to stand. Instead of being caught and helpless in the storm, imagine that you took safe refuge while you let the storm pass by. Imagine that you could step back and watch the storm from a safe distance, without being caught in it or swept away by it. Imagine that you had a wonderful, warm, water-resistant raincoat to wrap yourself in that made it easier to tolerate the unpredictable weather. And from this vantage point of safe refuge, you could feel greater ease, see greater possibilities available, and trust in yourself to get through this and even be more resilient because of it.

While my previous book focused on five tools to address the common mental habits that we all experience, this book focuses specifically on how we can work with life's challenges and the accompanying emotional unease, and what to do when it arises. Rather than needing to change your external and/or internal experience (which often you can't) or yourself (which is often a self-defeating path), it offers you six ways that you can shift your vantage point, the place from which you are viewing what is occurring. As you do this, as you relate differently to your emotional experiences, something begins to naturally shift on its own. One of the consequences of this shift, as you will see, is that you step out of adaptive survival circuitry and begin to have more access to your inner resources that were there all along. This book will show you how.

The Beginning of My Journey: Looking Back

When I look back over the past thirty years, it's not what I did that really stands out after all. It is who I met along the way and how each of those people changed my perspective, my understanding, of what it means to be human, to love and live and struggle and thrive in this human life. It is Hannah who I met as a young twenty-something in college, looking to broaden my experience working with people who struggle with mental disabilities. It is the house full of adults who I worked with for a summer in the group home near my hometown, showing up day after day and becoming privy to their lives. It is the folks I met in the psychiatric unit of a local community hospital on the 11:00 PM to 7:00 AM shift, waking them for their medications and listening with interest as I caught glimpses of their stories and struggles and observed what made them feel at ease.

When I first met Hannah, she was sitting across from me in a smoky coffee shop in town, near the group home where she lived. She was thin and disheveled looking, wearing a gray sweatshirt with coffee stains on it, hair stringy and thin for someone her age, cigarette in hand—and a pack nearby so at all times there was no break in this nicotine fix that clearly, she relied on. I introduced myself and explained that we would have the chance to meet once a week, to talk or spend time together in whatever way she wanted. Not prepared for what came next, I sat a bit stunned as she began telling me disjointed and hard-to-follow stories about how people were out to get her, how the devil visited her frequently, and how she was being secretly spied on by the government. While the stories she told made no rational sense, the theme of her delusions was about not being able to trust people. So slowly, I built up a trust with Hannah. I helped her to feel seen and heard and listened to. I let her know through our regular visits that I wanted to spend time with her, whether she made sense to me or not. I kept showing up. And once we'd built a trust, one of my favorite memories was taking Hannah on occasion to the music room at my college, where there was a piano. Hannah loved music, and while she didn't really know how to play the piano very well, playing the notes and making music became a way she could express herself and reconnect with something deeply joyful in her that made her feel vibrant and alive.

I remember Greg—a short man in his thirties, scruffy beard and scratchy voice, homeless for a time, displaying behaviors at the group home that I could only begin to understand as an unwinding from his traumatic past. Having lost his sight several years before, I was amazed at his courage to navigate in the world and touched by his deep compassion for his brother who lived with him. There was Frankie and Sarah—an unusual pair as a married couple—loving in their own tender way as they opened to guidance about how to perform basic daily functions that so many of us take for granted. And there was Robert, in many ways lacking self-awareness and without language, yet still communicating to me clearly in nonverbal ways that he cherished connection and care as much as any of us.

What I discovered in these experiences is the labels that fell away, the diagnoses that felt so insufficient, the boxes that were confining and oh so limiting. Hannah relaxed when I sat with her in the coffee shop listening to her stories, not validating the delusions she shared, but listening through the spaces to hear the pain that she suffered as a teenager, the longing that she felt to be seen and to feel safe. It wasn't the hallucinations that I tried to talk truth into, but the truth of her suffering that I tried to hold in the silence of my gaze and my simple presence.

Each day was a new adventure, opening my eyes to the depth of what it means to be human, opening my heart to help the challenges of another, pulling me to find the little things that made a difference. In the end, it wasn't my education that mattered; it was the way I smiled, the warm greeting, the welcome look, the soft tone, the acceptance that became the framework from which trust emerged.

*In this space, something unexpected happens, and even more so, as I discovered over the years with countless patients, when we learn to give **ourselves** this presence. As we do this, we relate to our own experiences in a new way. In the therapy room what I found was that through presence, connection, and ultimately*

helping others to be present and accept themselves right where
they are, something begins to shift.

I went to graduate school to become a clinical psychologist, and in part, I think, to find a solution to my own suffering, and to the suffering of others. I thought that I might figure out how to get rid of anxiety and depression and all the things that make people unhappy, how to change people and make them better.

I myself was (and still am) wired to be anxious and "type A" by nature. On top of this was a strong drive to be perfect in order to be accepted, and a need to (over)achieve in order to feel successful. After my mom died in a car accident when I was fifteen years old, I grappled with many strong emotions that I put away as I forged through high school, college, and graduate school without missing a beat. Through much of this time, I disliked myself in many ways. I had an unhealthy relationship with my body and felt inadequate compared to the unrealistic standards of what I thought I should look like. I developed an unhealthy relationship with food, often binging and then restricting food in harmful, self-defeating patterns in high school and college that led to shame and struggle. Outwardly I was highly successful, but inwardly I vacillated between stifling my emotions or feeling out of control with them. Through it all, I hoped to become a new, better, self-improved version of myself. I went to graduate school to study psychology, a field which, at that time, was very focused on psychopathology ("the scientific study of mental disorders"[3]). I wanted to understand what was wrong and how to fix it, in myself and in others.

But I discovered a few unexpected things along the way.

First, during my internship at McLean Hospital in Belmont, Massachusetts, I had the privilege of working with Dr. Robert Brooks—now a renowned expert on resilience. What Bob taught me is that we don't start by finding what is wrong with people, we start by finding what is *right* with them—we work from strength. We find their "islands of competence" (we *all* have islands of competence) and then we figure out how to help the other person discover this for themselves, to help them see their own strengths and to build on them. During a time when the study of psychopathology and mental disorders was a major focus of psychology training, Dr. Brooks introduced me to a new way of working with my patients that was quite transformative.

The second transformational thing that I encountered along the way was the practice of meditation and mindfulness. Mindfulness is a 2,500-year-old practice that in large part originated from the Eastern, Buddhist tradition. While my journey with and understanding of mindfulness continues to evolve and deepen, it has had a profound effect on both my personal and professional life over the years. There are many definitions of mindfulness. The first one that I encountered was from the teachings of Jon Kabat-Zinn, the founder of Mindfulness-Based Stress Reduction, who says that mindfulness is a particular way of paying attention: "on purpose, in the present moment, and nonjudgmentally."[4] One of my favorite more recent definitions of mindfulness (which I will return to in Chapter 3) is from meditation teacher Susan Morgan, who says, "Mindfulness is an alert, relaxed, nonjudgmental, non-self-referential posture of caring attention, as if a dear friend, wise elder, or beneficial presence is watching over the experience of well-being in this moment."[5]

For someone who was so used to being busy, driven, and on the go, this idea of slowing down in meditation to sit and observe my breath and eventually my thoughts, emotions, and physical sensations was quite foreign, and quite frankly uncomfortable at first. The last thing I wanted to do was sit when there was so very much to be done in any given minute. However, with practice and patience, I've gained tremendous benefits from observing my inner experiences in this new way.

As I learn to step out of the automatic pilot mode that I (and we all) so often operate from, and observe what is arising moment to moment, I begin to notice the mental stories that my mind creates, the ways that I live in the past and future so much of the time, the way that my worries create much added suffering for myself, and the disconnection that comes when I push away my feelings. I learn to watch what arises with a kinder attention, with an openness and acceptance, without trying to push away or change what is there. Mindfulness invites me to be present with what is here: the pleasant, the neutral, and the unpleasant, and to hold it in an expansive awareness that steps me out of my "small self" view. It offers me a way to embrace the preciousness of the moment and embrace the whole of life and the whole of myself, in all its messiness and muck. It doesn't mean that I don't work to improve things, but that I start by accepting what is here. From this mindful viewpoint, when I can hold my pain but not be swallowed up by it, when I can relate to my suffering from a half step back and through kind eyes, something begins to shift.

Hand in hand with my evolving journey with mindfulness came a third transformational learning in my life, when I had the privilege of working with several gifted therapists who incorporated mindfulness and mind-body practices into the therapy session. Having sought therapy in the past for myself (as the patient) through more traditional talk therapy, I was suddenly introduced to a more embodied experience. Rather than just talking about my experiences, I would bring attention to what was happening in my body and often use mindful awareness to connect with mind, body, and heart together to notice what was arising. In these deeper states of embodied presence, I would imagine opening the door and inviting different "parts" of myself to come into the therapy room—often parts that I had pushed away or that held emotions I had cared not to feel. "Miss Fuck You" that I introduced you to at the beginning of the book was one of these parts. (You will hear more about her in Chapter 7.) My therapist would invite me to take a curious look at who came in, and I would talk to and understand these parts of myself that I had pushed away in a way that allowed them to soften and feel heard and understood. In this safe space I allowed myself to make contact with and be with all of those painful emotions that I had tried so hard to suppress. I allowed myself to hold in juxtaposition both the joys of my life and the deep sorrows.

I allowed myself to hold my sadness and grief and anger and vulnerability, without needing to get rid of it. Instead, I would sit beside it like I would do with a good friend. The impact of this was profound, and it began to transform the relationship I had with myself, and the way that I sat and worked with my patients.

This book grew out of my personal experiences with mindfulness and mind-body practices to help me move through my own emotional struggles, and my years of practice as a clinical psychologist working with hundreds of patients to help them find greater ease amidst strong emotional challenges of all kinds. The six vantage points are a conceptualization and integration of principles that I've learned through my understanding of psychology, neuroscience, and Eastern wisdom traditions. This book is interspersed with personal vignettes and many short, practical exercises to help you learn and practice shifting with the six vantage points that I will teach you.

While this is not specifically a book about mindfulness, each of the six vantage points will help you cultivate aspects of mindfulness in your everyday life. You need not have any experience with meditation or mind-body practices to benefit from this book, but if you do have a meditation practice, my hope is that this book will offer you a helpful framework in which you may deepen your practice in ways that are enriching and nourishing for you.

What You Will Learn

As stated previously, this book is not about changing yourself, fixing yourself, or self-improvement to find happiness, though you might pick up any of a thousand self-help books to do that (and there are many good ones, by the way). This book is about shifting where you stand, shifting your vantage point, and how, when you do that, everything begins to change. It's about shedding the layers to uncover the essence at your core that has been there all along. It's about freeing yourself from the mental habits that have been keeping your life small. It's about shifting your relationship with your own suffering, and how, when you can relate to your suffering in new ways, things begin to change. It isn't about changing your circumstances (when you can't) or about changing yourself; it is about changing your relationship to what is already here, and the choices, possibilities, resources, and deep sense of well-being that become available when you do. This has been the gift of mindfulness for me, and of other mind-body practices. I am excited to share this with you! These six vantage points are foundational to well-being, and you will learn how to use each of them to create lasting well-being from which you can draw upon, no matter what life brings your way.

Important Guidelines for How to Use This Book

In the remaining chapters of Part One—Chapters 2 and 3—I provide an important framework for understanding why we react the way we do to our unpleasant emotions and become disconnected from ourselves and the whole of who we are, based on our evolutionary wiring, sociocultural and childhood histories, and other factors. By looking through the lens of our autonomic nervous system, I explain how each of the vantage points help us to shift from being stuck in our adaptive survival circuitry/"old operating system" to access our more newly evolved "thriving" circuits (our "newer operating system") that help deepen our "well" of well-being. We will explore the ways we disconnect from our bodies and hearts, and the important shift from "hole" self to "Whole Self." **I believe this information provides an important foundation and shift in vantage point right from the start by helping you understand your emotions in a new way. However, for those looking for less foundational background and who are eager to jump right into the vantage points and hands-on exercises, you might skim through these chapters and focus on Part Two and the six vantage points.**

In Part Two (Chapters 4 through 9) we'll explore each of the six vantage points: the anchor view, the child view, the audience view, the compassionate parent view, the mirror view, and the ocean view. Each chapter provides an explanation of the vantage point it is focusing on and is accompanied by personal vignettes and many practical and hands-on ways that you can experiment with shifting your vantage point through: 1) short practices, 2) questions for reflections (I encourage you to journal for these!), and 3) meditations (recordings are available at bethkurland.com/vantagepoints).

The anchor view will teach you how to find calm strength and stability in the midst of life's emotional storms. The child view will teach you how curiosity can be your superpower and forever change the way you meet and greet your emotions. The audience view will give you a new perspective so that your mental habits don't continue to run the show. The compassionate parent view will help you feel seen and heard by the one person who has likely been missing from the picture—your Self. The mirror view will help you see your strengths and discover the choices and possibilities that emerge when you start by noticing what is already here, already whole. The ocean view will offer a glimpse into the transcendent, explore the nature of awareness and spirituality, and help you discover what is possible when you experience an interconnectedness beyond the "small self."

NOTE ABOUT ACCOMPANYING AUDIO MEDITATIONS: In each chapter starting with Chapter 4, wherever you see the ear symbol ☺, you can find accompanying audio versions of these meditations at: bethkurland.com/vantagepoints.

There are several points I feel are important to emphasize. First, this book is not intended as psychological treatment or intervention of any kind and is purely for educational purposes, with the hope that it will enrich your life in many ways. If you are in need of psychological treatment, I encourage you to seek the guidance of a licensed mental health professional. This can be especially important if you are dealing with overwhelming challenges or trauma of any kind. This book will show you ways to bring ease to emotional distress but is not a substitute for professional help. Second, while my experiences with mindfulness inform much of this book, and through this book you will learn to bring greater mindful awareness into your life, this book does not address the rich Buddhist traditions from which mindfulness came or the teachings of which mindfulness are a part. There are many wonderful books on this topic written by people with far more knowledge on this subject. Please know that you do not need to have any experience with meditation or mindfulness or any mind-body practice to fully benefit from what this book has to offer. Lastly, while my previous book *Dancing on the Tightrope* might be considered in some way a prequel to this book, one does not need to have read that book to gain the full benefit from this book. They complement each other but offer different tools for you to bring into your life.

Questions for Reflection: Getting Started

- In what ways in your life do you feel that you are "spinning your wheels, stuck in a rut"? In other words, using effort to force something to change (perhaps yourself, circumstances you can't control)? How well is that working for you?

- What is your current relationship with emotional unease? When you encounter difficult emotional experiences involving anger, sadness, fear, frustration, disappointment, anxiety, and other unpleasant emotions, how do you tend to react? Do you tend to push away your feelings? Plow through and carry on? Get caught in your feelings and have them run the show? Respond with kindness and compassion to what you are feeling?

- Are there certain difficult emotions that you accept and others that you resist?

- In what ways do you feel like you need to change or improve yourself in order to have a better life? How well has that worked for you?

- What are the things that you already accept about yourself in all your human imperfectness? What is that like when you rest in this acceptance?

- Do the actions you take in your life tend to be aligned with who you are at your core and bring about a deeper sense of well-being?

- What do you do when you are upset? Do you have healthy ways of soothing or comforting yourself when you feel distress?

- Do you ever judge yourself for feeling how you feel or feel that you shouldn't feel that way? What does that inner dialogue sound like in your head? What does it feel like in your body when you think those things?

CHAPTER 2

You're Running on
an Old Operating System

How We Disconnect from Ourselves

We lose ourselves early in life. It is often a slow loss, an insidious one that creeps in without us having any idea of what is happening. Because of our early experiences, because of cultural conditioning, because of the messages we download unconsciously from the people and media around us, because of implicit societal messages, we think we need to be different, do different, or look different in order to be loved, accepted, and valued. At the core of this is a nagging sense of "not enough." This happens to most of us. It happens to the most accomplished of us, the ones who seem to have it all together, the outwardly successful, the doubtful, the warriors, and the wounded. It happens in part because we disconnect from our feelings and from the parts of ourselves that can offer us the greatest comfort. It happens in part because of our evolutionary wiring, because of the nature of childhood, because of our social conditioning, and in part because of the ways we disconnect from our bodies and hearts in an effort to protect ourselves. This disconnection is often a significant loss that comes at the cost of our well-being.

This chapter will explore the many reasons and ways we disconnect and will lay the foundation for reconnecting with our "well" of well-being.

What We Shove Away

To this day I'm still not sure why I shoved the button up my nose, but I distinctly remember doing it. Was it boredom, curiosity, the need to do something—anything—to distract myself from this strange place of learning where students were paddled when they did something wrong, and one student was even put under the teacher's desk and lightly kicked for misbehaving? I kid you not, this was the early 1970s, Wichita, Kansas, and while it is horrifying for me to believe it now, wooden paddles existed and were used well more than on one occasion during the year I spent there. Between this fear of getting paddled (and making sure I never did anything wrong to end up in trouble), fear of the tornadoes (yes, we had tornado drills instead of fire drills), and adjusting to this recent move from Michigan to Kansas, I recall an uneasiness during that year of first grade that may have had something to do with the button ending up in my nose.

Not realizing my strength, I shoved this little button up there pretty deep and was alarmed to discover that I couldn't get it out. It had completely disappeared into some unreachable crevice in my nose that I was unaware even existed. I recall the sudden and panicky feeling and the sinking feeling at the same time in the pit of my stomach when I realized I could not retrieve it. Not knowing what else to do, I raised my hand from my little wooden desk and asked to go to the nurse's office, a place that had become quite familiar to me during that year. The nurse called my mother and I remember the relief when she arrived to take me home for "not feeling well," something that I recall convincing myself reassuringly was not a lie. I never told anyone about the button. I was ashamed, embarrassed. In time, I forgot about it.

Until months later, maybe a year, when I had a visit with the ear-nose-and-throat doctor to follow up with me for a genetic hearing loss. To my surprise when he looked in my nose, he pulled out this hard white object. "A button, hmm, I wonder how that got there," he pondered out loud. I had almost entirely forgotten about it and now here it was, uncomfortably making a surprise re-appearance. I shrank in the chair, acting like I had no idea how it possibly could have gotten there.

Was it just the button, or my sadness, loneliness, and unease that got shoved inside with it that I was reacting to? This button was hardly the first, nor the last thing that I shoved away and hoped would be forgotten over the course of my lifetime. What else did I, do we, push away in the hopes that in time it will just go away? How often do we learn, at an early age, to put away uncomfortable emotions, to push things deep inside of us, thinking that somehow by doing so we won't have to deal with them again? How often do well-meaning people tell us to cheer up, "Wipe that sadness off your face," "Here, have some ice cream to feel better," or "Cut it out and shape up" when you're angry—without taking the time to listen to the pain underneath that is longing for expression, longing to be heard.

What about the messages we learn from society around us, and from advertising and the media—that if we just purchase this item or drink this Kool-Aid our lives will be better, happier, like the airbrushed photos of the perfect-looking people who entice us into thinking we too can have that idyllic life if we just buy in? And it is not just the messages and atmosphere around us, but within us, that innately drives us to put away our uncomfortable emotions. Our evolutionary wiring, our biological inheritance, plays a strong role in our pursuit of pleasure and avoidance of pain, because that was what helped our ancestors survive. But the pain we tend to avoid in our modern lives is not the pain of being bitten by a poisonous snake or being eaten by a tiger, it's the avoidance of emotional pains and hurts that we instinctually (and because we haven't been taught otherwise) push away in the service of our well-being.

The problem is, in the end that rarely if ever works. The button I shoved in my nose didn't disappear—it just lay dormant until such a later time when it could rear its snot-covered head. The emotional pains we stuff away, the feelings we suppress, don't go away, they just come out in other ways—perhaps as anxiety, or depression, or addictions, or distractions—that take us away from the richness of our lives. Research tells us that when we push our emotions away, this does not help us cope better in the long run but in fact has negative consequences for our well-being.[6] As the saying goes in psychology: "What we resist, persists."

The Habitual Ways that We Deal with Our Inner Emotional Life

Most everyone has their own habitual way of dealing with their inner emotional life. For me for many years, busyness was a way I could keep moving and not have to sit with all that was uncomfortable. I believe this began to some extent as a strategy after my mom died when I was in high school, to help me cope with what would have been, I feared, otherwise overwhelming grief. It was not a conscious decision, but I threw myself into my schoolwork and my activities without missing a day of school, or a beat. This busyness continued through college and graduate school and became a familiar and habitual way in which I lived my life. I became good at keeping my feelings to myself and being unaware of the way this disconnection was seeping into my life in other ways, in the form of anxiety and disordered eating. While I love being busy (still to this day) and find joy in much of what I do, it was in the busyness that I lost myself, became disconnected from my deepest emotions, and with it, the full aliveness that comes with holding the whole range of human emotions. And it was in the stillness that I rediscovered the deeper and more expansive parts of myself that allowed me to turn toward the whole of my experience and embrace all of it.

From my experience working with hundreds of people over the years, it seems to me that many people often fall into one of three camps, or some combination of these: 1) they are good at resisting and ultimately suppressing unwanted feelings; 2) they are largely unaware of or ignore their emotions and yet these emotions occur like a slow drip in the background, affecting their day-to-day lives in ways they don't realize, or 3) they tend to get swallowed up by their emotions, often fighting against them and reacting in unhelpful ways or feeling overwhelmed by their emotions. Often, people can vacillate between all three. I know I have.

These three ways of relating to our inner emotional experiences can lead to greater unease, anxiety, discontent, frustration, depression, numbing out, exploding, unhealthy habits, addictions, or just going through the motions but missing the full richness that is possible. The additional consequence of this can be that we then feel that we need to change ourselves or our lives in some way in order to feel better, not realizing that what we may need instead is to help these parts of ourselves that are holding these emotions feel seen and listened to in a new way.

Questions for Reflection: Handling Difficult Emotions

- What is your habitual way of responding to difficult emotions?

- What messages did you learn as a child about what emotions were okay to feel, express, and share, and what ones were not?

- Are there emotions or parts of yourself that you have shoved away in the service of your happiness?

- How well has that worked for you? What might you have gained and lost in doing so? In what ways did they make a reappearance—like my button—perhaps in unexpected or undesired ways?

- Have you ever had an experience of greeting your difficult emotions with kindness, care, and a listening ear? If so, how did that feel?

The six vantage points taught in this book offer an alternative to this more habitual way of reacting to life's challenges and our accompanying emotional discomfort. Each one allows us to be with our difficult emotions without pushing them away or getting swallowed up and swept away by them. This is fundamental to how the six vantage points can help us find greater ease and well-being, even amidst our suffering. When we are neither fighting nor avoiding what is here, when we are not struggling to change our inner experience or ourselves in the process, we open to deeper qualities of acceptance, care, and connection that can soothe and comfort our emotional distress. From this place we also have access to greater inner resources that naturally guide us toward wise actions in the service of our long-term well-being. In this way, we don't have to change ourselves or our experiences, yet something foundational begins to shift.

Each one allows us to be with our difficult emotions without pushing them away or getting swallowed up and swept away by them.

How Did We End Up Here Anyway?

Unconsciously I held my breath when I saw the caller ID. It was my son, and it was only minutes before that I had seen him back out of our driveway in his usual mad dash, wait-until-the-last-minute to leave for school frenzy. I answered with a bit of trepidation in my voice but was quickly relieved when he sounded okay and all in one piece. Still, his voice was concerned, saying he had pulled over because something was "wrong" with the car. He described that it didn't feel right, wasn't moving freely, and then he realized he started to smell smoke or like something was burning. Given he was a new driver and a male teenager, I was relieved he had the wherewithal to immediately pull onto a side street and call me, even though this would make him late for school. Minutes later I arrived on the scene, and I too smelled

the burning odor and wondered what could possibly be wrong,
since we had just had the car tuned up weeks before. I did a
quick walk-around inspection, and when nothing wrong jumped
out at me, I scooted into the driver's seat to give it a quick test
drive myself. Within seconds I discovered the problem: the
emergency brake was on, and he had been driving with it on for
at least a half mile down the road. No wonder the burning! No
car is designed to be driven with its emergency brake engaged.
It is only to be used for times when the car is stationary and for,
well, emergencies. But my son hadn't realized it was on. When
the brake was released, the car immediately returned to its easy,
smooth ride. (Whew, no permanent damage as it turned out.).
The other systems of the car could go back to doing what they
were supposed to be doing, without being overridden and in-
terrupted by this brake that was impeding it. Natural ease was
restored to the ride.

Without realizing it, we can go through much of our lives with our emergency brake engaged. Many people operate unconsciously from old, adaptive survival circuitry much of the time. These survival programs, which evolved over millions of years through evolution to help our species survive, have a lot to do with the habitual ways that we experience and react to our difficult emotions. These complex networks in our brain and nervous system were designed to protect us and help us survive life-threatening emergencies, to detect threat and danger such as sabertooth tigers lurking nearby, and to prepare us to mobilize resources to manage that threat by fighting or fleeing, or in some cases freezing. While not designed for some of our more modern-day challenges of day-to-day life as we now know it, these survival circuits often take over when we come up against challenges, acting like that emergency brake that was stuck in the on position even when it was not needed. Instead of a nice fluid, smooth ride, there is friction, tension, stuck-ness, and a jerky ride when we go through our lives with our emergency brake engaged. That creates unease and unnecessary wear and tear. We don't need to go buy another car; our car already has everything it needs. We simply need to learn how to release the emergency brake so that the other systems of the car can naturally do what they are designed to do and come back into balance.

Wired for Survival

One of the things that takes us away from well-being in this human life is that we are running much of the time on evolutionary wiring from over millions of years ago that helped our ancestors survive. The automatic, adaptive survival programs that we run on play a role in our reaction to life's events and they play a role in the second arrow of suffering that we experience.

In order to understand how we can deepen our well of well-being, it can be helpful to first understand how getting stuck in our old survival circuitry contributes to unease right from the get-go and can disconnect us from access to our Whole Self. Here is another analogy to consider:

Imagine for a moment that you have one of those original IBM computers from the early 1980s—you know, those big, clunky, heavy computers that at the time seemed quite revolutionary. Imagine operating throughout your day and life with this computer today. It would be slow, it would be inefficient, it wouldn't be able to do all the things that our more modern-day computers can do. If this was the only computer you had, you wouldn't be working or perhaps even living up to your full potential. At the time when this original computer was developed, it served an important purpose in transforming how information was processed, accessed, and shared. But over time, technology has evolved so much that forty-plus years later our new computers are capable of so much more, and they allow us to do things in our lives that we couldn't do prior.

If you only had access to that old IBM computer, imagine how limiting that might be. What if you didn't even realize that there were newer computers available, and you thought that this was just the way things are?

In some ways, it is as if we all operate from this old IBM computer more than we may realize. You see, some of the networks in our brain are wired to operate from old survival programs. While this is a normal and necessary happening to move in and out of these states as we go through our day, when we encounter difficult experiences many of us can get stuck in these threat programs and not have other ways of responding. **When we don't realize the access we have to our newer operating system (which we will explore in more depth in Chapter 3), we are cut off from tremendous inner resources that can help us navigate life's challenges and the accompanying difficult emotions we encounter.**

How Our Survival Wiring Contributes to Our Emotional Unease

The brain and nervous system first and foremost operate in service of our survival with the job of trying to keep us safe. Neural circuits in our brain and *autonomic nervous system* (the part of the nervous system that regulates involuntary processes such as heart rate, breathing, blood pressure, and more) are involved in constantly scanning our environment for cues of safety and cues of danger and threat, in an unconscious process called neuroception.[7] When there are more cues of threat and not enough cues of safety, we reflexively react in self-protective and defensive ways.

An important part of our survival circuitry has to do with this innate threat response. As you might imagine, back in the Stone Age, being able to detect external physical threats such as predators, and then having a way to respond to those threats, was essential for survival. Our *amygdala*, a small, almond-shaped structure in our midbrain, along with surrounding structures, plays an important role in scanning our environment for salient information and for what is familiar versus unfamiliar.[8] Other parts of our brain also (*temporal cortex, periaqueductal gray, and insula*) and our autonomic nervous system[9] (carrying signals from our body) act like a surveillance system.

When a potential threat or danger is perceived by the autonomic nervous system, neural circuits fire in response to allow us to mobilize in order to fight or flee (or, in some cases, freeze/immobilize/play dead). This makes good sense in that, according to Lisa Barrett,[10] our brain's most important job is to figure out how to best allocate resources to regulate our body and all its functions in a way that allows us to survive and be well. Mobilizing to escape a predator (ramping up all of our resources) or playing dead (shutting down our resources) when escape is not possible makes good evolutionary sense.

In our modern world however (and in places not in the midst of war), we don't typically face "tigers" or similar external physical threats. Instead, our threats tend to come in the form of other kinds of real or perceived challenges: day-to-day stressors of all sorts; worries about future "what ifs," feelings of self-doubt, feelings of not good enough, sickness and aging, juggling the demands of work and family, arguments with loved ones, work stress, relationship struggles, etc. It is not that these things are not challenging—because they often are. It is that our habitual automatic reaction to try and protect ourselves in the face of these "threats"—when we get stuck there—is not necessarily the one that will be most helpful in the long term.

In the face of these modern-day threats, our protection circuitry gets activated. While we may not literally fight or flee or freeze, our nervous system's response might lead us to a more modern-day version of arguing, exploding; engaging in avoidant or addictive behaviors; over-consuming food, material items or social media/electronics; feeling overwhelmed and getting stuck in procrastination; living in chronic states of anxiety; or even collapsing from emotional exhaustion or burnout. Even in the face of the very real threats that the COVID pandemic brought to so many, our more primitive automatic responses (e.g., for me, walking around in a heightened state of anxiety) were not necessarily the ones that helped keep us safer.

Another vestige of our survival brain, and one that plays a key role in how we process emotions, is that we tend to seek what is pleasant and avoid what is unpleasant. This was a biological survival strategy for our ancestors who needed to avoid external dangers like poisonous plants or getting bitten by a snake, and who needed to seek pleasant-tasting foods and sex for survival.[11] While this served us well in avoiding external threats, the carryover of this in our contemporary lives is that much of what we tend to avoid is the unpleasantness of our own inner experiences. We tend to push away emotions that are unpleasant, and we chase after feeling good in many ways, some of which don't always serve our long-term well-being. Modern psychology has shown us that the more we try to escape from our own internal sensations, feelings, and thoughts, the more we can get stuck and suffer in unintended ways.[11]

There are additional aspects of our evolutionary wiring that developed in the service of survival that tend to operate in the background of our lives like that old IBM computer. One is that our minds tend to spend much time in the past and future, and relatively far less time in the present moment. It was likely adaptive for our ancestors to be constantly thinking about the future or past to inform their every action. You can imagine that sitting around and smelling the roses may not have had as positive an evolutionary outcome as thinking and planning and worrying about where the next meal was coming from.[12]

Another mental habit is that we tend to get caught in mental activity involving self-judgment, self-criticism, and distorted thinking (often overestimating threats, catastrophizing, imagining worst-case scenarios, etc.). Having fears of messing up, being hard on ourselves for mistakes, being driven from a place of scarcity and "not good enough" may have existed in the service of trying to protect our ancestors from life-threatening situations and being ostracized from the tribe but leaves us feeling depleted in our modern lives.

An additional mental habit that contributes to our unease is that our brains have a negativity bias.[13] That is, we tend to focus on the negatives and overlook the positives. From a survival point of view this may have been effective, but when we view ourselves through this lens, we see all the ways we fall short and easily overlook our own strengths that are here to draw on.

The Consequences of Being Stuck in Survival Mode

When we are in the grip of our old evolutionary wiring and its accompanying mental habits (without the regulatory input from our newer operating system that we will explore in Chapter 3), here is a closer look at how this can contribute to our emotional unease and to our habitual reactions to emotional experiences:

1. Our nervous system becomes dysregulated. Our threat response often overfires in the service of trying to protect us, by perceiving danger when there isn't really danger (e.g., too much to do, traffic jams, feeling misunderstood), and/or by initiating the fight-or-flight or freeze (collapse/shut down) reaction when it may not be the most effective response at addressing the problem at hand (e.g., going into a state of panic when my computer crashes). In the grips of our stress response, when more primitive parts of our brain "hijack" our higher thinking centers, we experience tunnel vision, or our thinking becomes scattered and overwhelmed, and it is harder to see a bigger picture.

2. We spend much of our time thinking about the past and future, reliving or rehearsing unpleasant events that can contribute to anxiety, depression, and unease. We might be anxious about an upcoming meeting and worry about this for days, when there is little we can do about it, and yet it consumes much of our attention. We might ruminate for days or longer about something that happened that we are angry about, without realizing how much this is draining our energy and keeping our anger going. It is estimated that we spend about 50 percent of our lives thinking about something other than what is actually happening right in the present moment.[14]

3. We close ourselves off to our difficult emotions (or get hijacked by them); we push away what is unpleasant and try to cling to what is pleasant. In doing so, we resist our inner experiences and fight against feelings that are unpleasant. This resistance—to fight, suppress, or try to ignore difficult emotions—takes up tremendous emotional energy and doesn't leave room for comforting our own pain. When I am going through a difficult situation and ignore my feelings, it's like putting a lid on a pot of boiling water; it eventually overflows in one way or another. When I berate myself for feeling how I do, or tell myself I shouldn't feel this way, this certainly makes me feel worse. When we push away parts of ourselves that feel pain, hurt, or suffering, in an effort to protect ourselves, we often judge our own inner experience as weak, wrong, or something we shouldn't feel.

4. We create narratives that are often inaccurate, distorted, and self-critical, and we get entangled in these stories and thoughts as if they are absolute truth. For many years I thought that I wasn't enough, that I needed to look different, accomplish more, in order to be okay. Believing these thoughts contributed greatly to my emotional suffering. Even on a day-to-day basis, our mental chatter and inner dialogue can increase our stress and distress in ways we often don't realize.

5. We overfocus on the negatives not only in our lives, but in ourselves, and we under-appreciate all of our strengths and the things we do well. This leaves us feeling lacking, self-critical, and often falling short, and leaves us little access to the rich array of strengths that we have to help us meet challenges at hand.

Christopher Germer[15] describes that when the body's threat response is triggered by inner threats (challenges to our sense of self and/or emotional challenges), our fight-flight-freeze response (designed to deal with outer threats) is turned inward. Our modern-day version of fight turns into self-criticism; our flight response turns into isolation; and our version of freeze turns into rumination. In this way, we disconnect from ourselves and from the inner resources we have to comfort ourselves.

In this way, we disconnect from ourselves and from the inner resources we have to comfort ourselves.

So, in essence, as much as we suffer because of the many uncontrollable aspects of this human life, we suffer additionally because of our mental and biological habits. While our brain and nervous system are doing what they are wired to do and trying to help keep us safe, when locked in our threat response we are cut off from well-being. These networks of the brain and nervous system, operating from an old evolutionary program, can sometimes lose connection with the regulatory input of our newer operating system (which you will learn about). When this happens, we don't have full access to other inner resources that are available to help us meet our challenges.

It is important to note that our survival circuits are necessary and adaptive in many respects and perform essential daily regulatory functions. However, *being stuck* in our survival circuitry limits our capacity to access a whole range of wider inner resources that can enrich our lives. Importantly, while I refer throughout this book to our "older operating system" or "survival circuits" and our "newer operating system" or "thriving circuits" please know that these are metaphors to help understand what is happening inside our bodies and minds; it is not quite that simple or an either/or scenario. In reality, this inner wiring is quite complex and interconnected and these systems are constantly operating in tandem to various degrees as we move through the day. It is when these systems are in balance and we have a good amount of input from our "newer operating system" that we experience our deepest well-being.

The good news is that we already have thriving circuits, and they can help us immensely when we are dealing with emotional distress and unease of all kinds. When these thriving circuits are engaged, they help to keep our survival circuits in balance (rather than our survival circuitry taking over completely). This balance creates important regulation in the nervous system, allowing things to operate more smoothly. From this state of regulation, we are able to access more inner resources (e.g., perspective taking, problem solving, self-compassion, creative thinking, etc.) to deal with the challenges at hand.

These thriving circuits are not often what we default to though in the midst of emotional storms, so we need a little extra practice to find our way there. Also, our threat system is quicker to react than our thriving circuits, so learning how to access our thriving circuits is essential in the face of challenges. When we can understand how our brain and nervous system work, it empowers us and gives us increased choice to meet life's challenges with greater ease and well-being.

When we are caught in contraction, tension, stress, fear, self-criticism, denial, suppression of emotions, resistance, etc., we don't have access to all our tools. But when

When we can understand how our brain and nervous system work, it empowers us and gives us increased choice to meet life's challenges with greater ease and well-being.

we are in our natural state of openness, curiosity, care, compassion, and awareness, we can move through the world with much greater ease. When we are operating so much of the time stuck in our old survival circuitry, we are disconnected from possibilities that can help us find ease, comfort, and even peace amidst the challenges of this human life. We are disconnected from the deep well of well-being upon which we can draw strength and nourishment. **Each time you shift to one of the six vantage points that you will learn, you gain access to your thriving circuits. This book shows you how.**

Why You Can't Comfort Yourself when You're Running from a Tiger

The fact that we have this survival wiring and threat system is not in itself a problem. It is healthy, necessary, and adaptive in certain situations and helps us orient toward what is salient and may need our attention. Being able to mobilize is essential in situations where there are real threats, and we need some mobilizing energy to help us approach everyday tasks, accomplish goals, and stand up for ourselves when we feel wronged. Being able to know when to shut down, step away, or withdraw at times can be self-protective and skillful. Importantly, these survival networks have crucial regulatory functions in our body when we are not reacting to danger. Additionally, our survival networks and thriving networks work in tandem, allocating resources to try and keep our bodies functioning optimally.

But often, we spend large amounts of time with our threat system overactivated without even being aware of this. At the same time,

What our survival brain thinks is keeping us safe may actually take us away from a deeper sense of inner peace and ease.

our habitual way of reacting in the face of any threat does not always serve us in the most beneficial way. What our survival brain thinks is keeping us safe may actually take us away from a deeper sense of inner peace and ease. And when we are operating from an overactive or misinformed survival circuitry, naturally and adaptively, we tend to experience tunnel vision (it isn't adaptive to see the big picture when we are running from a tiger), we have less access to our higher cortical "thinking" networks, we experience greater tension physically and feel greater emotional distress.[16] While we have more newly evolved systems that help us experience care and compassion, we can't access this when we are in the grips of perceived threats that overpower our sense of perceived safety.

Even when our threats are very real (such as during the pandemic or dealing with an illness or loss in our life), our habitual and automatic survival responses, as stated above, may not always be the ones that are most adaptive. Here is an illustration of this.

Consider these two scenarios:

Version 1: It is smack in the early stages of the pandemic, a surreal, catastrophic global event that has stopped us all in our tracks. I wake up in a cold sweat, heart starting to race, very quickly pulling me out of my sleep and into the darkness of the room, alone with my thoughts. I am fearful about the uncertainty that abounds and find it especially challenging for someone who seeks such comfort in being able to control everything I can. My husband appears to be sleeping peacefully next to me, but I start to worry about his well-being, especially considering his work requires him to go to the hospital on a regular basis to see patients, some of whom may have COVID. My mind starts to race, jumping to worst-case scenarios and trying to find resolution, as if I have a handful of puzzle pieces and am desperately trying to put together a whole, coherent picture when there is none to be had. I think about the loss and fear that so many are feeling, and this only increases my anxiety. I replay clips of bad news in ruminating loops in my mind. My mind continues to play out future scary scenarios over which there is nothing I can do anything about. I try to block these out, attempting to stop the cascade of emotions that follow, but find that I am getting more upset with myself that I can't stop these emotions, and that now I am keeping myself more awake. I wonder what is wrong with me that I can't control my anxiety and just fall back to sleep for goodness' sake.

Version 2: I wake up in a cold sweat, heart starting to race and very quickly pulling me out of my sleep and into the darkness of the room, alone with my thoughts. My mind starts to race to the well-being of my family members, my community, and the world at large, and to fearful and catastrophic thoughts about all the "what ifs" that start to parade through my mind. I put a hand on my heart and the other hand on my abdomen as I take slow, deep, rhythmical breaths in and out to the count of five, imagining being rocked by these breaths. I bring my awareness to the warmth of the blankets weighing heavily on my body and the softness of the pillow that cradles my head. I feel the support of the mattress underneath me and invite my body to soften into it so that it is not quite so rigid, tense, and tight. I become curious about this anxiety that has come to visit me, yet again, in the wee morning hours. I notice the inclination to want to push it away and get rid of it, but I try to imagine it as a guest that I allow into my home to sit across from me in my living room, so that I can look at it with friendly eyes. I start to notice that my mind is running way into the future, and as it does, that my heart rate quickens, as if I am preparing to run from a tiger. I thank this primitive circuitry for trying to protect me but remind myself that I have more newly evolved ways to help me feel safe.

I invite something else to sit side-by-side with the anxiety that is now taking up a lot of space on my imagined couch: some caring, soothing energy, as if a loving parent is holding a frightened child. I see more clearly the way that my mind is creating much added suffering for myself through all its imagined future catastrophes, with which I of course cannot cope because they haven't actually happened. I remind myself of the refuge I feel when running through the woods nearby with its running streams and still lake. With my hand still on my heart, I imagine breathing out a feeling of compassion and care for all those who are suffering, as if it could reach them. I sense into something that is vaster and more spacious in this moment than my fear—the care and courage of so many, the interconnectedness of us all, and a sense of the awareness itself that holds all of it, the good, the bad, and the ugly. Residing there, I let the anxiety wash over me as my breath continues to rock me to a still, quiet place of rest.

In version one of the vignette above, you can see many of the mental habits we explored above played out in action: 1) my body was going into threat mode even though in that moment, I was safe in my bed; 2) my mind was wandering to the future and getting stuck there; 3) I was engaging in self-critical narratives about "What's wrong with me that I'm feeling this way?"; 4) I was trying to push away the anxiety; and 5) my mind was focusing on all the negatives. In version two, the mental habits are still there but I am not as caught in them and am able to relate to my emotional experience in a new way that brings me to a deeper place of peace.

Living through our global pandemic has given me ample time to observe my own threat response, which, like most people, had been turned on quite a lot. Me lying in bed, gripped by fear thoughts running through my head, heart pounding, playing out worst-case scenarios in a heightened state of arousal, was not helping me be safer amidst the pandemic. The fact that this happened from time to time was a normal human response, and in and of itself, not a problem.

But when caught in an old survival response, if that were to take over and be the only way that I could relate to what was happening in the moment, it could lead to increased suffering for me. Now, if I were being chased by a tiger, or dodging out of the way of an oncoming car, this fight-or-flight response would be highly adaptive. My heart rate would increase to get blood to my fighting muscles. My thinking would narrow so that my only focus was on escaping. I wouldn't have access to more newly evolved systems that could calm me, but I wouldn't need to calm myself if my life depended on fleeing. No need to relate differently to my internal experience under that circumstance. But in this case, while the threat of the pandemic was very real, my instinctual way to try and protect myself was not in fact protective.

When I could appreciate it's the nature of the mind and body to respond in this way, I could thank my old wiring for trying to protect me and then use the six vantage points (which you will learn!) to help me relate to what was happening in a different way, allowing for greater comfort and ease. More about this in chapters to come!

You Don't Have to Change to Change Everything: A Newer Operating System

We Already Have What We Need

The other day I was frantic, in a frenzy, looking for my keys to my office—the office that I hadn't been to in the almost two years since the start of this pandemic. I had put those keys away in a safe spot, in a spot I would surely remember. I am organized when it comes to things like this. I have a home for everything, and when things leave their so-called home—to be used, perused, modified, or otherwise—they make it back to safe return. So, I looked in all the potential places where I would store keys, where I would put something important, knowing someday I would want to access it again. Not in that cabinet. Not in that drawer. Not in my work bag. Not in my car. Maybe my husband took them—no, not in his possession . . . nowhere to be found. Getting more frantic now, feeling as if something could vanish in thin air and make you feel like you are losing your mind because you know that you put them in a safe place. And then, in a moment of clarity as the frenetic energy settled, I looked in my pocketbook in the pouch where I had always kept them, the place they had been for years, and with a sigh and a laugh, there they were waiting for me.

We spend so much time looking outside of ourselves, trying to find answers in all kinds of unlikely places, searching for that thing that we know is somehow here and yet it feels nowhere within sight. We can feel frantic in our search and let down when we come up empty-handed. But what if we were looking in the wrong place? What if we could discover that we have everything we need and it is right here, right now, within us? We simply forgot to look in the one place where it always has been—waiting patiently to be discovered.

We spend so much time trying to resist what is here or trying to change the things that we can't (the second noble truth in Buddhist teachings) and this drains our energy. We are putting our efforts in the wrong direction. It is like pulling and pulling a locked and bolted door to try and get outside, not realizing that there is a back door, and it is wide open, and we can just walk out.

Fortunately, in addition to our threat system, we also have a built-in "caring system"—more newly evolved circuits in our brain and nervous system that help bring us into connection with others and with ourselves. According to *polyvagal theory*,[18] developed by Dr. Stephen Porges, there are three pathways of our autonomic nervous system that evolved in an evolutionary hierarchy in the service of our survival. Our most primitive pathway, involving the dorsal branch of our vagus nerve, travels and winds from the brainstem to the stomach and responds to cues of extreme danger by protecting us with a freeze response. This immobilization response helped our reptilian ancestors survive threat by playing dead when faced with a predator. As mentioned above, in our modern lives we don't typically "freeze" per se, but this might appear as dissociating, being stuck in procrastination, numbing out, withdrawing from others, going into a kind of shut down or collapse mode in response to emotional upsets and perceived threats.

The second part of our nervous system to evolve was the sympathetic branch of our nervous system (also referenced in the previous section), which allowed us to mobilize (fight or flee) in response to threat. The most newly evolved part of our nervous system is the *ventral branch* of the vagus nerve, which travels from the base of the brainstem to the neck, throat, eyes, and ears and also has important connections with the heart. This ventral vagus pathway, also referred to as the social engagement system, with its ability to read cues from others' facial expressions and tone of voice, allows us to co-regulate (have one nervous system help calm and regulate another nervous system), process signals of safety, be in connection with others, be soothed and cared for by others, and ultimately, soothe and care for ourselves as well. Importantly, this ventral vagal pathway has connections with the *sinoatrial node* of our heart that slows down the heart rate and helps to downregulate our fight-or-flight response. When our ventral vagal system is engaged, it provides important regulatory energy that acts like a brake on our survival circuitry, allowing us to mobilize energy as necessary without becoming overtaken and diverting all our resources toward protection. With enough cues of safety and access to the regulatory energy of our ventral vagus, we are able to remain in connection rather than slipping into protection.

> *With enough cues of safety and access to the regulatory energy of our ventral vagus, we are able to remain in connection rather than slipping into protection.*

As much as external circumstances can present challenges for us and activate our threat system, our internal responses to our own emotions themselves can also feed the threat system. When we criticize ourselves for having certain feelings, or when we feel we need to push away feelings that might otherwise be too dangerous to feel or deal with, we are activating our threat circuitry. Self-criticism has been found to have similar effects as if someone else is saying those bad things to us.[19] Running from our feelings reinforces the message that this really is something big, bad, and terrible that needs to be avoided. And yet, often these strategies may have had some survival value for us when we were younger (if I am hard on myself, I won't mess up again and be dismissed/left out/yelled at/unloved). More about this later.

One key point here is that understanding our biological wiring offers us a subtle shift in vantage point right from the get-go.

One key point here is that understanding our biological wiring offers us a subtle shift in vantage point right from the get-go. When we are caught in emotions based on our threat system and can understand our propensity for these emotions to get activated, it steps us out of blame or shame or self-criticism for feeling what we are feeling.[20] This is part of our human condition! This is a part of our nervous system trying to protect us (whether from evolution or from childhood), and we can appreciate its efforts to do so. But it is empowering to know that we have more newly evolved systems that, when engaged, can often offer us better protection, ways to feel safe, soothed, regulated and connected, ways to see more creative solutions and act from a place of deeper values. This can lead to skillful means to meet our challenges. Understanding this more newly evolved system is a critical part of our journey toward greater psychological freedom, self-compassion, and well-being.

When we can learn to engage our newer operating system and invite in more cues of safety for our nervous system, there is more ease and possibility that becomes available. We are no longer stuck in our survival circuitry. **The six vantage points help to activate this more newly evolved system.** When we learn to shift our vantage point, we are also shifting our operating system and the physiology in our body. From there, we have access to a whole array of inner resources, possibilities, and behavior choices that weren't available in survival mode.

We already have all the hardware. No need to look elsewhere, outside of ourselves. We just need to learn how to access this newer system more of the time. We are ever-evolving creatures. This is the next step in our evolution journey!

CHAPTER 3

Getting to Know Your Newer Operating System

Wired for Connection

It was a hot August morning, and the full-on blue Arizona sky was like a vast canopy that covered us as we traveled in our silver sedan rent-a-car through the back roads outside of Sedona. Our GPS led us to a quiet, seemingly untraveled road, and then to another road that was all dirt and gravel. This must be the place, we concluded, as we proceeded to head down this dirt road looking for the trailhead. We had found a hike that seemed perfect for all four of us—not too long or vigorous, but that promised us beautiful vistas. I had expected to enter something that looked like a state park, with paved roads and clear places to park. Not only was this road not paved, but it was filled with huge boulders and became steeper and narrower the further we went. Perhaps a 4x4 Jeep could cross this terrain without issue, but certainly not our rental vehicle without even all-wheel drive. How the average tourist could make this trek was beyond me, but it appeared we were in the correct place. As the road stretched on and deteriorated, so too did my mood. I became increasingly anxious, thinking this was not safe, and I wanted to turn back. Unfortunately, by the time I spoke up there was no way to turn around and the only way forward was down. When our car went over a large boulder and tipped at a 45-degree angle, my daughter screamed from the backseat. Panic set in and I started flipping out. Fear completely took over and put me in a combined state of fight (yelling at my husband that we should never have attempted this) and flight (literally getting out of the car with my daughter and walking/running down the hill, not having the stomach to watch what might happen next).

My son, who must have been about thirteen at the time, remained calm and steady. Either unfazed by the fear that had overtaken my daughter and I, or able to overcome it, he saw the necessity of being a calm presence for my husband, who had to navigate the treacherous terrain. Glancing back, I saw my son get out of the car and bravely stand by my husband's open window as he guided my husband, turn by turn, a little left here, a little right there, past each boulder and through each rocky crevice until he could safely turn the car around. Then patiently and in a steady voice, he guided him back up the dangerous part of the hill, slowly, with an equanimity that was unusual for someone his age. Evaluating each boulder and assessing the best possible path with the least likelihood of the car capsizing, he provided my husband the step-by-step guidance needed to make it back to safe ground.

My nervous system, in the throes of a full-blown survival response, hijacked my ability to navigate this challenge, see a wider perspective, or consider any possibilities other than trying to escape an inescapable situation. I was cut off from my higher-thinking capacities, my ability to calm myself, and my ability

to help my husband who clearly needed guidance to find the best
path out of this quagmire. While it was not in truth a life-threat-
ening emergency, the fear of getting stuck and totaling the car
put me in a state of panic. From that place, I had access to very
few resources to help me manage. My son, on the other hand,
was operating from a much more regulated nervous system. Not
only was he able to override any fear to remain stable and an-
chored, but he was also able to stay in connection with his dad,
guiding him with his ability to see things from a wide angle and
with his calm, steady presence.

From an evolutionary point of view, as much as having a way to respond
to threats was essential to the survival of the species, so too, having a nervous
system that could process signals of safety, help us to feel safe and connected
with one another and soothe one another and ourselves was a biological imperative.[21] For our mammalian species, our caring system (or social engagement system) helped to ensure our survival. Being together and supporting
one another in one's tribe was essential for survival. Additionally, early mammals evolved such that their young were dependent on their mothers for
care. This attachment process of the young is critically dependent upon our
social engagement system—and on a parent nurturing its young. Without
this, infants would not survive. This same caring system also allows us to
self-regulate in the face of challenges, to comfort ourselves, and from this
calm place, to be engaged, curious, willing to explore and approach, and have
access to a fuller behavioral repertoire than when we are in the grips of our
threat response.

Emotionally, when our social engagement system is activated, through the
activity of the ventral branch of the vagus nerve, we feel safe and connected,
and we have access to a wide range of emotional responses including: "calm,
happy, meditative, engaged, attentive, active, interested, excited, passionate,
alert, ready, relaxed, savoring, and joyful."[22] Our compassion response is also
available, thanks to the activity of this ventral vagal pathway, allowing us to

reach out to help others in their suffering and communicate care through our soft eyes, tone of voice, and tilt of head. Importantly, this same pathway helps us to turn toward our *own* suffering with self-compassion. As Kristen Neff describes,[23] when we can activate our mammalian care system, we replace our threat response of self-criticism, isolation, and rumination with self-kindness, common humanity (sense of not being alone), and mindfulness—the three core elements of self-compassion.

And as nature would have it, there are also strong health benefits of the regulatory influence of our ventral branch of our vagus nerve. When our caring system is activated, oxytocin and endorphins are released, which help to reduce stress and increase feelings of well-being, safety, and security.[24] When we experience balanced input from the ventral vagus, not only do we feel safe and connected, but the other parts of our nervous system are able to do the jobs they were meant to do when not responding to threats. Just as police officers or firefighters may have essential jobs they can perform when they are not responding to life-threatening emergencies, so too our sympathetic and dorsal vagal systems have important jobs in helping to keep our bodies balanced and in homeostasis. Our sympathetic nervous system helps to regulate our breathing and heart rhythms. Our dorsal vagal pathway plays an important role in digesting our food, and in helping us rest and conserve energy and refuel. When our nervous system is in balance, we experience more optimal states of inner balance, and our energy and metabolic resources can be allocated toward rest, recovery. and growth.[25]

None of these physical or emotional benefits are available when we are in the grip of the threat response. However, as we learn to shift our vantage point, we engage more ventral vagal energy and these inner resources become available to us. Imagine unlocking a toolkit in which you could access calm, clarity, connection, compassion, creativity, self-compassion, gratitude, acceptance, equanimity, and an ability to see a bigger perspective, among other things. It makes sense that these qualities would not be available if you were fleeing from a tiger; but, when you rest in a regulated nervous system that feels safe, these qualities become possible to experience. **The six vantage points will help you unlock this toolkit.**

All Our Emotions Have a Purpose

Not only do we have a nervous system that evolved to help us survive as a species, but this nervous system allowed us to experience a whole range of emotions that had evolutionary value for our ancestors.

According to Dr. Paul Gilbert,[26] there is a three-circle model of emotions that helps to explain the origins and function of our emotions. Our most primitive system of emotional regulation, our threat system, is all about protecting us and keeping us safe, and emotions such as anger, fear, and disgust did just that. Anger allowed us to fight, fear helped us avoid dangers, and disgust helped us to rid ourselves of and avoid poisons and other dangerous things. In addition, emotions such as shame could be seen as self-protective in terms of removing oneself from the tribe when one behaved badly, to avoid further being ostracized. We evolved for this threat system to be always turned on. Our second system of emotions, our drive system, helps us engage in goal-directed behaviors and accomplish things, and involves emotions such as being driven, excited, and vital. While this system can involve positive emotions, it also involves high arousal, and operating too much from this system can leave us chasing after goals in a more stressed manner. Our third system of emotions, according to Gilbert, the soothing system, involves caregiving behaviors and emotions such as feeling safe, contented, and connected. This third system is the heart of where compassion lives, and it offers a very different quality of positive emotions than the drive system. In this system, Dr. Gilbert says that our bodies are in "rest and digest" mode, with our parasympathetic nervous systems and vagus nerve more active. It is in this system that we can calm threats, and where attachment of infant and mother can occur. Ideally, we need each of these systems to work together. Dr. Gilbert proposes that most of our emotional distress comes from an *underactivation* of our caring system, which many of us experience.

Dennis Tirsch,[27] building upon this model, describes that our threat system, which is protection and safety seeking, leads to narrowed focused attention directed toward the potential threat (and unable to see a wider perspective), tension in the body, and avoidant behaviors. Our drive system is reward-focused (wanting, pursuing, achieving) and also tends to involve more narrowly focused attention driven toward acquiring, and a narrow behavioral repertoire as we move toward what we want. In contrast, with the caring system, our attention is more open and receptive, allowing for flexibility in our perspective, greater capacity for empathy, and peaceful and prosocial behavior.

Barbara Fredrickson, a pioneering voice in the field of Positive Psychology, provides yet another evolutionary lens through which to understand positive emotions. In her groundbreaking book *Positivity*,[28] she shared research that supports why positive emotions (such as love, joy, gratitude, serenity, interest) were so important for our survival. While she describes how negative emotions narrow our thinking and action repertoire (as was necessary when our ancestors were faced with threats), she posits that positive emotions "broaden and build" our thinking and our behavioral repertoire, allowing for greater exploration, choices, and possibilities. According to Fredrickson, whereas negative emotions mattered more for our immediate survival (feeling anger and fighting a predator, or feeling fear and fleeing), positive emotions mattered more over time, across the bigger picture, by encouraging exploration, creativity, experiential learning, broadening our outlook, and allowing us to see possibilities that we wouldn't otherwise see. She explains how positive emotions build physical, mental, psychological, and social resources that help us experience greater resilience and well-being.

The fact that when we are under the influence and regulation of our more newly evolved circuitry we have access to a broader array of inner resources is an essential part of understanding why we don't have to change in order to change everything.

The fact that when we are under the influence and regulation of our more newly evolved circuitry we have access to a broader array of inner resources is an essential part of understanding why we don't have to change in order to change everything.

We already have this newly evolved circuitry. Once we learn how to engage it more consistently, we also have access to all the rich resources that it gives us. This includes being able to take a half step back instead of being caught in what is happening, being able to pause and access our inner guidance about what is most important to us and what is most needed in the moment, being able to comfort ourselves and others, being able to access heart-focused qualities that allow us to hold our suffering in a more self-compassionate way, and experiencing a greater sense of oneness and connection versus isolation.

All our emotions serve a purpose; they are not good or bad and there is nothing wrong with feeling any emotion. But many of our more depleting emotions are activated by old evolutionary pathways in the service of our survival. Our modern-day version of the fight-or-flight (or freeze) response is not running from or fighting a tiger (or playing dead), but it might look more like: perceiving a "threat" when you get in a disagreement and get very angry; worrying that people don't like you and staying in your room/isolating or sinking into despair; thinking about all the possible bad things that might happen in the future and experiencing anxiety; having your computer crash and going into panic/freak-out mode (I can attest to this one); fixating on all the things that you have done wrong and sinking into a depressed mood.

Our initial feelings are not a problem. Where often the stuck-ness comes in is in how we relate to what is showing up. Sadness is not a problem, but if we push it away or tell ourselves we shouldn't be feeling this, or if it becomes so consuming that we can't engage in our lives, then it becomes more problematic. Often it is the "second arrow"—that is, how we are relating to our emotions—that increases our suffering. Pushing away sadness may lead to anxiety in its place. Attaching negative narratives to our sadness might lead to depression.

Putting Your Unpleasant Emotions in a More Spacious Container

There is a teaching from the Buddhist tradition shared to me by meditation teachers that if you take a teaspoon of salt and put it into a cup of water, that water would be extremely salty. If you imagined drinking it, it might be hard to bear. But if you took that same teaspoon of salt and put it into a pond or lake, that salt would be hardly noticeable. It is the exact same teaspoon of salt, but held in the vast expanse of the water, the experience of that salt transforms.

When we can hold our difficult experiences and accompanying uncomfortable emotions within a vaster and more expansive container, it helps bring greater ease to whatever is there. This vast expansiveness can be most readily experienced when we access heartfelt emotions, when we connect with heart qualities such as acceptance, compassion, care, kindness, courage, etc. We don't have to change what is there. We don't have to try and change the teaspoon of salt (nor could we). We don't have to try to be different, try to push away our inner experiences, force ourselves to think happy thoughts to get rid of what is uncomfortable. In fact, doing these things may in the short or long term keep us stuck or intensify what is there. But when we can access genuine heart qualities and invite them to sit side by side with whatever is already here, something can relax inside of us. There is a felt sense of more space. We don't feel so swallowed up by whatever is happening.

The other day I found myself in an anxious state—not about any one thing but about many things all mixed together: the pandemic, my own aging and midlife landscape changing, my dad's aging, worries about the world, my kids' futures, etc. I have been working on recognizing when I am living from my threat system or my drive system (much of the time it turns out) and consciously activating my caring system. In this moment of becoming aware that my threat system was engaged, I made an intentional effort to pause and activate my caring system to help me, instead of staying in threat mode which was not protecting me at that moment. I put a hand on my heart and another on my abdomen, which felt soothing. I recognized this was a moment of anxiety, and in naming that I could step back to comfort myself. I thought about what was true *right now*: I was in the safety of my home and about to go for a walk on an inviting autumn day. I connected with feelings of love and care for the friends and family in my life who enrich my life and support me. I did not try to push the anxiety away, but on its own it softened and dissipated as I moved forward into my day, more energized and at ease.

If we consider our human tendencies and conditioned responses, they make sense from an evolutionary and biological perspective. For most of the past 300,000 years, early humans lived in environments with harsh and dangerous conditions that required a primary focus on survival first. It is only much more recently in human evolution that these conditions have changed, but our brains are still programmed to do what helped our species survive for so many years.

Thanks to evolution, we have access to more renewing emotions, we have a nervous system wired for connection, and importantly, we have a well-developed prefrontal cortex that gives us the ability to *observe* our own behaviors and to *see the consequences* of these behaviors in order for us to take skillful actions. This prefrontal cortex gives us the ability to align our behaviors with our deepest, heartfelt values in ways that serve our long-term well-being. Our prefrontal cortex is like the CEO who is able to see our larger mission and can orchestrate the steps necessary to align our actions with that mission. When we are resting in the safety of a regulated nervous system, that CEO can fully do its job.

When we are resting in the safety of a regulated nervous system, that CEO can fully do its job.

Learning to Shift Your Vantage Point

Learning to shift your vantage point helps you to access to this newer operating system with greater ease and consistency (rather than being stuck in threat mode). While it is common to move in and out of states of protection and connection throughout the day and week, when we can learn to invite in more cues of safety for our nervous system and find greater moments of balance between these states, this allows for growth, recovery, and thriving. You will learn six ways, or "moves," that help you to shift your vantage point in future chapters. Here are some of the things that become possible when you do so:

1. The *anchor view* is fundamental to helping your nervous system become more calm, stable, and regulated. As discussed above, when your nervous system feels safe, many more possibilities become available to you to help meet your challenges at hand with flexibility, open-heartedness, and compassion.

2. The *child view* encourages you to approach, explore, and investigate your inner experiences (uncomfortable emotions and difficult mind states) with curiosity and friendliness. Instead of being reactive, you become more mindful. It also helps you reconnect with childlike qualities you may have lost along the way (such as playfulness and creativity).

3. The *audience view* helps you see things from a wider angle and perspective, taking into account things you were not able to see before. It helps you step out of the small self view and into a larger Self view (more about that below), where you recognize you are not your thoughts or your feelings. This is an important shift in consciousness that helps you untangle and separate from your difficult inner experiences (emotions and mind states) that might otherwise run the show that we call our life.

4. The *compassionate parent* view allows you to meet your own discomfort, distress, and suffering with kindness, acceptance, and self-compassion. It invites heartfelt emotions to sit side by side with whatever you may be feeling, to bring greater ease and comfort no matter what the circumstance.

5. The *mirror view* allows you to notice your own inner strengths that are already here that can help guide you toward wise actions that deepen your well-being. It also reflects back to you positive qualities in yourself that you might otherwise miss when you are looking in other directions, that can support and uplift you.

6. The *ocean view* reminds you that you are not alone but in fact are part of a larger whole to which we are all interconnected. It reminds you that your larger Self is held in something vaster and more transcendent. It is our highest form of consciousness.

Missing Ingredients: What the Heart Has to Do with It

We get disconnected from our newer operating system for many reasons. In addition to our biological wiring, as we explored above, here are some other ways that disconnection can happen.

When I was around four or five years old, I remember the great excitement of the treasure chest. It was positioned right when you walked from the lobby into the entranceway of the restaurant, the one we would go to as a family on those Friday nights when Mom didn't feel like cooking and Dad had had a long day of work. The treasure chest seemed huge to me, and endless. On each outing I was allowed to reach my little hands deep into its depth, searching around excitedly for the plastic treasure that I would get to take home with me and savor for just that short bit, before it ended up lost under the bed or eventually in the trash without me realizing it was gone. For that bit of time before its disappearance though, it was mine to cherish and to play with and to entertain me at the table when my boredom and hunger would otherwise have gotten me hushed and shushed and told to stop whining. Years later, I would learn that this was cheap stuff, kid's stuff, hardly worthwhile—and I would lose interest in ever opening that chest to discover what was inside.

But it wasn't just those little plastic treasures that got lost in my childhood. I began to learn at an early age—as so many of us do—what was valued by others and what was not, what deserved praise and approval, and what didn't rise to the level of recognition and importance. Little by little I began to hide parts of myself, only showing the world what felt safe, what felt mainstream, what felt acceptable. I learned from an early age to be a good girl, to gain approval for what was valued, and to unconsciously put away the parts of myself that I didn't think others wanted to see, or that I didn't think others would accept in me. Little by little, those treasures of delight from the giant chest lost their enamor. The chest closed. The lid remained shut.

The achievements that got airtime from the adults around me—that was well worth expressing. The parts of me that were valued in the media and pop culture, in the classroom and in the public spaces in which I resided, those I could display like a badge of approval with bold black lettering. Even in my career, I was careful about what I shared with my colleagues and what I brought into the therapy room, lest it felt too "out there" in a time when meditation and mindfulness and body-based therapies were not considered "evidence-based."

But inwardly, something else was calling me. The playful, the childlike, the delightful, the silly, the creative, the messy, the nonsensical, the authentic—these remained hidden from view but not forgotten. Inwardly, and from the earliest that I can recall, I have been drawn to something deeper, more expansive, more spiritual, more elusive than my intellect would tell me I should focus on. There was a pulling, a tugging, a longing to connect with heart energy and body energy that got me out of my head and touched down into the authenticity of those places which felt like home. For so long I lived in my head, safely surrounded by my intellect. But I longed to be in my body, to explore my heart not just in my intimate and loving relationships, but in the very fabric of which I lived each day.

This heart energy is the hidden treasure, the one that we close off or learn at an early age (at least many of us) to put away. It is the heart energy that we often lose connection to in our pursuit to fit in, to feel accepted, to do what is expected, to be and do what we "should," to be "strong," to grow up. So eventually we stop lifting up that lid of the treasure chest all together and go about the adult way of things.

The Influence of Early Conditioning

As much as our evolutionary wiring can affect how we relate to our inner emotional experiences, so too our early childhood experiences and cultural conditioning can have a powerful impact on our conditioned responses as well. All our experiences and our subsequent responses to them are constantly shaping our brains' wiring (not to mention our underlying genetics and temperament that predispose us to certain ways of responding in the first place). But our early experiences in childhood have a particularly significant effect on the way that we learn to express and respond to our emotions, and the way that our nervous systems become wired. As children we naturally long to be loved and accepted (belonging is an important part of our "survival"), and we learn early on from our caregivers, teachers and others what we believe we need to do to gain love, approval, and acceptance. Often these beliefs are inaccurate at best, based on our limited perspectives. For example, we might believe "I need to be perfect to be loved," or "I need to not show anger in order to gain approval," or "I need to not be my authentic self in order to belong."

Because we naturally scan for threats and try to protect ourselves even at a very young age, early childhood experiences that are painful or difficult or traumatic can have strong influences on us that can be carried (often unconsciously) into adulthood. If something felt unsafe when we were little, we might form beliefs and reactions around what is safe to allow ourselves to feel. As an example, for myself, I was wired with a good bit of anxiety from birth. However, this was greatly heightened during my adolescence when my mom died in a car accident. The shock and trauma of that shaped my nervous system in ways that continued to carry forward into my adult life. Because of fear of future sudden loss, and in an attempt to protect myself from this, my coping strategy at that time was to throw myself into my schoolwork and try to control every aspect of my life that I could—as if by gripping very tightly and controlling everything I could, this would somehow stave off anything bad from happening again and avoid the pain of loss.

Even more typical experiences such as feeling the painful jealousy of a sibling who seems to be getting more attention, or being left out by a group of friends, or a parent who is managing enormous stress and yells frequently because of their own limited resources, can leave strong impressions on our nervous systems. Being both vulnerable at these young ages and limited in our abilities to fully comprehend and make sense of the world and others' behavior in it, we construct narratives based on our myopic views that are often inaccurate, distorted, and self-critical. In an attempt to protect ourselves, we often wall off parts of ourselves to try and protect our hearts, and we develop beliefs about ourselves and the world (e.g., I'm not good enough, I'm unlovable) that can influence our emotional responses and follow us well after our life circumstances have changed.

Interestingly, as Lisa Barrett Feldman[29] explains, our brains operate on a prediction model, taking into account past memories to inform future behaviors (both internal physiological responses in our bodies and external actions and behavior choices). In this way, our memories play an important role in our construction of our reality. When we encounter a current situation,

Feldman Barrett explains that our brain asks, "The last time I encountered something similar, what did I do?" Beyond our conscious awareness, it takes into account all our past experiences that it deems similar to the current situation in order to assess safety. It then organizes responses based on these past memories to anticipate future outcomes, all in the service of helping to regulate our bodies' resources to survive and stay well.

The problem is that sometimes, our perceptions and predictions may be inaccurate, and they may be outdated, especially if they are coming from childhood memories and circumstances that are no longer relevant. If you were humiliated by your first crush at age ten or had your heart broken at age twelve, it's possible that at age twenty when you want to start dating this feels too threatening and you might avoid putting yourself in this situation. Or at age thirty, if you allow yourself to start getting close to someone, if this feels "dangerous" due to earlier memories of getting hurt, you might fight or flee to try and protect yourself.

What I have found in years of working with people in therapy is that often strategies that may have been adaptive for a time and helped the childhood versions of my patients survive get carried forward into adulthood, even when these self-protective patterns are no longer adaptive or needed. For example, the child who learns "it isn't safe to show my feelings" in a chaotic home with an explosive parent might continue to hide their feelings away, even later in life when they are in a safe, loving relationship. Someone who got bullied in third grade for showing their authentic self by dressing up in an unusual outfit might not feel safe to express themselves long after the threat of the bully has passed, even into adulthood. Even for those who grew up in loving and supportive homes like I did, it is easy to misinterpret the behaviors of the adults around them and form beliefs about themselves that are inaccurate at best.

And so, we disconnect. We disconnect from our hearts. We disconnect from the essence of who we are—our true Self—all in the service of protection, trying to keep ourselves safe. These self-protective moves are meant to be of help, but often they move us away from the very well-being for which we long.

Questions for Reflection: Early Messages

- Take a moment to consider what messages you received when you were younger about how to deal with difficult emotions. Were you encouraged to express these emotions, or put them away? What early beliefs did you develop from these experiences?

- Whatever difficulties you may have experienced in childhood, what beliefs did you form about yourself at that time that may not be true or accurate (e.g., I need to be perfect in order to be loved; it's not safe to show my true feelings)?

- What are some of the early negative or misguided messages you received in your childhood that have formed into beliefs about yourself? Are these beliefs true? How much do they run in the background (or foreground) of your life? How have cultural and societal messages affected the beliefs you hold about yourself?

- If you have experienced racism, sexism, or systemic oppression of any kind, in what ways has this impacted your beliefs about yourself?

- In what ways are you aware that you protect yourself, keeping certain parts of you hidden because it does not feel safe to show these parts to others?

The Transformative Power of Heartfelt Emotions

It was the night before our trip, the one that would take us to California to watch my son and his college Ultimate Frisbee team play in the national tournament: a last hurrah for my son who was graduating, and a moment I didn't want to miss. The trip had been planned carefully and thoughtfully with our busy schedules in mind, so that my husband and I could fit in all the patients that needed to be seen and still set aside this time away for travel and fun. As we always do the night before such a trip, we got online to the airline website to check-in and print out our boarding passes. No problem for my husband, everything went smoothly there. However, when we went to check me in, there was no ticket listed under my name. Staving off any first inclinations of panic, I suggested we call the airlines, thinking there was just some technical mistake.

After being on hold for close to two hours we finally reached an agent who informed us that my ticket had been canceled, without notifying us, and apparently due to an error on their end. Surely there was something they could do to rectify this, I asked, explaining that I needed to be on that flight, and aware that there were first class seats available on that same flight. The agent, in a very matter of fact monotone, responded that in fact there was nothing they could do (unless we wanted to pay an additional close to $1000), and that we would have to find another flight (which would either require us to board an early morning flight and last-minute cancel all our patients without even having time to inform any of them, or would have us missing some of the tournament). Unsatisfied with our options, and quite frustrated at the situation, I asked to speak with a supervisor. Unfortunately, the supervisor seemed hardly concerned about our predicament and was even more monotone and dispassionate than the agent, repeating phrases robotically that only ramped up my anger.

By now I was highly worked up. It was close to midnight, I had no ticket, no great options, and no one on the other end who

seemed to give a darn that the airline had messed up and put
us in a bad predicament. Desperate for a satisfying resolution, I
called the airline back and waited on hold for yet a third person.
This agent that I reached was caring, understanding, and em-
pathic. They were truly apologetic about what had happened
and expressed this in a genuine way. My threat response, which
had been ramping up for several hours now, began to ease in the
presence of a caring person on the other end of the line. In the
end, and similar to the previous conversations we had had, this
agent was unable to offer any ideal resolution to this situation.
But they did offer a listening and understanding ear, and the
wish to be able to make things better. They didn't tell me to stop
feeling how I was feeling, and I didn't tell myself to "snap out of
it" and be happy. Yet somehow, in the presence of this person's
kindness, my anger and irritability dissipated. In the space of
feeling cared for, my threat response turned off and I was able
to think more clearly and consider the best steps forward. More
calm and clear-headed, I was better equipped to assess the situ-
ation and figure out how best to proceed.

Heartfelt emotions have the power to act like a bowl of warm water in which an ice cube is placed. In the presence of that warm water, the ice cube naturally melts and changes size or form. My anger and frustration, in the presence of someone else's kindness and care naturally transformed, without me trying to do anything. In the example above, this kindness and care came in the form of someone else's nervous system (their caring or social engagement system) helping to regulate mine (which was in a state of fight-or-flight). However, this can also come from within ourselves. When we are able to access heartfelt emotions and allow them to sit side by side with whatever we are feeling, those heartfelt emotions become a larger container in which our more difficult emotions can be held. It isn't about changing or pushing away our difficult emotions or *trying* to be happy; it is about what happens when our emotional distress and difficult mind states are held by something more vast, expansive, and transformative.

If we are to cultivate a deep well of well-being, part of that well is made up of heartfelt qualities and renewing emotions that we can draw upon to sit side by side with our difficult ones. We can bring curiosity to our anger, compassion to our sadness, comfort and calm to our fears. We don't need to put on a happy face to do this. We don't have to push anything away or fake it till we make it. When we generate heart qualities such as care, compassion, connection, curiosity, acceptance, trust, and gratitude, they become deep inner resources of our well of well-being.

Each of the vantage points helps you to access heartfelt emotions:

- The anchor view helps you cultivate feelings of safety, stability, courage, and trust.
- The child view helps you cultivate curiosity, friendliness, playfulness, and interest.
- The audience view helps you cultivate mindful caring awareness, and the widened perspective that goes along with it.
- The parent view helps you cultivate self-compassion, care, and acceptance.
- The mirror view helps you develop appreciation and gratitude.
- The ocean view allows you to experience more transcendent emotions such as awe, wonder, and equanimity.

Sitting on a Goldmine: The Missing Ingredient of Heart

Heart-based emotions don't just feel good, they have powerful effects on our brain, our cognitive capacities, and our behaviors. The heart doesn't tend to get too much airtime in many traditional psychology modalities. In the psychology world there has been a strong emphasis on trying to eliminate or reduce negative feeling states and mind states (anxiety, depression, obsessive thinking, etc.), but not so much emphasis on cultivating positive ones (joy, gratitude, acceptance, and other aspects of well-being). There is a long history in psychology of focusing on mental illness and psychopathology, but only in more recent years has positive psychology made some significant headway in terms of putting more value on one's strengths, being interested in what contributes to a meaningful life, and how to increase well-being.

In all my initial years of training and years of work to follow, I don't recall ever reading or hearing about the role of the heart, until I came across the HeartMath Institute.[30] In fact, to talk about the heart would have seemed (and may still seem to some) kind of "woo-woo" or touchy-feely in the context of therapeutic treatment. I became intrigued by the research of the HeartMath Institute because they seemed to be onto something that resonated deeply with me, that tied together scientific research with the unique role that the heart plays in emotional regulation, and the important role that heartfelt qualities play in one's physiological and psychological well-being. Essentially, HeartMath researchers discovered (as have others) that the heart is not simply a mechanical pump keeping us alive, it is a "highly complex, self-organized information-processing center" that has its own intelligence and acts like a kind of brain of its own.[31] Eighty percent[32] of the fibers of the vagus nerve are *afferent*—that is, they ascend from the body to the brain, and many of these fibers have connections between the heart and the brain. Through biochemical, neurological, biophysical, and electromagnetic means, the heart communicates vital patterns of information to the neocortex (the higher thinking centers of the brain) as well as to the emotional centers of the brain such as the amygdala, and to the brainstem.[33] These afferent inputs play a strong role in influencing our perceptions, cognitions, and behaviors. When the rhythms of the heart are *coherent* (a synchrony and harmony in the flow of information between the heart, brain, and different branches of our autonomic nervous system), we have much greater access to improved mental functioning and mental flexibility, an ability to see a bigger picture, increased problem-solving, increased access to intuition, increased resilience, higher emotional flexibility, and improved decision-making.

It turns out that we can influence the rhythms of our heart in beneficial ways through both intentional, regulated breathing, and by generating heartfelt and renewing emotions such as appreciation, care, compassion, and courage. Renewing emotions thus play an important role in our cognitive processing, behavior, health, and well-being.[34]

When we understand how to work with our body and access these heart qualities, so many possibilities become available to us that weren't there before.

And this is where we are sitting on a gold mine. When we understand how to work with our body and access these heart qualities, so many possibilities become available to us that weren't there before. It allows us to open the door to the thriving circuits. This is where well-being lives. But heartfelt emotions also reconnect us to the core of who we are, to our deepest values, our "true nature," to our essence and what makes us feel most alive. Most importantly, they connect us back to the person we often abandon along the way as we get lost in day-to-day stress and the emotional challenges that go along with it—our Self.

Each of the vantage points will help you reconnect with and strengthen important heart qualities that you may have lost touch with, qualities that are part of your thriving circuits, that will help you flourish.

Each of the vantage points will help you reconnect with and strengthen important heart qualities that you may have lost touch with, qualities that are part of your thriving circuits, that will help you flourish.

Activating heartfelt qualities is not about forced positivity or forced happiness. It is not about pushing away our uncomfortable feelings to be replaced by something else. But as we invite these heartfelt emotions to sit side by side with our difficult emotions, our experience can transform. Similar to how hydrogen and oxygen gas combine through a chemical reaction and form a new substance of water, so too, a kind of alchemy can occur when we invite heartfelt emotions to sit beside our difficult inner experiences. While one might consider happiness to be a heartfelt emotion, the heartfelt emotions that we explore in this

book are ones that are accessible, regardless of the difficulties we are encoun-
tering. These include, for example, care, kindness, courage, acceptance, and
curiosity, which can sit side by side grief, sadness, anger, irritability, and so on.

Mindfulness and Mindlessness

Mindfulness has been deeply transformative to me both in my personal
life and in my professional life with my patients, and not surprisingly, it is an
important element of the six vantage points. Mindfulness is a 2,500-year-old
practice that is part of Eastern spiritual and wisdom traditions, originating
in the Buddha's teachings as part of the eightfold path out of suffering. While
this is far beyond the scope of this book, mindfulness as a particular kind of
awareness and way of paying attention is foundational to many of the vantage
points.

Normally, due to the default setting of our brain, we operate much of our
lives on automatic pilot. We are surprisingly not aware of the present moment much of the time. Instead, we are commonly lost in thoughts about the
past, the future, or self-referential thinking. In an eye-opening study by Killingsworth and Gilbert,[35] thousands of participants in this study from around
the world received texts on their smartphones periodically throughout the
day, asking them three questions: 1. What are you doing right now? 2. Where
is your mind right now? Is it focused on what you are doing, or elsewhere?
3. How happy or unhappy are you right now? What they found is that close
to 50 percent of the time, our attention is occupied by something other than
what is actually happening. Additionally, this mind-wandering was a strong
predictor of amount of happiness (i.e., when our minds wander, we are less
happy).

If you think of a typical day, take a moment to reflect on how often you are
present to what is actually happening, and how much of the time you are lost
in thoughts. How about when you are showering, driving a car, walking in
nature, having conversations with others, or eating a meal? Even when you
are talking with others, notice how much of the time you are fully present,

giving that other person your undivided attention, and how much of the time you might be thinking about something you want to say, or perhaps thinking about other things entirely.

Mind-wandering, besides taking us away from some of the precious moments of our lives (the ones that are *right here*), can also increase our suffering by pulling us into unhelpful narratives about ourselves (often distorted, inaccurate, or self-critical ones); unhelpful imaginations about what might happen in the future; or mental reruns about the past that we can do nothing about. Not only does this mental activity typically occur, but importantly, *we don't realize that it is occurring.* It happens so automatically that it is often outside of our awareness.

Mind-wandering is part of our evolutionary wiring, as is the inner chatter that is often distorted and self-critical. When we are caught in this, we are the opposite of mindful. Additionally, when we are in the grip of strong emotions, we often are not mindful. Frequently, as discussed earlier, we are pushing our emotions out of awareness or being hijacked by them and swallowed up in what we are feeling.

Mindfulness and the Role of Heart

Mindfulness offers us a kind of antidote to living from these default states of mind-wandering. Mindfulness involves some of our higher brain structures such as our prefrontal cortex and thus I consider it part of our more newly evolved "thriving" circuits versus the more reflexive and automatic responses of the lower brain stem. Engaging in this kind of awareness allows us to step out of and back from our thought stream and our difficult mind states and emotional states. By being able to witness and observe what is happening, without getting pulled into or identified with or swept away by what is there, we are no longer victim to our automatic reactions and can be more responsive to what is happening, with greater choice. It is like the difference between being caught in the middle of a storm, being carried away by the strong winds, and watching the storm from the safety of your home.

In some ways, I think of mindful awareness like being handed a flashlight in a dark room. Imagine without the flashlight that you are trying to get across the room. In the pitch black, you would likely be tripping and stumbling along the way. If someone hands you a flashlight the room suddenly becomes illuminated. You can see more clearly. The obstacles are still there, they don't disappear, but you are able to navigate with greater ease.

Mindful awareness allows us to notice the mental habits and inner chatter and inner emotional storms that we are caught in. Once we can see more clearly what is arising from the vantage point of safe and stable ground, there is the ability to respond with many more possibilities than when we are in survival mode, on autopilot, being carried away by the storm.

So, what does the heart have to do with any of this? Let's look again at some definitions of mindfulness that I mentioned earlier. One of the well-noted definitions of mindfulness as it has been adapted in the Western world is from Jon Kabat-Zinn, who says that mindfulness is "the awareness that arises from paying attention, on purpose, in the present moment and non-judgmentally."[36] For many who practice mindfulness from both Eastern and Western traditions, there is a sense of this awareness as neutral, simply observing objectively (e.g., noticing thoughts, emotions, the breath, physical sensations in the body, etc.).

Bill and Susan Morgan, mindfulness practitioners and teachers who have deeply and extensively studied the Buddha's teachings and whom I am fortunate enough to have studied with, teach something a bit different. They emphasize the importance of heart, which they talk about as an often-missing ingredient in mindfulness practices.

In his book *The Meditator's Dilemma*, Bill writes about how we are wired for both survival and happiness, but because of our evolutionary hierarchy, survival tends to triumph and in doing so, the mind "looks for trouble" in the past and future. "When balanced mindfulness is present, however, the negativity bias is disengaged, and this is when we have the capacity to develop new neural pathways, more conscious and less self-defeating mental patterns. In order to do this, we need the aid of a supportive inner environment."[37]

As an important ingredient of creating such a supportive inner environment, Bill writes that heart qualities are essential—and yet they are an often missed or overlooked part of the meditator's experience. Some of the heart qualities that he emphasizes that are important to develop include: relaxation and ease, playfulness and delight, gratitude and wonder, and warmth and tenderness. When we cultivate these qualities as part of our inner "holding environment," he explains, we are creating a nurturing relationship with ourselves, in which negative feeling states can be "held," and in the presence of which they naturally dissipate.

Additionally, Bill writes and teaches about the importance of strengthening positive affect (something encouraged within Buddhist teachings). Because these positive emotional states don't always arise on their own, we can practice intentionally calling them up through imagery and memory within our meditation practice, remembering times we felt warmth, tenderness, care, and other regenerative emotions, and re-experiencing it in the present moment in this way. Far from forced positivity, this involves finding genuine positive feeling states and inviting the mind to rest there.

As we know from HeartMath research, this not only feels good, but it has far-reaching implications for our mental, emotional, and physical well-being and psychological flexibility. One study that looked at the effects of practicing loving-kindness meditation (repeating short phrases of loving-kindness to oneself and others in one's mind) five days a week for seven weeks found some remarkable changes. Compared to those in the control group, participants who did this experienced, perhaps not surprisingly, increases in daily experiences of positive emotions. What is more surprising, however, is that this in turn led to an increase in personal resources (such as increased mindfulness, increased social support, decreased illness, greater sense of purpose), which predicted increased satisfaction and decreased depressive symptoms over time.[38]

In addition to heart qualities contributing to an inner holding environment, Bill and Susan Morgan teach that they also inform the lens through which we observe what is arising moment to moment. Rather than simply observing the present moment (whether pleasant, unpleasant, or neutral) from a dispassionate lens, when we access these heart qualities within the experience of mindful witnessing, there is a more caring, open-hearted quality in the noticing. Imagine the connection and warmth you might feel in watching a small child who is a member of your family playing in the sandbox. You are not blankly watching the child the way you might watch a speck of paint on a wall. There is an attitude of care, friendliness, and interest toward this child. This is the attitude that mindfulness helps us to cultivate.

As shared in the previous chapter, Susan Morgan has a definition of mindfulness which captures this well: "Mindfulness is an alert, relaxed, non-judgmental, non-self-referential posture of caring attention, as if a dear friend, wise elder, or beneficial presence is watching over the experience of well-being in this moment."[39] From this vantage point, through the eyes of a loving presence, this quality of mindful attention shifts the very nature of our experience. Through such a lens, our experiences do not change, and yet they are nonetheless transformed. Our relationship to what is happening shifts, while the contents of what is happening might remain unchanged.

We will work with this with each of the vantage points, learning to bring caring, mindful, and heartfelt qualities to all our experiences and thus shifting the very nature of those experiences. **Each of the six vantage points will help you activate heart qualities that are an essential part of mindful awareness. And each vantage point offers you a place to be aware from that cultivates this mindful view.**

Questions for Reflection: Exploring Your Inner Heartscape

Let's take a few minutes to explore your *heartscape*—the landscape of your heart.

- What does the landscape of your heart feel like right now? Is it loving and supportive there? Harsh and self-critical? Is it contracted? Expansive? Something else?

81

- Think about things you used to love to do as a kid. What were those things, and what emotions did they evoke in you? As you think about this now, how does your heart feel?

- What opens your heart—someone you love, a pet, seeing suffering in the world, standing over a breathtaking vista?

- How do you best express your heartfelt emotions—through words, gestures, acts of service, something else?

- What kind of music moves you? Notice the difference between different kinds of music and what your heart energy feels like when listening to each type.

- What heartfelt emotions do you experience most easily (e.g., compassion, kindness, love, courage, acceptance, joy, awe, wonder, appreciation, gratitude, etc.)? What evokes these in you? Which do you experience less often?

Try going through some typical activities in your day as if operating from the heart (even if just for a few moments at a time). When you drop awareness down into your heart (rather than your head) and drink a cup of tea, eat a meal, take a shower, or make your bed, what do you notice? How about if you intentionally focus on connecting with your heart before having a conversation with someone you care about?

Another Missing Ingredient: The Body

It was near the end of yoga class and up until now things had felt familiar and comfortable. There were the usual sun salutations, the standing pose sequence with triangle, warrior, twisted warrior, and side angle pose. There was the standing balancing sequence ending with tree pose, a posture that had early on become one of my favorites. I found something particularly stabilizing about envisioning myself as a tree, with deep roots growing out from the soles of my feet down deep into the earth—even if it was just one foot that I was balancing upon.

But before the end of class the teacher offered us something new to try, something we had never done before in class: a headstand. The thought of having my world completely turned upside down and balancing on my head was both exhilarating and terrifying at the same time. Because this was our first time trying this, we each claimed a little piece of wall that we could literally fall back upon. I positioned my head between my hands in the shape of a triangle, my head forming the top of the triangle and each palm one of the bases of the triangle. Up my legs went, wobbly and shaky, uncertain of where or how to be. Up and down, up and down I went, as I fell out time and again, like a pendulum between earth and sky. I remember the effort, the striving, the determination to stay steady that only seemed to backfire with an equal and opposite force. Finally, there was a moment when the effort fell away, when I stopped striving and just allowed myself to sense into the still point of nothing supporting my legs, sensing into the letting go and trusting of this upside-down posture. In that place of no effort, I discovered a moment of balance. It was beautiful. It was amazing. It was a sense of simply being and not needing to do anything, right in mid-air.

Over time as I practiced that posture, I became familiar enough with that place of effortless freedom that I could find my way there with less and less shakiness, and more certainty and confidence. What I came to realize about headstands is that there is a precious triad of stability necessary. The balance does not come from what is happening with my legs, but it starts with creating a stable foundation upon which everything else is built. That stable foundation has three essential points: the top of the head, and each palm. The weight is equally distributed at each point, and from that base of stability one can literally turn one's world upside down and remain deeply rooted. If balance is off in any of those three points, if weight is unevenly distributed, things go south very quickly. But from that solid triadic base, things flow and the seemingly impossible becomes quite possible.

That power of three has stuck with me. A stool of three legs has stability that would not be possible with two, and even less so with one. With three solid points as a base, tremendous support is available, and steadiness becomes a given. So it is with this remarkable thing we call the human being. When we can connect with our mind, heart, and body, this creates a strong anchor of stability from which we can firmly stand and find balance. We can have our world turned upside down and somehow still, find steadiness within. But take one of these points away and we fall out of balance; we lose our full potential. If we are fully in our heads (as so many of us are) but are cut off from our heart energy or from our bodies, we lose that stability. Likewise, if we are fully in our bodies but don't have access to the ways that our minds can steady us, we lose our strength. When we learn to operate from this magnificent triad, finding balance in all three systems, this foundation becomes a tremendous support and a place to return, even and especially when things get turned upside down.

It is not just our hearts that we often disconnect from, but our bodies along with it. We learn to live in our heads much of the time. We learn to operate from the neck up, to lose touch with the amazing signals and sensations and physical and intuitive experiences that are known in our physical being. We learn this because of our biological wiring that keeps us stuck in our wandering minds so much of our lives. We learn this because of experiences when we feel shame about our bodies. We learn this because there are painful sensations that we would rather push away. We learn this because listening to our bodies is not taught, or appreciated, or understood the way that intellect is. Somewhere along the way, we stop trusting this remarkable, intelligent body that holds tremendous wisdom. Another treasure becomes inaccessible, another treasure lost.

In my many years of experience working with people of all ages and from many walks of life, it is rare that I come upon someone who has a healthy, loving relationship with their body. It certainly took me many years of my life to find my way there myself. Many people outright dislike their bodies and have animosity toward this thing that operates with such amazing precision and complexity that it is hard to fathom or fully appreciate how so many systems must operate in balance to keep us alive in any given moment. Many people have a love/hate relationship with their bodies, sometimes taking care of it and other times punishing it for its human imperfections. Yet others don't pay much heed to their bodies at all, living as if in the attic space of their home, not realizing there is a whole ground level and foundation that they hardly visit. The problem is that, when we disconnect from our bodies, we disconnect from one of our most valuable resources.

In her book *Yoga for Emotional Balance*,[40] Bo Forbes writes about the intricate connection of mind and body, and the power of the mind-body connection for emotional health, well-being, and healing. She describes how the way our minds filter experiences and see the world has direct effects on our body, and how the information our body takes in and stores can powerfully influence the mind. Like a complex dance of partners, the heart and circulatory system, the endocrine system with its hormones and glands, the immune system, the musculoskeletal system, and the nervous system all communicate with one another in ways that make mind and body inseparable when it comes to emotional experiences. The good news is that as we learn to work with the body through movement, breath, and embodied experiences, this can have powerful and positive influences on our emotional states and on our well-being.

Questions for Reflection: Relationship with Your Body

- In what ways have you disconnected from your body?

- Have you had more of a love or hate relationship with your body?

- Do you listen to your body's signals in helpful ways, or do you ignore these signals, or alternatively become consumed by these signals in ways that take you out of balance? What body signals are you most aware of? What ones do you notice only once in a while?

- Are there things that you have stopped doing because of self-consciousness about your body?

- In what ways do you care for your body?

- When do you most feel connected to your body, aware of its inner experiences?

- If your body could speak to you, what would it tell you about its needs?

Reconnecting with Our Bodies to Find Our Stable Triad

The power of the heart and body in mental wellness has been underrated. From my many years of my own therapy, as well as my many years of sitting with my patients, I believe that we don't heal with our heads; instead, healing is an *embodied* process. "Talk therapy" underrepresents what is going on, and the name is misleading on the surface. When two people sit together in a therapeutic relationship, there is a kind of co-regulation of nervous systems that occurs, with the therapist, through their body language, voice tone, gestures, and other verbal and non-verbal cues, helping to regulate the nervous system of the patient, helping that person feel seen and heard, creating an atmosphere of trust and safety, and often creating corrective experiences in this way that allow for healing to occur.

Additionally, from my personal and professional experiences, there are many powerful mind-body healing modalities and practices that go far beyond talking (such as working with the breath and gentle body movements, using guided imagery and guided visualization, mindfulness meditation, etc.) that play an important role in the healing process. Over recent years, body-based therapies have become standard and considered essential in treating trauma.

Everyone's journey looks different. My own experience of reconnecting with my body and learning to listen to the wisdom of my body came in the form of yoga, dance, discovering the joy of movement (beyond just exercise to manage my weight), mindfulness meditation, and working with many gifted therapists and mind-body healers who understood the importance of the triad: mind, body, heart. It is an ongoing journey, of which I am still learning. No matter the modality, having embodied experiences is essential in bringing about transformation. In order to feel whole, to deepen our well of well-being, we must reconnect with our bodies, which are the home to our soul, the essence of who we are. The body holds tremendous wisdom if we will only stop long enough to listen and attend to its signals.

Each of the six vantage points offers you an embodied experience. Shifting your vantage point is not simply an intellectual exercise, but one that involves the body as a vehicle for experiencing, learning, and healing. Bringing heart qualities along as well allows us to have a more deeply embodied experience, and in so doing, to experience an integration of that stable triad—mind, heart, and body—which can help support us with whatever challenges we are experiencing.

Questions for Reflection: Getting Comfortable in Your Body

- In what ways do you feel most at home in your body?

- What kind of movement do you find most enjoyable or pleasurable?

- What kind of experiences help your body feel most at ease, relaxed, and calm?

- What kinds of activities make you feel most alive and energized?

What sensations feel most soothing/comforting for you: a hot shower, feeling sunshine on your face, a warm blanket, a cool breeze, etc.?

What bodily states help to bring about feelings of well-being (calm, relaxation, ease, playfulness, etc.)? When do you tend to feel this most?

Practice for short moments living from the body. Drop your awareness down from your thinking mind and into your body. Walk around doing typical tasks while staying embodied, for example, folding laundry, having a conversation, going through e-mails. What feels different or similar?

The Shift from Hole Self to Whole Self

Ray's Story. On this day, when I opened my door and invited Ray in (as she liked to be called), I could see that we were in for a rough ride. Her mother, accompanying her as she often does at the beginning of a session, looked agitated and worn down. Ray immediately sat in the furthest corner of the couch with her hooded sweatshirt pulled tightly around her face in an act of protection, eyes averted downward, and with her body slumped down and contracted, as if prepared to field a gut punch. It was clear after a few minutes of interchange between her and her mom that Ray was escalating exponentially into extreme thinking and self-hatred, rage, and dark thoughts. I thought it best if Mom stepped outside in the waiting room, and she gladly took the cue.

I sat with Ray, quietly at first, as she started to rant about how she hates her mom and her whole family, and how she is no good, stupid, and doesn't deserve to be here. Without trying to talk her out of anything she was saying (which would have only made her dig in further), but also not colluding with her self-denigrations and distorted thoughts, I acknowledged and named the pain underneath her words and held a space for it. Knowing how dysregulated her nervous system was, in full fight-and-flight mode, I tried to keep mine steady and calm through soft voice and caring eyes, helping her feel seen and heard. In time, picking up my cues of safety, she began to settle—her mind, her body, her agitation.

What happened next amazed me, as it always does, though I've seen it time and again with Ray and so many others. In the settling, it was as if another person took the place of the one who had walked in the door. This "new" person sitting in front of me was deeply wise beyond her years. She sat taller and looked at me directly through wide-open eyes. She told me how a part of her has been feeling strong fear as she faces a major transition to a new high school, and she worries about whether she will fit in and be accepted there. She told me that she thinks she is trying to protect herself from potentially getting hurt, and from feeling the sadness and loss that sits at her core. She said she doesn't really hate her mom, but sometimes she feels that mom doesn't always understand her. The wise Ray sitting in front of me was able to see a much bigger picture than the one who had earlier walked into my office. From this more regulated place, we were able to talk together about who and what might help her face this challenge ahead, talk about ways her family could support her, and things she could do to support herself. When her mom came back in at the end, she was able to express herself clearly and appropriately to her mom and receive her mom's care that had been there all along. From this more whole and interconnected place, she walked back out into the world facing the same challenges she had come in with, but with a new, clearer lens through which to look.

In my experience sitting with hundreds of patients over the years, and from my own many years of therapy, I have come to see that we have what I call a "hole" self and a "Whole" Self. The hole self is our small self; it is made up of the many parts of us that we identify with as who we are, especially in times of challenge. This hole self often feels "not enough" and has a chronic sense of "something wrong, something missing." The hole self is caught in a narrow, limited view and cannot see a bigger picture. It is our default, the place we revert back to when things get difficult, and when younger parts of us that hold painful memories are triggered by current situations that remind us (often unconsciously) of earlier experiences.

Small self operates from the survival brain, in the service of trying to protect us, often in misguided ways. This sense of not enough and something wrong may have had some evolutionary value for our Stone Age ancestors, who needed to be on high alert and for whom messing up could cost them their lives. Small self often holds painful memories from childhood (such as losses and embarrassment) and gets triggered easily when things happen in our adult lives that have some flavor of an old experience. This sense of not enough and something wrong or missing is understandable from our early childhood experiences. From our limited childhood viewpoints, we could not possibly have understood how Mom and Dad fighting wasn't our fault, how Mom's yelling after a long day didn't mean that we were bad, or that the kids being unkind in school didn't mean that we were unlikable or unworthy.

Small self feels contracted, constricted, and closed off. I think of it as "hole" self because the small self often is stuck in ruminations, worries, and self-judgments, and has the sense of "something wrong" and "not enough"—a hole within us. Also, when small self is present, we often feel isolated, alone, overwhelmed, anxious, uneasy, as if we are stuck in a hole from which we can't see a way out.

When we are acting from small self, we are cut off from an ability to see a bigger picture or access our more newly evolved caring circuits and all of the inner resources available to us. We are stuck in our old operating system, and the limitations that come with being in a threat response. When we identify with hole self as who we are, we don't realize there is anything outside of it. We feel isolated, alone.

However, we all have a Whole Self that is here, that is always with us. When Whole Self is online and present, there is more expansiveness, a sense of more space, and an ability to see a bigger picture. From Whole Self we can take a mindful view of things instead of being lost in a myopic view. Whole Self is a more embodied self, connected with mind, body, and heart—and connected with an inner wisdom, an inner knowing, about what is best for our well-being. Whole Self operates from our caring circuits, with our more newly evolved operating system online so that we can access our fullest potential and all the possibilities available to us. When we are stuck in hole self, there is suffering; when we shift to Whole Self, there is greater ease and well-being.

There is an entire field within psychology called Internal Family Systems Therapy (IFS), of which I have been strongly influenced through my own many years of personal therapy, and through my studies and work with my patients. IFS, developed by psychologist Richard Schwartz, posits that our psyche is made up of sub-personalities or parts, and that there is a larger, capital S "Self" which oversees them all.[41] Often these parts are younger versions of us that get frozen in time due to big T and little t traumas that occur in our childhoods, when we had limited understanding to make sense of the world. These parts often operate in the service of protection, but in fact they can keep our world small, our emotional responses to adult challenges disproportionate, and our behavioral repertoire limited, rigid, and inflexible. Much of the work in IFS is helping these parts of us feel seen and held by our capital S Self, the way a loving parent might hold a small child who is suffering. In the presence of the loving parent, the child is soothed. When this happens, instead of our parts running the show, they can learn to relax, become integrated versus separate, and let our Self take over, living from a sense of greater connection, wisdom, and wholeness. "Miss Fuck You," who I introduced at the beginning of this book, was one of my parts who I got to know well, and to love and care for the way I would care for a child in pain.

Each of these six vantage points will help you shift from hole self to Whole Self. They will help you connect with mind, body, and heart qualities. They will help you develop greater access to mindful awareness and operate from your newer caring system rather than your survival/threat system. Without needing to change anything about your life situations or about yourself, these six vantage points will help you to move from suffering to greater ease. You will discover why you don't need to change, and yet how, when you shift your vantage point, everything begins to change.

> *Each of these six vantage points will help you shift from hole self to Whole Self. They will help you connect with mind, body, and heart qualities. They will help you develop greater access to mindful awareness and operate from your newer caring system rather than your survival/threat system.*

From Contraction to Expansion
(of Body and Heart)

Frenetic is how I describe it: that familiar buzz like a glimpse of the hummingbird that pauses in midair, wings flapping so rapidly that they are barely visible to the naked eye. Buzzing here and there, I wonder if there were points where my feet hardly touched the ground: back and forth to work, driving my kids to sports and rehearsals, packing lunches, volunteering with a bunch of second-graders as they wiped their noses and cautiously spelled out words on a page that they were proudly able to vocalize with some fluency now. In between I would train for triathlons, short ones at first, and then longer ones. In between the space of—well, not much—I would run ten miles followed by a swim in the lake, or drive forty-five minutes to practice with the team, and then back to lift weights before picking up the kids, the groceries, or the dirty laundry that didn't make it into the hamper.

My therapist at that time would talk to me about slowing down, about doing nothing, about giving myself more space. Ha. Sitting? Silent? Just sitting there, not accomplishing anything? I wrote my dissertation by sitting for stretches of ten to twelve hours with a cat on my lap and not even a coffee to propel me forward. What a strange concept, this sitting and doing nothing.

After the knee pain, and the anxiety of whether this injury would take me out—and oh, the panic of not being able to have my beloved exercise to fuel me—I ended up in the MRI machine. Yes, that dreaded place for many, the tunnel of terror, where you are literally frozen in a space capsule with loud pounding noises hammering around you. For me it was revolutionary. It was the first time that I couldn't do anything, and in the not doing—well, there was my breath, breathing, breathing space to see the rush and whirl and pressure of my frenetic life. It was a meditation space, one that became increasingly familiar—not the MRI capsule (though I ended up there more than once)—but the stillness itself, the kind that I look forward to now when I take my seat on the cushion, watching and waiting to see what and who will show up.

Grief has a way of seeping through the cracks, and, given space, it becomes undammed, unblocked—freeing life energy that has been trapped and looking for a way out, sometimes for years or decades. In the stillness, the anxiety loosened as I discovered underneath it the sadness that longed for a voice, the anger that shut itself off like a valve jammed tight, that just wanted a listening ear, someone to sit beside it and say, "I hear you, I hear you." In the stillness, the fear showed up in familiar places: the tight chest, the pressured breathing, the too-high shoulders. Without the usual channels to shut it down, it began to show its many faces, creeping out at first from the shadows, and then sitting beside me more easily, even casually once it trusted I would listen. Sometimes it was the little girl who didn't understand why her parents needed to have another child and didn't feel enough in her little and then later adolescent body. Sometimes it was the adolescent, terrified at the loss of her mom, and more terrified that life could change in an instant when one car loses control in a split second. Sometimes it was the older self, watching her daughter walk confidently onto the school bus for the first time with her blue dress, backpack falling off her shoulders and little wave as she hopped on the bus to take her away to a world that no longer involved me keeping her safe; or my son, running off after the soccer ball and the knowing in my heart that this too— this moment of motherhood as I know it—is as fleeting as it is lovely.

Breath in, breath out—spaces between the breath—and in those spaces an opportunity, to open the heart just a drop.

Spaces between the breath: in the spaces become opportunities to notice the longing glance of your child, or partner, or the inner child wanting to be seen; to see the moment as it is, not as you imagine it to be; to catch that last ray of sun as it bounces off the water droplets and retracts into a cascade of falling colors. There is the space to unwind, not only tight muscles, but stories that started as explanations, attempts to understand the world through small eyes, but that became beliefs, entrenched in the kind of cement that leads to conditioned and unintended actions, repeated over and over in unconscious ways. As these stories unwind, there are the loosened threads from which we can weave new narratives, more accurate ones, that strengthen and support us in lasting ways. Sometimes in the space there is nothing at all; the kind of nothing that becomes a welcome friend amidst the chatter of the incessant "monkey" mind. Nothing. No thing. In these fleeting moments of awareness, no attachment to stories or objects, feeling connected in this body and resting in pure space-less, timeless consciousness, Awareness opens her arms wide and welcoming as if to say, "rest awhile" and "home at last."

As we end this chapter, I want to share with you a simple but powerful body signal that you can begin to pay attention to, to provide you with valuable information about whether you are in survival mode or thriving mode, whether you are operating from hole self or Whole Self, whether you are in a state of unease, or whether you are tapping into your well of well-being. This has to do with paying attention to whether you are experiencing a state of contraction and constriction in your body and around your heart, or whether you are experiencing more of a sense of expansiveness and openness.

When we are in survival mode, we tend to experience contraction, constriction, and narrowing, both in our physical bodies and in our emotional experiences. As Bill Morgan writes: "We humans, wired to be vigilant, scanning for threats, anticipating catastrophe, engaging in fight or flight—habitually push and pull and steer and orchestrate our experience. This leads to mental and physical tightening, a psychophysical clenching."[41] This kind of clenching makes sense in the service of protection from an evolutionary perspective. Tight muscles are primed and ready to fight or flee at any moment. Contraction in our bodies is an attempt to protect our internal organs from harm in the face of life-threatening danger.

When our newer operating system, our social engagement or caring system is turned on, we tend to feel a sense of expansion in our bodies and around our hearts. In this more open state, we are free to explore, learn, create, and connect. There is often a "lightness" that people describe when they are experiencing heartfelt qualities that bring them into connection with others or with themselves.

When we are in a state informed by fear or threat (whether our nervous system is perceiving "danger" from something external to us, or internal, such as a fear of not being good enough or being in a state of self-criticism), messages are relayed between our body and brain that narrow our vision and cause our bodies to contract in protection. When we are experiencing more heartfelt emotions, in states of non-fear and non-threat, we open up, we expand, there is a sense of spaciousness within and around us. More possibilities become available that were not before so obvious.

This simple dichotomy—of expansion or contraction in the body—can be an immensely helpful piece of information, part of our body's wisdom that can guide us toward well-being. As we pay attention to these habitual contractions and invite in experiences that offer us expansion, we can learn a good deal about what nourishes us. This natural expansiveness and spaciousness that is ours to experience creates its own natural reward and helps us wire in these new patterns of well-being more consistently. **Each of the six vantage points will offer you embodied experiences to shift from a felt sense of contraction to a felt sense of more relaxation, ease, openness, and expansion.**

Questions for Reflection: Contraction and Expansion

- Begin to pay attention at any point in the day: Is your body contracted, tight, or tense? If so, where? Is there a feeling of more openness, spaciousness, or ease? If so, where? What do you feel around your heart—contraction or expansion?

- What are signs in your mind, body, and heart that you are in your old operating system? What kinds of actions suggest you are in your old operating system?

- What are signs (in your mind, body, heart, and behaviors) that you are in your newer operating system? What kind of actions do you tend to take when your newer operating system is online?

Here are some examples of signs to pay attention to:

Body: tense, dis-ease, contraction, tightness, shallow breath, nervous versus at ease, relaxed, calm, openness, expansiveness.

Mind: close-minded, narrow focus, tunnel vision, rumination, worry, scattered, unfocused, resistance, not enough, self-critical versus open-minded, creative, focused, equanimity, acceptance, seeing a bigger picture, sense of enough, self-compassionate.

Behavior: engaging in unhelpful behaviors, unhealthy behaviors, stuckness (inability to move forward), behaviors that disconnect or isolate versus behaviors that nourish well-being, healthy behaviors, behaviors that bring one into connection with others.

Heart/Emotions: fear, anxiety, worry, irritability, stress, anger, defensiveness, frustration, hopelessness, dissatisfaction, depleting emotions versus joy, appreciation, gratitude, calm, peace, satisfaction.

Why You Don't Need to Change to Change Everything: A Word About Change

When we are operating from our newer operating system, when our nervous system is in a state of safety and connection, when we have access to renewing emotions to sit side by side our difficult ones, when we are starting from a place of already whole, when we are working from strength rather than from lack, and when we can meet our difficult inner experiences with mindfulness and self-compassion, new possibilities become available. From this place, I have seen profound changes take place. Most always these changes take place as inner shifts, and sometimes the inner wisdom that emerges ends up leading to outer shifts as well. I have seen people make significant behavior changes that support their well-being, and even that change their lives. Some people have left unhappy or unhealthy relationships, they have set boundaries with family members so that they are no longer drained and depleted by them, they have made job changes that have moved them from burnout to fulfillment, they have changed their relationship with food and developed a healthier lifestyle, they have developed more loving and connected relationships with their loved ones, they have stopped living in the grip of anxiety and gone after things that matter to them, they have found peace from their traumatic pasts, have stopped engaging in addictive behaviors, or no longer feel gripped by incessant mental ruminations that were taking away from their lives.

When you learn to shift your vantage point, you will experience greater inner ease, and from that place, choices may emerge that lead to profound behavioral changes. This is not the starting point but often the consequence of shifting one's vantage point. I invite you to discover all the possibilities that await and see the natural changes that emerge when you begin by accepting yourself right where you are, right here, already whole.

Recap:

Each of the six vantage points you will learn will help you to:

1. Calm your survival circuitry and activate your thriving circuitry—
   different networks of your brain and nervous system that, with many
   of our modern challenges, can actually help us feel safer, connected,
   calm, grounded, and able to find ease and see more clearly.

2. Cultivate well-being no matter what you might be feeling or experiencing.

3. Awaken heart qualities in you that can sit alongside whatever you are experiencing, that help to bring greater ease.

4. Connect with embodied experiences that expand and shift your relationship with your inner world, that bring a greater sense of wholeness, spaciousness, and possibility.

5. Shift from identifying with your hole self and instead help you to live your life as your Whole Self.

PART TWO

The Vantage Points

CHAPTER 4

The Anchor View: Finding Stable Ground

In the midst of winter, I found there was,
within me, an invincible summer.

—Albert Camus

It was early on New Year's morning when I got the phone call. I had been in a sound sleep and when I saw my son's name on my caller ID, I knew this wasn't just a friendly "Happy New Year" phone call. My heart had already revved up before saying hello, but it continued to rev up further as my son proceeded to tell me that he was experiencing weird and concerning medical symptoms. He isn't an alarmist, and for him to wake my husband and I at this early hour meant there was reason to worry. I'm not sure if I was more aware of my heart beating furiously or my muscles shaking uncontrollably, but somehow, I managed to get myself dressed and in the car within a matter of minutes, as my husband and I hurried to pick up my son from his friend's house and rushed him to the local emergency room to determine what was going on.

Knowing that I couldn't stop my anxiety but wanting to be a calm presence for my son, I did the next best thing: I turned to the one stable thing I could find—my breath. My breath had been a steady companion for me during my daily meditation sits, and so here it was again, discoverable in this stormy turbulence of anxiety, fear, and uncertainty. Just this breath in this moment, breathing in, breathing out, one. Mind starts wandering to worst-case scenarios. Coming back when the winds of fear seem ready to blow me over, breathing in, breathing out, two. Just this breath in this moment, the moment that was actually here, which was us sitting in a small room within the ER, with a caring doctor running tests to discern whether there was truly anything to be alarmed about. Breathing in, feeling the coolness of the air at my nostrils, slowly exhaling, and feeling the warmth of the outbreath as I tend to my son and my own nervous system at the same time. Three, four, a hundred times and more—feeling the rise and fall of my abdomen, my lungs, coolness of the in breath and warmth of the out breath.

Sometimes no news is good news, but sometimes it leaves unanswered questions and more strange symptoms. And so it was over the next month, a bumpy road that culminated in an MRI to rule out something bad, something unthinkable. Probably very unlikely, but still, the anxiety. . . . Each time finding my breath, helping to steady me, helping me to ride the waves of uncertainty.

On that final day as I waited for the MRI results even my breath was hard to follow, with my mind running away like an escaped convict to places I did not want to go. Everything was probably fine, but still, but still, but still . . . the fear. Knowing I could not sit still and wait, knowing this storm was powerful even for my breath, I walked, and walked, and walked. I focused on the feeling of each foot hitting the ground, solid earth beneath me, just one steady step after another. Just one step at a time, moving nowhere in particular. This foot supported by stable ground, and this one held by the solidness beneath me, sending calming messages to my sympathetic nervous system that was operating in overdrive. In the end the MRI was normal—an enormous relief, a chapter closed, an invitation that my worries could be put to rest. So grateful for this news. Grateful too for my anchors that steadied me through the worst of the storm.

Why Do We Need an Anchor?

Picture that you are in the middle of a storm at sea. You are out in the water, going for a swim, and suddenly, unexpectedly, this storm swoops in. The winds are whipping up. The rain is pelting. It is hard to see clearly. The waves are high and rough, and the undertow is getting stronger. What do you do? If you ignore this storm, pretend it isn't happening, surely there will be potentially harmful consequences. If you try to fight against the storm and the powerful waves, you will exhaust yourself without changing the nature of the situation. If you remain in the middle of the storm without any support, you may be swept away. Suddenly you notice a small boat anchored very close to where you are. It is within your reach to get to it, and you grab onto the rope that is connected to the anchor. The anchor is deeply embedded in the ocean floor. It holds the boat safe and secure. The rope you are holding travels deep down below the surface of the water, to where there is stillness far below. Holding on tightly, from the vantage point of the anchor, you can watch the storm and observe the turbulence at the surface without being swept away by it; and you are also connected to the deep stillness of the water far below you, where the anchor lies. You can climb into the safety of the anchored boat and ride out the storm. This creates safety and stability, a sense of calm within the storm. From this safe vantage point, the storm can come and go without taking you along with it.

For many of us, the habitual way that we are wired to deal with life's stressors and challenges does not involve approaching things from a calm, centered, anchored place of stability. Life has inevitable storms, whether the minor day-to-day hassles or the bigger challenges that we encounter.

At the core of many meditation and mind-body practices is the focus on learning to calm and steady the body and nervous system. Because of the nature of our human bodies, because of the perceived threats that we face on a regular basis, big and small, and because of our evolutionary wiring, our nervous systems can easily become dysregulated.

The Role of the Nervous System

As discussed in the earlier chapters, the nervous system acts in the service of our survival first. A very helpful way to understand the emotional dysregulation we often experience, and the antidote to this dysregulation through the anchor view, is by looking through the lens of the autonomic nervous system. Let's review briefly so that this really makes sense to you.

According to polyvagal theory developed by Stephen Porges,[43] our most primitive part of our nervous system to evolve as a system of defense against threats was the dorsal vagal branch of what is called our parasympathetic nervous system. This unmyelinated nerve played an important role in protecting our ancient species by allowing for immobilization (the freeze response) in the face of life threat. Think about an animal playing dead or a turtle pulling into its shell to get an idea of that most primitive response. In our modern lives, this might take the form of isolating, withdrawing, or shutting down when things feel overwhelming, or in more extreme situations, feeling frozen and unable to move, dissociating, or collapsing.

The next part of our nervous system to evolve was our sympathetic nervous system, as we explored in earlier chapters. This system involves complex communication between the brain and body via both electrical signals and

hormones and enabled our ancestors to mobilize in the face of threat by either fighting or fleeing. We experience this in our modern lives as our classic
stress response that can take many forms and intensities, either of the more
aggressive flavor (e.g., anger, frustration, rage), or of the anxious flavor (e.g.,
fear, anxiety, panic).

Finally, as discussed in the previous chapter, our most newly evolved part
of our nervous system, the social engagement system, involves activation of
the ventral vagus nerve (a myelinated branch of the vagus nerve that origi-
nates in our brainstem). This nerve had an important role in evolution and
enabled our mammalian ancestors to feel safe, soothed, calm, and connected
so that infants could attach to their caregivers, and people could feel supported by others in their tribes. Importantly, unlike our reptilian ancestors,
mammals developed the crucial capacity (via the vagus nerve) to perceive
cues of safety and signal cues of safety to others, letting them know it is safe
to approach. Having a nervous system with the ability to respond not only
to cues of threat but to cues of safety allowed our mammalian ancestors to
socially engage in essential ways to promote our survival.[44] This connection,
and the accompanying calm and safety experienced in the nervous system,
became an important part of our evolutionary inheritance. Unlike other animals, this ventral vagal response and its ability to co-regulate (one nervous
system helping to soothe another) is a biological imperative[45] for us humans
to not only survive but thrive. It is from this place of nervous system safety
that we are free to explore, create, and experience more expansive emotions
such as care, joy, compassion, and appreciation.

One other aspect of our physiology that is important to understand is that
our brains and nervous systems are constantly engaged in a process of *neuroception*. Unlike *perception*, neuroception is the process by which our brain
and nervous system constantly scan for cues of threat and danger and for cues
of safety, outside of our conscious awareness.[46] Based on this incoming information, bodily responses are mobilized to respond to the situation at hand.
When there are more cues of safety than of threat, we are free to connect with
others, problem solve from a broadened perspective, and think creatively.

When we experience more cues of threat than of safety in a given moment, we experience sympathetic nervous system mobilization (some variation of our fight-or-flight response). Such cues of threat could come from outside or inside, and in our modern lives might include such things as a stressful situation in our environment, uncertainty or unpredictable circumstances, an argument with someone, self-critical thoughts, or worries of the future, just to name a few. In situations where our fight-or-flight response is insufficient to cope with the challenge at hand, we may go into a dorsal vagal shutdown, collapse, or withdrawal.

From Out of Balance to Greater Balance

While all of that is going on behind the scenes in our nervous system, what we can experience emotionally is being thrown off-balance, feeling distress, and dis-ease. In the midst of life's challenges, emotions such as anger, fear, anxiety, frustration, irritation, and worry can show up as part of our primitive operating system, in a first-line effort to protect us. While those emotions can provide us helpful information that there is something for us to pay attention to, *if we remain stuck in a state of dysregulation*, we can't meet the challenges at hand effectively. When our nervous system is out of balance and we remain stuck there (i.e., too much sympathetic nervous system or dorsal vagal activation, and not enough ventral), it's hard to think clearly, see possibilities available to us, and take effective actions.[47] Resisting our emotions (trying to push them away through fight), or trying to ignore/escape them (through flight), or getting swept away by them entirely (often leaving us immobilized or stuck), are the common go-to reactions in the face of difficulty.

When we can anchor our nervous system the way we might anchor a boat at harbor in stormy waters, this stability provides greater safety in the storm and allows us to ride it out without getting swept away. Having an anchor allows us to help our nervous system return to a state of balance, where we have access to more ventral vagal energy.[48] As we shift back into this newer operating system, more possibilities open up as our perspective widens, and we develop greater resilience to weather the storms. While we can't stop the storms, there is a deeper trust in our ability to handle them, and a greater emotional and behavioral repertoire becomes available. We no longer have to live from fear, anger, or despair. Self-compassion, comfort, care, and courage become available to support us. We no longer have to react in unhelpful or unhealthy ways (e.g., lashing out at others, getting frozen in panic, or engaging in addictive behaviors). From an anchored place, we can take more wise and skillful actions, even if just to comfort ourselves or seek support from others.

When our physiology shifts from our adaptive survival mode to our socially engaged thriving mode, a host of inner resources become available to us that were not otherwise accessible in a in a state of protection.[49,50] I think of this like unlocking a treasure chest and suddenly having access to riches that are already within us but had been previously hidden. Some of these riches that become available from the anchor view (when the ventral vagal branch of the nervous system is engaged) include perspective, clarity, caring, calm, contentment, confidence, courage, creativity, competence, compassion, and so much more.

Surprisingly, most often we are not taught how to take this anchor view. Other than being told to "Take some deep breaths" (without further instructions on how best to do this), we are often left on our own to flounder. Growing up we were likely told what *not* to do—"Stop fussing, stop complaining," or told to "Calm down"—but not shown *how* to do this. Being able to take an anchor view and anchor ourselves and our nervous system is so basic and fundamental to our well-being; yet most of us have little formal experience in how to do this.

There are many ways we can learn to anchor ourselves, and you will have an opportunity to experiment with different approaches in this chapter.

When we take an anchor view as we come up against emotional challenges of all kinds, this vantage point impacts four different areas of our inner experience:

Body: It gives us access to more ventral vagal energy (the most newly evolved part of our nervous system) which helps us to feel more inner balance, steadiness, calm strength, and regulation. Also, when our heart rhythms are regulated, this sends calming messages up to the brain allowing for the trickle-up effect of thinking more clearly and seeing a bigger perspective.

Mind: Anchoring the mind in something that focuses it in the present moment (e.g., the breath; an image that evokes a felt experience of calm; the feeling of the feet on the ground) helps to steady our thinking. Rather than running amok to the past and future, the mind is able to stay steadier in (or return to) the here and now, which is the only place we truly live and can make decisions from.

Emotions: An anchor doesn't make difficult emotions go away, but there is more ease and stability available to sit side by side whatever difficulties are present. Also, we have access to greater self-compassion from this steady state, which is immensely helpful to be able to meet any challenge.

Behaviors: Rather than being in reactive mode and impulsively acting out of a survival instinct, when we hold an anchor view there is more ability to pause, assess the situation, and choose wise and skillful actions that will serve our long-term well-being.

A Word About Resistance and Why We Don't Have to Change

We are wired to resist unpleasant experiences. This mental habit informs so much of our lives, and so much of our emotional suffering. We often want things to be other than they are. We fight against what is, especially when it isn't what we want, or when it feels unpleasant. Also, we try to hold onto and cling to things which are pleasant but that will inevitably not last. This is a recipe for suffering as well. Both these modes of resisting "what is" make us suffer, clinging to certain experiences and pushing away others. As alluded to in the previous chapter, this is foundational to the Second Noble Truth in Buddhism (the First Noble Truth states that there is suffering as part of our human condition; the Second Noble Truth states that the cause of our suffering is clinging and craving).

The anchor offers us a place to stand where we need not cling to that which we can't control (struggling to hold onto passing pleasant experiences), and we need not push away or resist our unpleasant inner experiences that arise (trying to get rid of unpleasant feelings). It allows us to find safe ground and a sense of stability from which we can watch the storms and let them pass. It is not about trying to resist or fight against what is happening, but allowing what is there to pass through without becoming entangled in the struggle. Difficult emotions have very strong energies, and without an anchor we are at their whim to be tossed and pushed about. **When our goal becomes finding a safe place within ourselves, rather than trying to change that which we can't, our energy is freed up to handle whatever is here with greater resilience and ease.**

A Word About Self-Compassion

Think about a time when you were really upset about something and then talked to a good friend about what was bothering you as this friend just listened with caring attention. In the presence of a caring, non-judgmental other, our nervous system naturally calms. This is a process called co-regulation. It turns out that we can learn to offer ourselves this kind of care, and in doing so, it has soothing effects on our nervous system.[51] When we experience self-compassion, it is like sitting next to that good friend, except the good friend is *you*. In the acknowledgment of your own pain, and in the wish that you not suffer, the body tends to settle and calm. We will have an opportunity to work with this more in later chapters of this book but know that when you shift into the anchor view, you are opening the door to this self-compassion through your more regulated nervous system.

Importantly, Deb Dana teaches that when we are anchored in ventral vagal regulation, we have access to self-compassion. She says: "Self-compassion is an emergent property of our ventral vagal system. And when we move out of ventral vagal into sympathetic and dorsal, we lose the capacity to have self-compassion."[52]

Meditation teachers Bill and Susan Morgan emphasize the importance of creating an "inner holding environment" that allows us to work with difficult emotions and mind states. Without this inner holding environment, we can be easily swept away by strong emotions and mind states that we experience on a regular basis by nature of being human. Before we can do anything else, they teach that we must establish this inner holding environment as a safe container from which to hold whatever arises. One way we do this, they teach, is to assume a posture of caring attention toward ourselves, as if a dear friend or wise elder is looking over us and our well-being. We then drop from the head into the body to "ground, breathe, calm, settle and soothe" our physical bodies. From this inner holding environment, we can then take the important step of being able to notice and name when a difficult emotion is present.[53] This ability to find some inner stability in our bodies and nervous system is something we will practice in different ways in this chapter.

Discovering an Anchor View

Have you ever had the experience of waking up on the "wrong" side of bed where you are feeling cranky, irritable, anxious, or stressed? From that place, the littlest things might bother you, and you might anticipate "This is going to be a stressful day!" Or maybe you wake up feeling down, and the day ahead seems bleak and unfriendly. Then perhaps something happens that shifts your mood: you get a hug from your partner, talk to a friend on your way to work, go for a walk in nature, or receive a smile from a passerby. Suddenly your mood shifts, and you feel hopeful, at ease, happy, or content. Nothing has changed in your life circumstances. It is still the same day, with the same events unfolding. But as Deb Dana suggests, the world can look very different when different states of our nervous system are activated.[54]

Susan Kaiser Greenland[55] offers a fun exercise to help understand how settling our minds and bodies through mindfulness meditation can be helpful in shifting our view. While she uses this with children, I find this helpful for adults as well. She likens the mind to a bowl of water and adds baking soda to a bowl of water to show how stress and strain can make the mind cloudy. She then demonstrates that if we stop, settle our bodies and feel our breathing, and rest our attention on the water, over time the baking soda settles, and the water becomes clear. The baking soda doesn't go away but the clear water reminds us that we can see more clearly as we pause. Taking the time to calm and settle our bodies and minds allows for this kind of inner settling, from which we can see more clearly how best to manage our stress in a way that is consistent with our values.

When we can access ventral vagal energy through the anchor view, the lens through which we look becomes clearer even though nothing has changed outside of us. When our physiology changes, our lens changes, what we see changes, and the inner resources that we have access to increase, as well as our capacity to hold our own suffering.

An Added Benefit of Taking an Anchor View

Our nervous system is designed such that it responds to immediate threats, and after those threats have passed, our nervous system is supposed to return to balance, to homeostasis—the resting state we were in before the threat occurred. From this place of balance, each part of our nervous system can step out of survival mode and take on a more regulatory function. These important regulatory roles, such as digestion and immune functioning, allow for deep restorative moments where emotional and physical healing can occur.[56] In our modern lives we often miss these opportunities for reset. The anchor view helps us to find our way back to baseline, to homeostasis and balance.

Shift Your Vantage Point:
You Don't Have to Stop the Storm; Just Make Sure to Grab an Anchor.

Warm-Up—Using Imagery to Find Home Base

The morning was pristine, it was glorious: the new coat of snow so thick that you could sink in and not even know where the ground started and the soles of your shoes ended. The sun was so brilliant that it literally bounced off the white coverlet and sparkled like gems in every square inch of white fluff. On a whim, I grabbed my snowshoes—the ones I had purchased for $50 at Costco last year and that had been sitting in my garage ever since. I dusted them off, threw them in the back of my car and headed down the road not more than a mile, to the entrance where the trailhead appeared—the open space before heading into the wooded wonderland. I buckled up my snowshoes over my boots and, like a little kid let loose in a candy shop, I ventured into what was truly uncharted territory. Oddly, not a soul had yet walked or trudged or sloshed or skied on this trail, so it was mine, all mine to forge forward as if calling me to come and play. Not far into the path the pond came into sight, still and inviting to the eye, beckoning more than just a glance as the eyes vacillated between frozen ice and partially melted surfaces. I marveled at the wonder of this glorious moment in this tiny plot of earth on this giant planet spinning through empty space. Here, the trees in all their grandeur were my friends; the rocks, my refuge to rest, the sun my companion who had come out to play, and, the silence of all but the crunch of my boots the music *that soothed my soul. Home at last, I plopped down on a giant boulder, sunk into the snow with a laugh, and savored this moment of being alive and of the deep peace that awaited my visit and welcomed me with open arms.*

When we can access ventral vagal energy, it's like being in the comfort and safety of home. I will refer to this as finding "home base" or our "green zone," as neuropsychologist Rick Hanson writes.[57] Once we become familiar with how home base feels and practice going back there again and again, even in small moments at a time, we can help ourselves return there more easily (eventually even amid challenges). This home base becomes our anchor view from which we can look out and see what is needed. Without an ability to find our way here, we flounder and risk getting swept away by the big waves that life brings.

There is no one right way to find one's home base, so this chapter will offer you many things to try to discover what is most helpful for you. One way to get a sense of this green zone energy is through the use of imagery. Here you will practice through the modalities of writing, and then guided imagery, engaging your senses. Imagination can be extremely powerful because when we imagine something, it can activate similar parts of the brain as if we were actually experiencing that event.[58]

Practice: A Safe Place Anchor

Part One: Writing About Your Safe Place

Take a moment to think about, and write about, a time and place when you felt calm, relaxed, safe, and peaceful. It could be sitting in a comfortable room in your home in front of a warm fire, being in a beautiful place in nature, visiting a spiritual setting, resting on a rock in the sun, or soaking in a warm tub. You might even think of a place you would like to go to, or imagine a made-up place in your mind, so long as when you think about this place you have a sense of ease and calm.

Take five minutes and write about this experience in as much detail as possible, as if you are there now.

Part Two: Meditation/Visualization of Your Safe Place ·

Once you have finished writing, take a few minutes to visualize yourself there now. Make this experience as real as possible in your imagination. **If you like, you can follow along with the audio meditation which can be found at bethkurland.com/vantagepoints.**

Engage as many of your senses as possible to create an experience of being there now. Picture sights, shapes, colors, textures, light and shadow. Imagine sounds in this place, even if subtle, or perhaps the sound of silence. Call to mind sensations against your skin—is there warmth, coolness, gentle pressure, softness, firmness, or other sensations? Perhaps there are aromas that you are aware of as you picture yourself there. Make this a multi-sensory experience and an embodied experience in any way that is available to you. Notice what happens in your body when you imagine being in this place. Do you feel more ease, relaxation, a sense of calm? Does your heart rate slow down slightly? Do you feel tension releasing or a sense of expansion or lightness?

Notice any heartfelt emotions that are present for you. Do you feel centered, content, peaceful, present, serene, accepting, in awe, trusting, inspired, replenished, grounded, or something else?

Note how this feels in your body and heart-mind. Let this feeling sink in and become familiar, so that over time you may find it more easily and return to it again and again.

When I lead patients through this short exercise people often report noticeable shifts in body states, mind states, and emotional states within a matter of minutes—even though nothing in their external environment has changed.

Practice becoming familiar with this "place" in your body-mind, this felt sense that you tapped into. This is your home base. It is part of your deep well of well-being, and it is not dependent on external circumstances or you trying to achieve anything for you to find your way back here. This state already exists in you, as part of your direct experience. It is just a matter of learning how to find your way back there more intentionally.

See if you might choose a word, image, phrase or feeling in your body that represents this home base. For me, I need only call up an image of being in the woods to re-experience this, or to think of the word *surrender*. Whatever you choose, see if you might imagine revisiting this home base for short moments throughout the day: perhaps several minutes when you wake up, sometime midday, and again before you go to sleep. Associate a feeling, image, or word with this state of being so that you can, over time, more easily find your way back there, like a landmark on a map.

Once you find your way to your home base, take a look out from that vantage point and notice what things look like from this anchor view.

Anna's Story: Anna was a CEO of a large company and found that the demands of her job and managing hundreds of employees had her keyed up and on edge much of the time. The pressure of deadlines and constant meetings left her feeling drained during the day, and she started to have difficulty sleeping at night. While she was effective at what she did, she found herself stressed and anxious in a way that was taking away from her being able to enjoy her work and home life.

When I asked Anna if she could think of a time when her nervous system felt deeply relaxed, she immediately said that she feels this way when she sits in her backyard with her dog. I led her through a few minutes of guided meditation, and she was able to imagine herself in this setting with her beloved pet beside her, and very quickly began to experience a feeling of calm within. Her body remembered this kind of letting go, softening and ease just by calling up this image in her mind. She was surprised at how quickly she could shift from feeling tense and stressed to feeling more at ease. She committed to using this exercise several times throughout her day for several minutes, especially prior to meetings. She reported feeling more clear-headed, centered, and present when she did this; also, when moving forward from this anchor view, she felt more capable of effectively solving problems.

Anchoring Through a Circle of Care

Startled out of my sleep, heart racing with unnamed anxiety that I can't place, I anticipate another restless middle-of-the-night episode. So curious that my body is experiencing anxiety before my mind can even figure out what of the many things to worry about that it should rest its attention on. These have become familiar during what is now well over a year into the pandemic. Thankfully, so too are my middle of the night meditations that I remind myself to do. Closing my eyes again, I begin to picture myself surrounded by my circle of care: people in my life who I feel loved and supported by. Sometimes I picture my friends, sometimes my family and loved ones, and sometimes I surround myself with spiritual teachers who comfort me with their wisdom and inspiration. As I focus on this circle of care, I feel my nervous system start to settle and my heart rate slow. There is a sense of connection that transcends the room I am in and fills my heart space with ease. Darkness no longer feels unsafe and instead becomes a thick velvet blanket which envelops me and allows me to slip back into rest.

As we've discussed, the ventral vagal branch of our nervous system helps bring us into connection with others and allows us to feel soothed by their presence. While being in the presence of caring others has a calming and regulating effect on our nervous system, a next best thing is to *imagine* being in the presence of caring others. Our minds can be very powerful, either directing us toward worry or toward comfort, toward fear or toward ease, and we can learn to generate this comfort as a felt sense in our body-mind-heart. As we do this, our physiology changes, as does our emotional state.

When we access a sense of feeling cared for, or a sense of protection and safety being in the presence of others, this helps to activate our ventral vagal response. In doing so, Deb Dana states that some of the outcomes of this response include a change in heart rhythms with reduced stress and lower blood pressure, an increase in immune functioning, improved mood and sleep, more joy, compassion, aliveness, and life satisfaction, and reduced depression and burnout.[59]

Rick Hanson[60] talks about building up a sense of an inner "caring committee" as both a way to help soothe and comfort ourselves, including the younger parts of us that may be fearful or hurting, and as a way to counter our natural inner critic. I find that intentionally calling up this inner caring committee is a powerful way to anchor myself and my nervous system to help me face emotional challenges. When we can look out from this anchored place, we are better able to effectively meet the challenges at hand.

Meditation: Circle of Care

Call up a single moment of care and connection. Think about a time when someone—a family member, friend, acquaintance, teacher or mentor, pet, or other showed you kindness, care, or compassion. It could be a simple moment—a kind word, a listening ear, a gentle hand on your shoulder, or a kind act. As you call this scene to mind, recall how it felt to be in the presence of this person, and to be the recipient of this care or moment of kindness. Notice the area around your chest, your heart center, and sense what it feels like there. Imagine breathing in kindness, care, and support of the person you are picturing. Let that care fill you up, as if a warm light filling you from head to toe and surrounding you. Let go of the specific memory and continue to bask in the energy of care, the way a plant might take in the nourishment of the sun.

Now picture a circle of care surrounding you. This could be made up of people—real or imagined, fictional characters, animals, spiritual guides, or religious figures—or perhaps aspects of the natural world (e.g., experiencing the trees as your friends or the mountains as a source of deep comfort and stability). Imagine that you are surrounded by this circle of care and support, and that whatever difficult emotions you might be holding, you are not alone. Let yourself take in this care and support in a way that allows your body to soften and feel a sense of ease. If it is helpful, imagine comforting words and voices (e.g., *You're not alone; you've got this; you'll get through this*), and facial and body gestures (a hug, a hand on your shoulder or back, warm eye gaze, or smile) from those around you. Notice how your nervous system responds to this and make note of any sense of ease or relaxation in your body and mind. Know that you can call this up during your day, and as you do, you create important cues of safety for your nervous system and an anchored view from which to see the world.

Anchoring with Breath

I recently came across a YouTube video titled "What it looks like beneath a crashing wave."[61] It has beautiful cinematography that captures the view of a crashing wave from below the surface of the water. Besides the sheer beauty of the photos, what struck me most was the sense of stillness and calm below the tumultuous surface. While the energy and intensity at the water's surface was wild and crashing, just several feet below the water was a sustained calm, untouched by what was occurring above it.

In my experience, finding and focusing on the breath can be like sensing that stillness underneath the rough waves of our strong emotions. The breath can be like a steady base of stability that helps to anchor us when difficult emotions might otherwise pull us out to sea. When we focus on our breath as it comes in and as it goes out, we immediately do several things: we drop our awareness into the body and away from the narratives of the mind; we bring our focus to a present moment experience, thus anchoring the runaway mind; and we utilize the body's natural system of regulation to help bring the branches of our nervous system into balance. You will have a chance to practice different ways of using the breath to help anchor you, thus creating another kind of home base from which you can steady yourself and look out from.

(One important caveat: for some people, focusing on the breath triggers cues of threat rather than cues of safety. This might be true if you have a breathing condition, if you have anxiety about body sensations, or if you have experienced a trauma. If focusing on the breath in any way dysregulates you, please skip this section.)

Meditation: Mindful Breathing

For this exercise, the invitation is simply to focus on the sensation of breathing, to observe your breathing the way you might observe the breath of a sleeping child (with an attitude of care). You are not trying to alter or change your breath in any way. Simply feel the natural rise of the inhalation and the fall of the exhalation, like waves coming in and out at the ocean's edge. The mind will naturally wander, and when it does, simply direct your attention back to your breath. Taking the perspective of watching a sleeping child allows you to step back and be the observer of your experience, rather than being caught in it. Return again and again to the sensation of just this breath coming in, and just this breath going out, and as the mind wanders, simply direct it back to the sensation of breath. Don't try to control your breath; let your breath guide you on its own journey toward deeper calm as it shows you the ways that it may want to settle, deepen, or slow. You might observe a natural way that your body softens and tension releases with each exhalation, shoulders dropping and belly softening. You might notice a natural expansion of your lungs and chest as you breathe in. Observe this flow of life, as if each breath was precious (of course it is, but we lose connection with this). Be curious about the slight pauses at the top of each inhalation, and at the bottom of each exhalation. Feel the movement of breath and at the same time, the deeper stillness underneath the surface.

Notice any calming effects in your body and around your heart of following your breath in this manner. As this inner calm becomes familiar to you, the breath itself can become your friend, something that is always there to return to when you start to feel dysregulated. Once you sense more stability present in your body, look back out at the world and notice how you might see things from a different perspective.

Practice: Affectionate Breathing

Affectionate breathing is a core practice of the Mindful Self-Compassion program developed by Christopher Germer and Kristen Neff.[62] It takes mindful breathing and adds an intentional heart quality of affection and care through its guided instructions. At the beginning, there is an invitation to put your hand over your heart or anywhere on your body that feels soothing, as a reminder to bring not only awareness, but affectionate awareness to noticing the breath. This position, of putting the hand on the heart (and often the hand on the abdomen) offers a gesture of care toward oneself that has been shown to help soothe and calm the nervous system.[63] The instructions of affectionate breathing also encourage one to give over to the breathing—to let the body be breathed, and to have a sense of the whole body being gently rocked and caressed by the rhythm of the breath. You can find variations of this practice on Christopher Germer's website (chrisgermer.com), and further guided meditations on YouTube by Christopher Germer and Kristen Neff.

Once you practice this affectionate breathing and feel its effects in your body, you can find your way back there more easily even in short moments throughout the day.

Practice: 1:1 Breathing

This breathing focus exercise encourages regulation of the nervous system through smoothing out the breath by making each inhalation approximately the same length as each exhalation in a 1:1 fashion. Research has found that taking approximately five seconds for each inhalation and five seconds for each exhalation (or six breath cycles per minute) helps to bring the autonomic nervous system into balance.[64]

You might experiment with this now but be sure to find a rhythm that feels comfortable for you without trying to force, strain, or exert effort. Let your breath naturally regulate by breathing in and out to the same count, whether it be five, four, three, or whatever feels best for your body. See if you might match the in-breath and the out-breath and let your breath settle there. You might imagine your breath like waves at the ocean, coming in and going out at the ocean's edge. If it helps, you might count silently to yourself as you breathe in and out. Notice how this kind of even in-and-out breath feels in your body.

Practice: Heart-focused Breathing

Beginning with the 1:1 breathing, you might now add in a heart quality to the above breathing. Start by breathing in and out to a similar count as above. As health psychologist Kelly McGonigal teaches with Heart Breathing,[65] you might imagine that your nostrils are in the center of your chest and you could sense breathing in and out through your physical heart. Breathing in this way, McGonigal explains, has a balancing effect on the autonomic nervous system as well as inducing a balanced, grounded feeling state from which we can act with greater compassion and responsiveness to whatever is in front of us. As you imagine breathing in and out through your heart center, or center of your chest, feel the natural expansion of your chest and lungs with each breath in, and a natural softening and letting go with each breath out. Feel the energy flowing into your heart with each breath in and feel tension dissolving with each breath out. Notice as you do this that your breath may naturally slow down and deepen.

To add a further heart quality, you might call to mind a positive, regenerative emotion such as care or appreciation. Think of someone or something that you care about and continue to focus on this as you breathe in and out through your heart center. HeartMath researchers[66] have studied this practice of combining heart-focused breathing with a positive emotion in what they call the Quick Coherence Technique. Doing this has been found to quickly shift heart rhythms into a more "coherent" state of increased heart-rate variability—a measure of physiological resilience and well-being. It is from this more coherent state that we can best make decisions, problem-solve, be creative, and experience life with more ease and balance.

Practice: 1:2 Breathing

When told to "Take a deep breath," most people emphasize, exaggerate, and increase their inhalation (sucking in air), so that it is quite a bit longer than their exhalation. If being done to calm down, this will likely backfire, because as we accentuate our inhalation, we are revving up the sympathetic nervous system, which may make someone who is already anxious, angry, or upset feel increasingly agitated. When we are feeling anxious, angry, irritable, or frustrated, it can be very helpful to learn how to slow down the exhalation, making it longer (up to twice as long, but mostly what feels comfortable) than the inhalation. Understanding the physiology a bit more can be helpful. When we inhale, our heart rate naturally increases. When we exhale, our heart rate naturally slows down. When we accentuate our exhalation, it is similar to tapping the brakes of the car; it has a slowing and calming effect on the nervous system. Because this response is mediated by our vagus nerve, this slow exhalation and the subsequent slowing of the heart rate is referred to as the vagal brake.[67]

Try this: let the breath come in naturally through your nose. Now, take your time with your exhalation, so that it is a few counts longer than your inhalation. If you breathe into the count of five you might breathe out to the count of seven or eight. Invite your body to release any tension you are holding with each exhalation, softening your jaw, facial muscles, neck, and shoulders.

You might now experiment with breathing out through pursed lips, as if gently blowing out through a straw. This can feel very soothing for many people and allows one to extend the exhalation. Do this for a minute or more and notice how your body feels. For an added visualization to try, as you breathe in through your nose you might imagine climbing the ladder of a slide at a playground, and as you exhale through pursed lips you might imagine going down a very long slide.

Practice using this slow exhalation when you are experiencing a challenging situation and you want to anchor yourself. Once you drop your anchor and regulate your nervous system, you are in a much better place from which you can look out, see more clearly, see a wider perspective, and choose what might be most helpful. Remember, when our nervous system is anchored in ventral vagal safety, the lens through which we look changes and along with it, our mindset, emotions, and behavior choices change as well.

> *Remember, when our nervous system is anchored in ventral vagal safety, the lens through which we look changes and along with it, our mindset, emotions, and behavior choices change as well.*

José's Story: José came to me because he had three small children at home, and he was struggling with his patience and parenting. While intellectually he knew that his toddler was not intentionally misbehaving to get him upset, he found himself getting very triggered and reacting in ways that were not in line with who he wanted to be as a father. We worked first on shifting him out of blame and self-criticism to understanding that this was his nervous system reacting to perceived "threats." Given the chaotic environment he grew up in, his toddler being out of control was especially triggering for his nervous system and evoked a feeling of being unsafe (even though intellectually he recognized this was not the case). We worked on helping José to develop an anchor view, by dropping his imaginary anchor using slow exhalations. He practiced this first thing in the morning, on his lunch break at work, and before he walked into the door at the end of the day. He became familiar with feeling anchored, stable, and safe in his body. Eventually he was able to use this breath when he felt himself getting triggered with his toddler. Only when his nervous system was regulated and from this anchor view was he able to remind himself of that which he already knew that his son's behavior was not personal but simply reflected his developmental age. From here, he was able to access his higher intellect to override his old, conditioned reaction and make choices that were more aligned with who he wanted to be as a dad.

Anchoring with the Body

The path of gravel and stone peeks itself out of the winding up-hill street aptly called Ridge Road. It calls to me like a voice from my past, inviting me into the woods of pine tree and rock, of shady comfort and glimmers of sun falling on the pond like jewels that remind me of what I came here for. What I came here for—and what falls away—is the stress, the to-do list, the needing to perform, to be "on," to be what is expected. On this path I hear the sound of my feet running past old, deep roots that reached their gnarly hands into the earth well before my life even began, towering over me like a protective shelter that welcomes me home. In this space my body flows like a dance, bouncing between earth and sky, sounds of dirt and water and wind taking me on a journey away from the autopilot that so often becomes our lives. I feel my heart pounding, breath quickening, heat and sweat rising and washing over me—reminding me I am very much alive, reminding me of the refuge I have not just in this wooded sanctuary, but in the inner sanctuary that is my true home.

For many people, movement can be an effective way to find one's home base from which they can calm their nervous system and take an anchor view. My body feels most at home when I am moving through space, whether running or walking in the woods, moving through water, on a yoga mat, or on the dance floor. If you love to move, you might find that certain activities are particularly calming or centering for your nervous system. But even the very simple movement of walking (and even in a small, indoor space) can be an effective anchor when done in a meditative way. I offer guidance for a short walking meditation below. Additionally, using the body itself as an anchor in a seated position can be a powerful way to find one's home base. I offer a few suggestions for doing this that you might try.

Practice: Walking Meditation

Pick a small space indoors or outdoors where you can walk back and forth, or in a circle. As you start, bring awareness to the soles of your feet, and just stand still, feeling the contact of your feet with the ground and earth beneath you. Feel the force of gravity keeping you grounded and feel a sense of solid ground beneath you giving you a strong foundation of stability. We often take this for granted, so take a moment to sense into this stability and appreciate the way your body takes in and processes this information, sending calming messages to your nervous system as you feel a solid foundation under foot. Now begin to walk, slowly and mindfully, feeling the contact of each foot along the ground as it hits the ground beneath you from every angle. Continue to notice the ways you are rooted to the earth with each step, and let your body take in this proprioceptive feedback. As you notice the mind wandering, bring it back to the sensation of each foot contacting the ground.

As you do this, add some heart qualities by imagining with each step that there is an anchor of stability, keeping you safe, grounded, and present. Invite this feeling of safety and stability into your body.

Seated Meditation: Growing Roots

This is a common exercise I use for my clients that helps them feel grounded, stable, and offers a felt sense of safety. From this anchor view, it is easier to look out and have a sense of being able to manage challenges at hand.

Find a comfortable seated position if you are able. Begin by bringing awareness to the places where your body is contacting the surfaces that are supporting it. You might start by focusing on the sensation of your feet resting on the ground. Notice the sensation in the soles of your feet and the feeling of your feet resting on firm and solid ground. Begin to move awareness up your body to any places where your legs, buttocks, and back are being supported by the chair or surface you are resting upon. What does it feel like at each of those touch points? What sensations do you notice in your body (firmness, softness, warmth, coolness, gentle pressure, something else)?

Now bring awareness back to your feet and imagine that there are roots, like the roots of a tree, growing out from the soles of your feet and spreading far and wide into the ground and earth beneath you. You might imagine that your body is like a strong, healthy tree above ground, and that these roots keep the tree stable and secure. The roots provide nourishment for the tree, and you might imagine with each inhalation that as you breathe in, you draw this nourishment up through the roots and into your body. These roots can represent your own inner strengths, and the support and care of those around you. Feel the strong foundation of these roots as you continue to imagine taking in nourishment through your roots. Know that this foundation supports you and gives you strength. On each exhalation, you might imagine drawing the nourishment of the sun or a soothing warm light of your choice down into and through your body from head to toe. With each exhalation, have a sense of this nourishing light spreading throughout your whole body, giving you strength, courage, and a sense of stability. Bring awareness back to the soles of your feet, to your roots. Know that even with passing weather such as rain, wind, snow, and other storms, these roots keep your tree firmly supported and stable, remaining strong yet flexible to ride out the storms. Come back to a feeling of being supported, held by the surfaces that you are resting upon. Open your eyes when you are ready.

Practice: Change Your Body, Change Your Mind

In this exercise you will experiment with shifting your muscle tension and posture, and seeing how that affects your viewpoint. You will do this using version one first and then version two, comparing what is different with each experience.

Version one: To begin, think of something that is routinely stressful in your week. Hold that in mind as you slump over, collapsing your posture as if you are starting to curl into a ball. From that slumped over posture, tighten and squeeze all your muscles (face/jaw arms, legs, chest, stomach) with mild to moderate intensity as you say to yourself "I'm so stressed, I'm so stressed." Notice how the experience feels in your body. Notice what emotions are present.

Version two: Now, you will repeat that except this time adjust your posture so that you are sitting upright and relaxed. Roll your shoulders up and back so that your chest is open. Do your best to relax and release any tension from your muscles while you remain upright and open. Hold that stressful situation in mind and say to yourself "I'm so stressed, I'm so stressed" while encouraging your body to remain in a relaxed, open posture with ease in your muscles. Notice how your body feels and what emotions are present. What shifts when you look back out at the situation that was stressing you out?

I find, as do many people I have done this with, that is it much harder to feel stressed when my body is in an upright posture and relaxed. This is because, as mentioned previously, about 80 percent of the signals from our body go up to our brain, with only 20 percent of the messages coming from the brain to the body. Upright posture[68] and relaxed muscles[69] send cues of safety to the nervous system, providing feedback to let the brain know that all is well, there is no danger. These are powerful body changes we can work with as part of the anchor view.

Practice: Putting It Together

Here are a few initial suggestions for what to do when you experience difficult emotions and mind states that can help you to take an anchor view:

Step One. Remind yourself that your nervous system is acting in the service of trying to protect you. Thank it for trying to do its job but recognize that this is part of your old operating system and while this will help keep you safe from life-threatening emergencies, it isn't always the most effective way to manage most modern-day challenges.

(Note: I found this helpful the other day. I noticed myself starting to get anxious about some financial matters. I noticed myself going into my habitual tight, contracted, anxious place, and caught myself. I reminded myself that this was my body trying to protect me from a perceived threat, but in this case, my nervous system going into a high state of arousal and anxiety was not going to be the most useful response to address the issue at hand. Once I named this, something relaxed in me and made space for a different response.)

Step Two. Activate your more newly evolved social engagement system and ventral vagal response (i.e., find your home base). Use one of the suggestions from this chapter (e.g., slow exhalations or compassionate breathing, imagery, calling up your caring committee, soften muscle tension, etc.) or come up with what works best for you. Stay as long as needed with step two until you feel a shift or settling in your body.

Step Three. From this place of increased regulation and nervous system settling, look back out at the situation at hand and notice if your perspective has shifted in any way, or if there is greater ease or "breathing space" to be with what is here. From this anchor view, ask what might be most wise or skillful for how best to proceed or care for yourself.

Finding our anchor view is our first and most foundational move when it comes to working with difficult and strong emotions. When we can find our ground and look out through a regulated nervous system, more possibilities become available to us.

Anchoring the Mind in the Present Moment

By the time I sat down at the small round table adjacent to the other small round tables on this fifth floor in the quiet, brightly lit space filled with collective anticipation, I was feeling a good amount of anxiety. My daughter, eighteen years old at the time, had been rolled away to the surgery room where I, of course, was unable to go. Seeing her in a hospital johnny, hearing about how she would be essentially put into a deep sleep, going over all the risks and possibilities of what could go wrong, and having to sign a consent for things to proceed, had been difficult. The waiting felt excruciating.

It was the first time one of my children needed surgery. While not life-threatening, my threat response was on high alert even despite the friendly faces of the staff trying to make my daughter and I as comfortable as one could in this situation. As if time had no boundaries, the flashbacks came unexpectedly and did not help matters—the ones of my mom's hospitalization after her accident—the one from which she did not recover or regain consciousness.

I had tried to be prepared for the waiting, as I try to be prepared (for better and worse) for most things in my life. My backpack was stuffed with my computer, my mindful magazines, two books I had started reading and hadn't had the chance to get beyond the first few chapters of, and my pen and journal, featuring pages filled with ponderings and reflections and dreams I remembered and scrawled down in the early morning hours. While my plan was to engage myself in activities that would trick my ruminative mind into a redirect, it didn't work. I found that I couldn't concentrate on anything. An hour and a half—that's what the doctor estimated the surgery would take—seemed like an eternity in this strange time warp of space and clock time.

And so, I began to observe the workings of my mind, the mental chatter that I had become familiar with noticing in my many meditations sits in the quiet and safety of my comfy green couch.

(Hardly the same as the firm chair that held my now rigid, clenched body.) Focus on the breath, focus on the breath. . . . Let it anchor me and let me return to it when my mind tries to pull me away. Noticing, noticing. At first, I am swept away in my thoughts, trying to swim upstream in a torrent too strong to resist even the most robust swimmer. Keep watching the thoughts come and go, come and go. Back to the breath, my anchor: just this inhalation, just this exhalation. This breath in this moment.

Then some curiosity: Isn't this interesting to notice my mind jumping into mental rehearsals of things which had not actually happened and the accompanying tightening in my body and quickening of my pulse with each scenario played out in my mind. How curious that this mind creates suffering for me far beyond what is actually happening in this moment. Like a wild stallion, running forward, running backward, I watch from stable ground.

Taking a half step back I begin to see the way that this is not a new pattern for me, this way of the untamed mind. I cannot stop it! It's far too powerful in this moment—and yet there is some space between me and it. Breathing in, breathing out, my peripheral vision begins to expand, to include the woman in the blood-red dress with her matching handbag resting on her lap, staring out into space and then glancing anxiously back at her watch. And the man with the gruff beard and soft voice, whispering into the phone nervously. And others, many others that had no name but yet were part of this shared community of "waiters." No longer just me in this expanse of space, I am with other parents, waiting for their children who too have been wheeled away into unknown territories. Coming back to my breath, it is no longer just me breathing; it is the whole room breathing collectively. Breathing in, I send myself compassion, breathing out, I send wishes of well-being to all who surround me. Breathing in, I feel my feet on steady ground. Breathing out, I feel the vast expanse in which we are all held—our fears, our worries, our restless minds—held in the outstretched embrace of humanity.

The anchor view can allow us to stand on steady ground, even while the mind runs amok in circles around us. The anchor view becomes a vantage point from which we can watch the workings and mental habits of the mind while remaining stable, like a rooted tree standing strong against a storm. In the above example I was focusing on my breathing as a way of steadying myself from my swirling thoughts. I didn't try to stop my swirling thoughts; I simply noticed them from a different vantage point. Having something in the present moment to focus on (my breath) allowed me to observe from safer ground, even when my worry thoughts tried to pull me away. From that vantage point, my peripheral vision also expanded and allowed me to feel more a sense of connection with others around me.

Practice: Present Moment Activity Anchors

Being able to have an anchor in the midst of the would-be runaway mind is an important skill that allows us to deepen our well-being. Any activity that brings you into the present moment, that engages your attention, and that allows you to take an anchor view and look out from stable ground even as you might observe the mental gyrations of the mind, can be considered an anchor. This might be as simple as folding laundry, doing a jigsaw puzzle, pulling weeds in a garden, cooking, or doing something else with your hands or body or mind. While there is nothing wrong with more passive activities such as watching TV (and those can be helpful at times to distract the runaway mind), such activities do not have the same mindful quality that allows us to feel anchored and practice returning again and again to the present moment and a felt sense of stability.

Write down a few activities that can be helpful anchors for you during times of distress or unease, things that allow you to be present in the moment. Rather than thinking of these activities as "distracting" yourself from your mind, think of your mental ruminations as the distraction that takes you away from the present moments of your life that are right here. Choose any of these activities as a kind of meditative practice. If you notice your mind is running away with worries or stressful thoughts about a situation you can do nothing about, engage in the activity of your choice and bring as many of your five senses to that activity. When your mind begins to wander, which it will again and again, simply come back to the experience of whatever you are doing and engage as fully as possible in it.

Putting It All Together

Practice: The Anchor Box

Health and performance coach and polyvagal expert Michael Allison talks about creating a metaphorical "container of safety"[70] that is filled with practices, inner resources, and strategies (e.g., postures, gestures, rituals and routines, breathing exercises, imagery, etc.) that we can use on a daily basis to bring greater cues of safety to our nervous system and into our day.

In this exercise, you will create an actual container of safety by making an "Anchor Box" for yourself.

Find a box of whatever size of your choosing, perhaps one that is pleasing to the eyes or that you can decorate. Fill this box with any things that can be helpful anchors for you, filled with cues of safety for your nervous system that help you find your way back to home base, to the green zone. Think about things that engage any or all your senses. Some ideas include aromatherapy, candles, photos, inspirational quotes or humorous ones, stress balls, notecards with reminders to yourself such as writing down different breathing techniques to try, special rocks, spiritual card decks, clay, art supplies, etc.

Alternatively, or in addition, you could create a special music playlist for yourself that helps you find home base, with music tailored toward creating calm, peace, trust, serenity, playfulness, joy, courage, or any other embodied emotions that you might want to cultivate.

Another idea is to create a file on your computer and write down any exercises from this chapter or other things that help you find your anchor. Have it easily accessible so you can pull it up and choose what you need as you go through your day. There is no one right way to do this. See what modalities work best for you and be creative and playful.

Meditation: Mental Rehearsal Using the Anchor View

Once you have a sense of how to find your way back to your home base, you might experiment with a little bit of practice to find your way back there. Using any of the exercises above, see if you might find your way to home base right now. Reacquaint yourself with this feeling in your body. Find an image or word or a sensation you can recreate that invites that home-base feeling state into your heart-mind-body and helps you to feel anchored.

Now, picture yourself going through a typical day where something stressful happens. Imagine that stressful event for a moment, enough to get a sense of it. Now, see yourself accessing your newer operating system by shifting your vantage point and dropping your anchor using any of the tools in this chapter. Envision yourself finding your way back to home base and a more regulated nervous system. Sense how this feels in your body and picture how you might go forward into the day from here.

This kind of mental rehearsal can help you find your way back to your anchored vantage point more easily in real-life situations. While it can be used at any points in your day, you might find this especially helpful right at the beginning of the day, before you even get out of bed. Rehearse how you might return to your anchor today when life's storms will try to send you adrift.

Then, as you go through your day, notice what anchors are most helpful and effective for you. Make a note of this and celebrate even very small moments of shifting your vantage point to the anchor view. Notice small ways that anchoring yourself changes your inner experience and how you show up for subsequent moments in your day.

CHAPTER 5

The Child View:
Curiosity Is Your Superpower

*A mind that is stretched to a new idea never
returns to its original dimension.*
—Oliver Wendell Holmes

*It's one of those just right days where the sun feels like a yummy
bath of warmth and bubbles that you just want to immerse
yourself in. The birds are singing in a little back and forth aria
that sits just in the background, enough to register in the body
and lift the heart into a feeling of lightness if you stop and notice.
I'm sitting in my outside sanctuary of trees and shrubs, smiling
at these outdoor companions that have kept me company for so
many days through this pandemic, and years and even decades
as children have grown, have gone out on their own, come back,
and now once again are leaving. How curious to have this space,
this pause in my busy life that has felt strangely busier than ever
during this most isolating year of my life. How curious to notice
that as things slow down, as I have open space for the first time
in what feels like months, that familiar tightening creeps in. It
starts in my chest as an unconscious constriction of muscles and*

breath, then feels slightly fluttery and unsettled, like energy that doesn't know where to go or how to be. Then the pressure comes, the feeling that I must take action, be productive, get something accomplished in my free time. And the thoughts: there must be something I can do with myself, something that needs to be done, something to check off my to-do list. Deeper the voice calls: not good enough, you need to do more. How curious, I find, that this familiar friend continues to knock at the door, wanting to come in and take charge, just at the moment I choose to kick my feet up and savor this moment of pause.

In the background, the butterfly settles on the rhododendron, the one that was partially eaten or, shall I say, mutilated—by the starving deer one late winter of crazy snowstorms thirty inches deep, and aching arms from shoveling again and again in unrelenting fashion. I was devastated when I saw the damage to this favorite plant, the one that lights up with bold purple as if to announce to the world, "I am here, I am beautiful, come let me brighten your world for just awhile." What happens to the soul, the essence of the small child who is us? The one who is beautiful like this flower, the one who starts off bold and open to the world but learns early on that it may not feel safe to feel beautiful, learns not to trust its own beauty. And so, we shrink, we close our blooms, it is safer hidden away, sometimes even invisible. And some years the deer are ravenous, and they do what nature demands, only to leave you sad and wondering if ever your plant will grow back and survive this harsh reality that is the living world.

Yet my plant did recover, with time and fertilizer and a little hope and some love from the sun. And today, just for a moment, this butterfly lands on a glorious bloom to drink before it is on its way to its next rest stop. I watch as the magnificent wings expand—yellow and black painted in splatters of color—and then as the wings contract around its tiny body, as if to protect its heart for just a moment before it widens and opens to the world again. In this dance of opening and closing, the rhythm just right, the timing precise enough to take off in an aerodynamic feat called flight.

Perhaps this is how we protect our hearts, closing around ourselves as if to give a hug, and then expanding as if to say, "I am here, I am beautiful," with just the right synchrony that we too can lift off into flight.

Why Do We Need a Child View?

It is so easy to get caught in our habitual way of things, to be caught in our automatic pilot going through the motions, playing out old conditioned and wired-in patterns of thought and behavior without realizing we are doing so, even when those old patterns no longer serve us. Often, those patterns have been there for a long time and come from a place of fear and protection, from our nervous systems trying to protect us by going into survival mode, and habitual ways that we learned to constrict to try and protect ourselves from feeling hurts of various kinds. For me, one of those old patterns is the drive to be busy, accomplishing and *doing* all the time, with some irrational sense of not feeling "safe" if I slow down, pause, and do nothing (as if in the doing nothing *I am not enough* in some way, or something bad will happen if I slow down and let my guard down).

When we bring curiosity to these old patterns, when we can learn to lean in and turn toward our inner experiences and our accompanying thoughts and difficult emotions with the curiosity of a small child—rather than pushing away what is uncomfortable, turning a blind eye to what is there, or being swallowed up by our emotions—possibilities open up. As much as we experience pain due to things that happen in life that we can't control, we suffer greatly because of the mental habits that we get stuck in.

Only when we bring curiosity to those mental habits can they begin to loosen their grip, creating the possibility for something else to arise in its place. If I am never able to see the ways that I constrict and contract and put internal pressure on myself to accomplish and achieve as I go through my day, those patterns will continue as automatically as a robot performing a predetermined task. When curiosity and friendliness touch into and turn toward these patterns, there is a space which opens up to see more clearly and work with what is there in new ways. In the seeing of these old patterns and noticing the ways they keep me stuck, I make a shift from my old operating system to my newer operating system. In seeing the ways that these habitual patterns no longer serve me, the ways that they are trying to protect me but are outdated, I invite in a new way to be. These qualities of curiosity and friendliness, which are foundational to mindfulness, help me make this shift. With practice, they can become your superpower.

Learning from Young Children

Young children are naturally curious and have an innate propensity to explore their world, moving toward and picking up objects that they investigate with all their senses. Initially, before we are conditioned otherwise, there is an openness to experience the world with few likes and dislikes. A spoon or a cardboard box or a shiny dangling object draws our attention with eager curiosity. There is also a natural openness to turn toward what is in front of us rather than close off to it.

The child view invites us to rediscover this curiosity that often gets lost through years of conditioning.

One of the things we can get curious about is our own inner experiences, thoughts, and emotions. Remember, we have an evolutionary predisposition to avoid what is unpleasant, and that includes our own uncomfortable emotions, thoughts, and unpleasant sensations in our bodies. Curiosity and other childlike qualities we will explore here in this chapter can help you work with these challenging emotional energies so that they are not suppressed, but instead can be given room to arise, be felt, and pass through without getting stuck. When we bring these qualities to what is arising before us, this helps us to unhook from unhealthy patterns that no longer serve us without trying to change.

Judson Brewer's work[71] illustrates the power of curiosity to bring about significant changes to the habits that we get stuck in. In one classic study working with cigarette smokers, he taught a group of smokers how to bring mindfulness and curiosity to their smoking habit. Rather than having them try to exert self-control to attempt to stop smoking, or to intellectually think about all the reasons smoking is bad for their health, he simply had them get very curious and pay attention to what smoking feels like, tastes like, how it makes them feel, etc. He never asked them to stop smoking, just simply to notice everything they could about it. Paying attention in this way resulted in a kind of paradox. When smokers were willing to turn toward their experience with curiosity rather than trying to control their experience, they naturally discovered there were things they didn't like about it (e.g., disgust of the smell) and were more willing to give up the habit on their own because of this.

Order of Business

Importantly, establishing our anchor view is often essential before we can take the child view. Only once we have established a safe home base and sense of stability and an idea of how to find our way back to home base can we venture out safely and be more exploratory. Then, when and if we start to get overwhelmed, we can come back to home until we are ready to explore once again. This is immensely important to our foundation of well-being. This allows us to operate in a zone of safety that keeps our nervous systems from swinging too far and going into overwhelm or shut down.

If you watch a very small child exploring a new environment, you will often see just this pattern with their caregiver. In this case, the caregiver provides the anchor. The child will venture out, explore something new with curiosity, and then will return to their caregiver to re-establish a sense of safety and connection before venturing out again. From that reassuring anchor of touching base with a stable caregiver, the baby feels safe to go out and continue exploring the world. So too, when we have an inner anchor to return to, we can find the courage to turn toward our inner experiences more easily, with curiosity and friendliness.

The child view invites us to cultivate and reawaken natural qualities within ourselves that can help us be present with our inner experiences and can also help us navigate the difficult ones with greater ease. These qualities of curiosity, friendliness, interest, playfulness, creativity, and humor are part of our well-being toolkit that we can draw from in times of difficulty.

Learning to take the child view is about reconnecting with these open-hearted qualities. Just as a quick experiment, picture a moment when you were curious about learning something new, or a time when you felt friendly toward someone, or felt wonder and awe. Notice how this feels in your body, particularly around the area of the heart. Is it closed or open, constricted or more expansive? How about a moment of playfulness, or a time you were being creative? When we have access to these childlike qualities, there is a natural openness around our hearts and a connection with ventral vagal energy from our nervous system. When we can approach life from this open-hearted place and these qualities are accessible for us to draw upon, we are setting up the conditions in which difficult emotions can be seen, felt, and responded to rather than being suppressed or overwhelming us.

Taking a child view does two important things. First, it allows us to be curious about our inner experiences and see through friendly eyes the ways that habitual, protective patterns may keep us in survival mode. Second, it offers an important step in learning to hold our own emotional unease with compassion. We can't do this unless we can turn toward our inner experiences.

Imagine a small child who is in distress. We wouldn't likely ignore that child, tell it to "Suck it up" or make the child go away. Yet we often do that with our own inner experiences. The first step in helping this child in distress is of course not walking away or turning your head and pretending that child isn't there but turning toward it and seeing it through kind eyes. The child view teaches us how to do this for ourselves. For most people that I have talked to, both one-on-one and in large audiences, self-criticism comes easily, and self-compassion is extremely difficult. The child view allows us to dip our toe into the waters of self-compassion in a way that feels like a doable first step for many people.

What each of these vantage points is really doing is helping us to be present with our inner experiences of thoughts and emotions in a new way, changing our relationship to them in a way that moves us in the direction of ease, support, comfort, and less suffering. Each vantage point also helps us in shifting out of our old operating system and into our newer operating system.

The child view sets up the conditions for this to happen. Just as a plant needs certain conditions in which to thrive, so too does our inner life. These attitudes of curiosity, friendliness, playfulness, and so on that you will practice here are part of those conditions.

This chapter will help you to bring curiosity and other childlike qualities toward your experiences. It will also invite you to reclaim childlike parts of yourself that you may have closed off or put away in the service of protection along the way.

Shift Your Vantage Point:
You Don't Have to Change Your Experiences—
Just Get Curious.

Part One: Cultivating Curiosity and Other Child-Like Qualities

Armed with my large stainless-steel pot and one of my oversized metal spoons that I grabbed from the top kitchen drawer, I headed outside the back door toward my outside sanctuary, my fenced-in pool area and garden of shrubs and bushes and tall, transcendent forest friends that had become my sense of deep peace through the ups and downs of the warm weather months. I had seen a fox recently, in the far edges of our yard, too close for comfort given I walk this yard often up to the start of the woods. To be honest I was a little scared—no, a lot scared, to run into this creature when it was not on my terms. Having Googled what to do if you run into a fox, I had discovered that they don't like loud noises, and thus the pot and spoon that somehow gave me at least an illusion of safety, should the fox make another unexpected appearance. That, along with the secure gate of the fence that I closely carefully behind me.

I had settled into my favorite spot under the awning, with ample shade and a cool breeze to add a just-right feeling for my meditation practice. Closing my eyes, I settled in to await what thoughts would arise in my mind. Sometimes wanting to peek my eyes open to take in the beautiful nature around me, I slit my eyes just enough to see her eyes staring back at me, no more than ten feet away. Yes, it was the fox, the one I had feared for these weeks since I had spotted her. Slowly, stealthily—holding my breath now, I scooted on top of the granite bar countertop beside me, at a safe enough distance and high enough that surely, she couldn't reach me. At first, I started banging and clanging my pot; what a scene if my neighbors would have happened to notice!

But as I paused and got a closer and more curious look, I saw something that was not at first apparent from my place of reflexive fear. This creature was scared: she had found her way into an unfamiliar space and was simply trying to find her own way back to safety. She was beautiful, with gray reddish fur and a strong tail with spotted black markings. She was no different than I, just trying to make her way in this world safely and find her way back home.

And so, I began to relax—to watch with further curiosity as she wandered about trying to find a way out of the fence, persistent, pacing, poking. I rooted for her and felt a sense of relief and happiness for her as she discovered at last how to find her way back out to her forest home.

And so it is with our fears, is it not? With our thoughts—the narratives we create in our own mind—the ones that keep us up at night and follow us in the wake of day. When we bring curiosity to them, when we can take that half step back and truly see them for what they are, perhaps they loosen their grip and become no more scary or powerful than that beautiful fox that wandered into my backyard on one cloudy day at dusk in July.

Warm-Up Practice: Getting Curious and Cultivating Interest

Begin by choosing an object that you find pleasant (a flower, a stone, a piece of fruit, a painting, a favorite piece of clothing, etc.). Imagine approaching this object with curiosity, as if discovering it for the first time. Notice the following four dimensions of your experience as you explore this object and spend at least a minute or more with each one:

Physical sensations in your body. Notice the senses of touch, sight, smell, sound. Notice how your body feels inside as you engage with this object through your various senses. Be curious about the area around your heart. Is there contraction, expansion, ease, spaciousness, something else? Is your nervous system in the green zone, or somewhere else?

Thoughts. Notice the thoughts that you have about this object. Try to pay attention to your inner dialogue as closely as you can. Notice any ways you appreciate, like, want, or crave this object. Be aware of memories that may arise, or thoughts about the past or future related to this object.

Emotions. Notice how this object makes you feel. Pay attention to any nuances in your emotions and name the emotions present as accurately as you can (e.g., happy, satisfied, appreciative, grateful, calm, peaceful, joyful, relaxed, etc.).

Behaviors. Notice any ways that this object may make you want to act in a certain way. Does it encourage you to savor it? Does it inspire you to take action in some way? Does it invite you to ingest, rest, contemplate, relax, smile, share, etc.?

Now, repeat this exercise two more times, next with a neutral object, and finally with an unpleasant or less desirable object. See what shifts or changes in your experience of each of the four dimensions. Simply notice without judging your experience. (I recently had the opportunity to practice this with a big, scary-looking black rat snake that was slithering in my flower beds.)

Practice and Meditation: Stop, Drop, and Get Curious

Taking this same curiosity and interest as you brought to various objects in the exercise above, begin to bring these same qualities to emotional experiences that unfold during the day and week. (Be sure to pick ones that aren't too strong or overpowering.). As you notice unpleasant emotions sneaking into your awareness, stop (pause) and drop your attention down into your body with curiosity. Make note of body sensations, thoughts,

Use the accompanying meditation to practice stopping, dropping inward, and getting curious.

emotions, and impulses to behave or act in a certain way. Use the accompanying meditation to practice stopping, dropping inward, and getting curious.

For example: "Isn't this interesting that when I just got angry at my partner my whole body started to tighten and constrict; I had a sense that I didn't want to let go of this thing that is bothering me and feel calm . . . I wanted to hold on to a sense of being right. I felt a strong impulse to fight back, even though I knew he didn't mean what he said, and my emotions felt disproportionate to the circumstances."

"Isn't it curious that when I'm about to pick up the phone and call X, I start to feel this tightness in my stomach and my breathing becomes quicker. I have a sense of feeling anxious and feeling small at the same time, kind of like I want to shrink away. It makes me want to put off this phone call and go turn on the TV."

Practice: Deepening Your Observation

For this exercise I suggest you have a notepad handy for several days and write down your observations. Begin to notice your habitual patterns as you go through the day. Which ones move you toward well-being and which ones move you away from well-being? See if you can notice with curiosity as many things as possible that move you in the direction of well-being (e.g., took time to call a friend; took a few conscious breaths before walking into my house after work today; left myself extra time this morning and felt less rushed and more at ease), and notice too as many things as possible that move you in the direction away from well-being (ruminated about why X never called me; started feeling dread about my in-laws coming next week; overate and felt lousy afterwards).

- Bring curiosity to when you shift into survival mode. Think about a time when you felt that this week. How do you know you are in your old, protective operating system? What are your body's signals (contraction, tension, increased heart rate)? What are your emotions (irritability, anxiety, fear, anger, frustration, hopelessness)? What does the inner chatter of your mind sound like (does it start to ruminate, worry about the future, forecast bad things to come; is it critical or self-critical)?

- Now, bring curiosity to when you are in a state of well-being, in your green zone, i.e., when you are accessing your newer operating system. What are your body's signals, your emotions, the inner dialogue in your head?

Cultivating Friendliness

Imagine that you were the manager of a hotel, but you weren't taught much about hotel hospitality or how to greet or interact with your guests. You did just fine with the pleasant guests, the ones who came in with a smile on their face, who were polite and went about their business easily. You would interact with them courteously and enjoy getting to know them, even during their brief stays; but when it came to the more difficult guests, well, that was more of a challenge. These were the guests who came in all disgruntled, angry, or untalkative, the ones who complained and carried on, the ones who didn't neatly follow the rules, or who gave you grief about the littlest things. Imagine if, when you came across those guests, you would either ignore their issues, get into escalated and heated exchanges, or implore them to leave and send them home. You might speculate that if you did this frequently, you would start to lose some business and your hotel would not be thriving.

Now imagine that just down the road was another hotel, and the person who managed that hotel had learned a thing or two about how to greet and interact with all kinds of guests. This hotel manager had learned that when they had a disgruntled or difficult guest, they would make sure to wait until they were in a calm head space to have a conversation with this guest. They would listen openly to what the issues were at hand, try to understand this other person's perspective, not take their behavior personally, and respond with compassion to come up with an appropriate response. They would welcome each visitor with warmth and openness, even if they didn't take a liking to them, giving each person whatever he or she needed to feel most comfortable. This hotel was thriving due to its management style.

What if you thought of your emotions–all of them—as just energy moving through your body, set in motion by your nervous system to offer you information. If you understood your emotions in this way, what might change for you? How might you be able to respond more skillfully or with greater ease?

Practice: Notice and Name (and notice who is doing the noticing!)

What emotions are you most friendly toward? What ones do you tend to be less friendly toward? Which do you not allow in the door?

As you go through your day, notice and simply name whatever feelings come through the door.

Then, when you think of it, bring curiosity to what these emotions feel like in your body. What happens when you are frustrated? What does your body feel like? Your mind? How are you inclined to act? (The other day I got stuck in traffic. I often just get caught up in the stress of this, but I stopped to be curious about "who" was showing up. *Oh, this is what frustration feels like in my body, when I get all tight and contracted. This is what it feels like when my mind gets all narrowed and starts to think angry thoughts.*).

Give your emotion an affectionate name: *Oh there's Mr. Irritable showing up again even though I thought he was not in the neighborhood today.*

Experiment with being friendly toward your emotions when you notice them. You might come up with a greeting as if each emotion is a character or child and thank them for the information they are providing. (For example, *Hello, Fear! Thank you for showing up and trying to protect me as I'm walking into the restaurant to meet this new person. I see that you're trying to be helpful, but it's okay to relax a little. I promise you there are no tigers in there. I've got this but come along if you must.*)

Willingness

Young children tend to be open and willing to turn toward new experiences before self-consciousness and fear of being judged sets in, and before they have come to deem certain experiences as desirable and others as undesirable. That doesn't mean there aren't inherent fears and temperamental issues that come into play but watch very young children and you will see an innocence and willingness to approach things that gets lost as we get older.

Fairly early on in life, we develop aversions to things and resistance toward that which we don't like. As we've touched upon in previous chapters, this includes our own uncomfortable emotions. One problem with this is that suppressing emotions doesn't work so well in the long run. Another problem is that many things that we may want to do in life require us to be willing to tolerate some amount of emotional discomfort (e.g., tolerating some anxiety to speak in front of people; tolerating cravings to make healthy food choices; tolerating fear of failure to launch our creative ideas in the world; tolerating fear of rejection to initiate meaningful connections with others).

I have an aversion to dead animals. I don't think I'm alone in this. My neighbor has had the not-so-good fortune of hearing me shriek, scream, and carry on many a time when I have had to clean out various dead rodents from our pool skimmer basket. This is an extremely unpleasant task for me, in part because it saddens me to see any once-living thing dead, and also because it completely grosses me out. Recently I've been experimenting with willingness. What would it be like to approach this task with some willingness to tolerate discomfort, rather than resisting it kicking and screaming (literally)? Either way it must be done. Doing so resisting and carrying on only drains me of energy. What I have discovered is that lately I have been able to turn toward this unpleasantness with greater openness. Rather than contracting and recoiling, I have been able to relax my body and accept this experience as simply what is. I have been more willing to experience some discomfort and bring curiosity to my own reactions, rather than try to avoid what I am feeling. More ease is available when I do this.

Notice when you are resisting experiences. Notice when there is some willingness to turn toward something uncomfortable and feel something unpleasant in order to do something that is important to you. Notice when there is openness present, even in an uncomfortable situation.

Practice: Getting Comfortable with the Uncomfortable

In this exercise you will practice getting curious about what is uncomfortable (instead of trying to avoid it).

Pick something small that creates some discomfort for you: going up and saying hello to someone, getting up on the dance floor when there is only one other couple out there, approaching a task that you have been procrastinating for a while, making a phone call you've been putting off. See if you might be willing to do that feared or avoided thing while bringing your emotions along for the ride. See if you can turn your attention to your inner experience and watch it with interest. You might practice first doing this in your imagination, mentally rehearsing this, and then try it in real life. Of course, be careful to pick something that feels doable and won't be overwhelming for you.

Advanced Practice: Dropping the Story

Often when we experience unpleasant emotions, we attach a narrative to that experience. If someone experiences a breakup of a relationship, they not only feel sadness, but they likely have a series of thoughts, beliefs, and stories that go along with that (e.g., There must be something wrong with me, I'm not attractive enough, I'm not loveable enough, etc.). We easily get caught in our heads, in the mental ruminations of our mind that can often increase our suffering. Even with minor irritations there are thoughts that get attached to those experiences (about ourselves, others, and the world).

Interestingly, in the world of polyvagal theory, story follows state.[72] When our body responds to some kind of perceived threat, we then create a story to explain and make sense of the physical sensations we are experiencing in our bodies. In other words, there is a physical disturbance at the level of the nervous system and then the higher structures in our brain create a narrative about this. Sometimes, these narratives can then keep us locked in states of threat well after the situation has passed. Being able to recognize the state separate from the story can be very helpful in loosening the grip of our stories and their accompanying emotions.

In this exercise you will practice dropping the story. Like a very small child who does not yet have language, you will move into the body so you can experience the physical sensation of your emotions through your senses, trying to disconnect it from any story your mind is trying to tell you.

1. Find your anchor (from the previous chapter) and take a few minutes to ground yourself and find some stability within.

2. Pick a recent unpleasant emotion that you experienced (irritation, frustration, anger, disappointment, etc.), or if possible, do this as the emotion is arising in the moment. (Start with something that is not too intense. Do not do this with anything traumatic or that may overwhelm you.).

3. Notice the tendency of the mind to want to go into story, to start creating interpretations, judgments, explanations, beliefs about the event. As these thoughts come up, imagine letting them go the way you might release helium balloons and watch them float away in the sky.

4. Drop your awareness into your body and see if you might be willing and curious to notice the emotions that are there as sensations moving through your body. Think of your emotions as energy moving through you. Follow the flow and movement of this energy in your body. For example, if I just had a frustrating phone conversation, I might notice agitated energy, a jumpy feeling around my chest, energy radiating out and down my arms making my muscles tense, and a kind of tightening around my heart. As I pay attention further,

I might notice pulsing sensations in my belly and a feeling of static in my head.

5. As necessary, go back and forth between step one and step four, coming back as often as needed to feel your anchor of stability, then dipping your toe back into the physical sensations present in your body. Invite in slow, deep, and steady breaths throughout so that you are giving breathing space to whatever you are feeling.

6. End this exercise by returning to your anchor for a final time, resting there, and noticing what is present.

Part Two: Reclaiming Lost Childlike Parts

When I was four years old, I remember sitting nervously on the edge of my blue bedspread with the fluffy velvet blanket and asking my babysitter the same question every night she tucked me in: Was I good, bad, or rambunctious? Oh, I so desperately wanted to be good—to have my parents get the good report card so in my mind they would be proud of me, so they would approve, so, to my four-year-old mind, they would love me.

The young version of me used to dance around the living room table to "The Unicorn" song, her free spirit alive like the joy in these daffodils bursting forth from the soil—opening their petals and shouting, Here I am, I am beautiful, and the whole world can see me, and I am here for the world to see. Come, savor my deep yellow, heartfelt yearning for connection; come dance with me!

And then slowly, little by little, the petals began to close up. First it was the time when she internalized the message that good girls don't get angry; and that the noise that she is making is disturbing the needed quiet in the room. Later she was silenced when she tried to close the bathroom door to get privacy but was misunderstood as slamming the door on her teacher walking in, and she felt confusion and shame for getting yelled at. Everybody sure liked when she was well-behaved, and boy did she get approval for those good grades from all of the adults in her life.

So, she began to sit up straighter, to laugh a little less. "Don't look so serious, Beth," people would say. But she had become an excellent student. In fact, she nailed it in the department of how to get approval from authority figures and those you love. And eventually there was no more dancing around the living room at all; it was replaced by the barre, and ballet class, and the structure and control that she became oh-so-comfortable with.

We learn early on to put away whole parts of ourselves. We learn what we need to get approval, what parts of us are desired, how to get attention, and what parts of us are unacceptable. We start to put away the time when we were laughed at for spilling our milk on the way to our desk and it splattered all over the teacher's shiny black shoes; or the time when we tripped trying to make it to home base and lost the game for our team; or brought home the boyfriend with the ripped jeans and stand-up hair and tattoos who was less than acceptable to your parents' higher standards, or the D that you got on the report card that you crumpled up and later buried in the backyard, along with the shame. . . . Little by little, these parts of us get shoved behind the door, and the door becomes locked and bolted and maybe it becomes an impenetrable vault, and we forget that we even have the key.

You know, the most memorable talk I ever went to by a psychologist was one where he talked about how family vacations are overrated, and how his own kids were running amok and he couldn't control them, and he completely lost it. Here I was, trying to be the perfect student, the perfect psychologist, the perfect mother, and I thought, Thank you, Lord, I was finally given permission to not be perfect. I was given permission to just be human.

It wasn't until later, much later—when the walls began to fall away; when the tears became steady and then eased; when the love of life screamed out from inside and tore up the dance floor like a fire gone wild, like a spirit unleashed—that the four-year-old girl knew the answer to the question that she had asked so many years ago.

Was she good, bad, or rambunctious? Hell, she was rambunctious—only this time, she sang it out at the top of her lungs!

Questions for Reflection: Young Parts and Early Childhood

- What messages did you get as a child (from your parents, the media and cultural messages, school, etc.) about who you should and shouldn't be?

- What parts did you push away, close off, hide, forget about, or abandon?

- What parts of you are messy, imperfect, or maybe hadn't been seen by others, and went underground?

- In what ways have you built up protective walls that you are aware of, that developed from early childhood experiences?

- Have you had opportunities in your adult life to reconnect with some of these parts of you that got put away early on in your life? If so, how have they expressed themselves? Where have they found a home?

Often as we grow up, we lose our childlike playfulness, creativity, and our silliness/sense of humor. Each of these qualities can be an important resource in deepening our well of well-being and can be there to draw upon in times of difficulty.

Cultivating Playfulness

We sat in the kitchen eating chocolate chips: me digging my little fingers into the bowl and dropping the chips into my mouth, as many as I could fit, and She with her soft, bigger hands taking a few chips at a time and savoring them one by one.

It was an innocent time, a carefree time, a simple moment. The cookie batter sat on the counter, waiting to be dropped by table-spoons on the baking sheet, but ah, it wouldn't miss those extra chips anyway, would it?

She was busy in a way I didn't understand until much later in life when I had my own kids. She had her full-time job, and her kindergarten kids on the weekend at the temple, where I would later help come into the classroom and make Shrinky Dinks art for the Jewish holidays. She had her volunteer meeting, and oh the carpools—driving three kids back and forth to activities, sometimes during her lunch break which was the only time she would have had for herself.

But for now, for this moment, it was just she and I in a moment frozen in time, with the smell of Toll House chocolate-chip cookies emanating from the oven and a sense of safety and peace that little girls lucky enough like me get to experience.

There were other innocent moments: like collecting all of her shoes and pretending to sell them to her in my store, or the hide-and-seek games we played with the lipstick, or when I was older the word games of trying to guess each other's five-letter word, or the day we sat on my brother's bed and laughed so hard I almost wet my pants.

Later, in my adolescence and beyond, I would have other moments: by her hospital bed, by her gravestone, in the temple where the eternal flame of the candles burned brightly by her wooden box, and the odd comfort of staring into the light, dancing with aliveness, consuming the air.

At fifteen I would pick myself up, never miss a day of school, get perfect grades, laugh with my friends, and become a high achiever in all things academic and in life, while beneath the surface something inside of me began to close up. And, for a while, go silent.

The sound of silence can be haunting, it can be beautiful, it can be filled with solitude. For me, the silence was rigid. It had firm walls and doors that didn't open, tight narrow passageways, and rules that needed to be followed.

But there were always the windows. There was always the light, the sunlight dancing in the breeze, the sunlight, without which there could be no shadows.

When, after all these years, I look to see what is here—it is the moments after all, the playful and precious moments of life. These moments, this moment: this precious celebration of everything that is right here. When the black hole collapses lifetimes into single points in time, this is what is left. It is all complete; it always was. I just needed to discover it for myself.

Questions for Reflection: Your Playful Self

- What memories do you have of playing as a child?

- What kind of play did you most love to engage in as a child?

- In what way have you disconnected from play and playfulness in your adult life?

- Think about a time when you remember playing as a child. Call it to mind in some detail. What does your body feel like when you call this memory up? What emotions are present in this experience?

- What do you do as an adult that you would consider playful?

Practice: Creating Playful Moments

Create some moments this week where you can unleash some playfulness. Perhaps you might blast your favorite music and dance around the kitchen while doing dishes; run through the rain barefoot and let yourself get drenched; or sing at the top of your lungs in the shower.

Consider how playfulness might help you manage stressful times. When my kids were little, we would make games out of boring tasks, like have a race to see who could get dressed first or see if we could get all the chores done before the timer went off. On those days when we did this, things went a lot more smoothly. How might you introduce some playfulness into one of your daily routines? Try something out this week and see in what way it impacts your mood and the ease with which you go about your day.

Practice: Tracking Mental Habits Playfully

Choose a mental habit (or other habit or reactive pattern) that you tend to get stuck in. Examples of such habits might include: being self-critical, going into stress mode over minor irritations; focusing on all the negative things in your day; getting caught in "what if" and catastrophic thinking, etc.

How might playfulness help you look at your mental habits? Can you come up with a game to notice these habits? Maybe put a rock or a penny into a jar for every time that you catch yourself in a mental habit or make a fun sticker chart to keep track of this the way you might have as a kid. Celebrate this noticing. This is not about berating yourself for starting to fall into (or falling into) this mental habit, but about making much of the fact that you noticed it was happening! This is where change lives.

Practice: Tracking States of the Nervous System

You might pick colors to represent each of the three states of your nervous system (e.g., green to represent the green zone of when you are calm, safe, and relaxed; red to represent when your fight-or-flight system is activated; and black to represent when you are in more of collapse, overwhelm, or shutdown mode).

Come up with a fun way of tracking how your nervous system moves in and out of these states as you go through your day. Perhaps use colored markers and make a chart, or draw a map of each day, or color in pieces of a pie chart. Bring as much curiosity and playfulness as possible to this activity.

Alternatively, you could come up with a fun way to track being in your old operating system versus being in your newer operating system. Perhaps make a list of all the qualities you are aware of experiencing when you are in your old operating system (irritability, frustration, anger, contraction, tightness, overwhelm, fear, etc.), and when you are in your newer operating system (connection, calm, safety, openness, etc.). Pretend to be a detective and be playful about catching yourself when you are in one state versus another and earning points for doing so. You might also make note of what helps you shift out of your old operating system into your newer one. Perhaps, give yourself bonus points for being able to do that.

Cultivating Creativity

There is a place, deep within, where creativity thrives. Like a hidden treasure waiting to be uncovered, it gets masked by the drip of seemingly unending stress that we think keeps us alive. When the fears and worries and stresses of the day subside, something arises that calls to our very nature, calls to take us home. This homecoming happens only when we feel safe, nurtured, connected, seen and heard by others, and by ourselves. In this tent of safe-keeping, inspiration becomes the fire by which we gather, with its light reminding us that we were always home.

Creativity, along with the childlike qualities named above, become available to us when we can shift into our newer operating system and when we have a handhold in the green zone of our nervous system. When we can access creativity, this can not only be nourishing in and of itself, but it can help us find creative solutions to challenges that we might not otherwise be able to see when we are stuck in survival mode.

We all have creative ways of expressing ourselves in one way or another. Some of us enjoy creating with our hands (crafts, delicious meals, knitting, woodworking, playing music), some enjoy creating with our bodies (dancing, singing, acting), or with our minds (writing, creating new ideas, inventions).

Practice and Questions for Reflection: Strengthening Creativity

- How do you express yourself creatively?

- What did you used to do as a kid to express yourself creatively? Did you stop doing this thing? If so, why? (E.g., sometimes people stop expressing themselves creatively because of fear of negative evaluation.)

- If you gave yourself free rein to express yourself creatively in whatever way your heart desired, what would you do (as silly as it may feel)?

Set aside some time this week to do something creative, whatever it might be. Put it on your calendar to make sure that it happens. Notice what comes alive in you when you do something creative. What emotions do you experience?

Think about a time when creativity helped you to solve a problem of some kind or helped you through a difficulty. During the height of the pandemic when we were in lockdown, my husband, who had not typically done much cooking, decided to learn to make pizza. He threw himself into this endeavor and became quite creative, experimenting with all kinds of crusts and toppings. Not only did this become a fun hobby for him, but it helped him get through a difficult time (and his pizzas continue to be delicious and as good as any I have ever tasted!).

How might you call on creativity in your life when you are experiencing difficult emotions or facing challenges?

Finding Humor/Silliness

When my daughter was little, she had a fear about two things: sitting on the toilet/flushing her bowel movements down the toilet, and having her toenails cut. These things brought her a good deal of anxiety, and led to some struggles that I wasn't sure how to allay. Trying to find a way to lessen her distress, I decided one day to make up a silly story about a man and his family who lived in the toilet bowl. As I began telling the story I started to elaborate on other characters with funny descriptions, some of whom had very long toenails that they never cut and that scared their neighbors because they were so very long. Somehow the humor of the whole thing brought some ease to her fears, and it became a regular ritual whenever she sat on the toilet or when I had to cut her toenails, that I would tell the adventures of these characters. The laughter and humor of these stories completely shifted her experience of these once-feared events.

Another struggle that emerged was her not wanting to go to bed at night. When I would lie with her in bed at night, we would make up stories about a character she named Ruby, who was really a mischievous version of herself. I would usually play the role of Ruby who would often misbehave and want to get into all manner of trouble. She enjoyed playing the parent role, trying to help Ruby settle down, and ultimately telling Ruby that it was time to go to bed. This silliness that we engaged in became a helpful space in which she could work through her difficult emotions and find a way to be with them, without being shamed or judged for her feelings and trepidation.

Practice: Strengthening Humor

Can you think of any times when the circumstances were challenging but you were able to access humor to help you through?

What role has humor played in your life?

Who do you feel most safe with to be silly?

Look for a situation in which you can bring some humor or light-heartedness into a difficult or frustrating situation. Bring some curiosity to how your inner experiences can shift even when your outer ones don't. As an example, I was in the airport with major flight delays and getting very irritable. We finally boarded a plane, sat there for hours, and then had to disembark and wait for a new plane. My patience was thin, and I just wanted to get home. But somewhere along the way I became curious and started to notice other people around me, light-hearted and joking around in the midst of this frustrating ordeal. I started to see the humor in the situation and started joking around too. It completely shifted my mood and my ability to handle the situation.

Can you notice how the inner state of your mind, body, and heart creates your experience of what is happening in any given situation—not the actual events themselves? Two people might be in the same situation and have very different experiences. Taking a child view creates the inner conditions from which our outer experiences may seem a bit more manageable and bearable.

Childlike Wisdom

The musty smell of the tall brick apartment building stands out in my memory, as if I could find my way back there in a flash, being catapulted back in time to a seemingly other life. In this other life I recall the adults around me frequently speaking Yiddish, the yellow walls of the small apartment where my grandmother and grandfather lived, and where we celebrated holidays together crowded into their small kitchen with the big round table; the small toys and trinkets I used to look forward to playing with upon my arrival. As a young seven-something, I recall that going up and down in the elevator was the highlight of an afternoon, as if a ride at Disneyland could be as exciting. Even more than this was the thrill of riding the elevator by myself. On this particular day I was taking my usual ride up to the third floor, waiting for the doors to open and for me to hop off, as I always did. But this day was not a usual day. In fact, something quite odd happened. When the elevator came to a seeming stop, the doors opened and to my confusion I saw the floor above me—I was caught in between two floors. Knowing something wasn't right, but not knowing how to fix this, I started pressing the down button, anxious to get back to someplace familiar. But instead, I felt a jolt and for a moment, my body froze in space. The elevator stopped moving and so did I. I was stuck and alone in an elevator shaft somewhere in the Bronx, New York, in the United States, on the North American continent, on a spec of planet Earth.

And isn't that the way? We are going along just fine, in our usual patterns, when something unexpected happens and we get stuck, thrown off, sometimes unable to move, unable to find our way. Frozen in fear, we often panic. Caught off guard, perhaps hurt or misunderstood, or unable to make sense of a situation through our young eyes, we close down. We contract. We do what is instinctual.

But my seven-year-old self knew something that my adult self has forgotten so many times. All by myself, and not knowing what else to do but able to read, I pressed the "help" button. And then I waited.

Calmly. Patiently. Hearing the man's voice on the other end of the intercom, I relaxed into the knowing that help was on the other side. I trusted into the comfort of a voice whose owner I could not see.

I was safe. I was okay. There was someone on the other side of the intercom, and with a little finagling I would become unstuck and find my way to where I needed to be. Instead of panicking, I waited. Instead of doubting, I trusted that someone would help. I don't know why, but I knew I would be okay.

Fear gets in the way. Fear makes us panic, knowingly or un-knowingly. Fear causes us to close our hearts in an automatic, self-protective fashion, like shutting a door on a possibility for something else that we can't see is waiting patiently outside.

But what if, on the other side of the intercom or space, there is a loving, reassuring voice? What if that voice tells you that you are not alone? What if that voice offers comfort even when life jolts you? What if that voice is your own?

Questions for Reflection: Your Wise Self

- Sometimes as young children we have great life wisdom that we can lose connection with as we get older. What were some ways you were wise as a child?

- What life wisdom did you have back then that helped you navigate life's challenges?

- How might you reconnect with that wisdom?

Meditation: Dropping into the Wisdom of the Heart

Get into a comfortable position, sitting upright if you are able with your feet on the ground. Imagine taking an elevator ride and dropping down from your head, from your mind, and into your body. Have this elevator take you down to the bottom floor, to where your feet are resting. Take a few moments to gently press your feet into the ground, feeling the solid ground and earth beneath you. Notice sensations at the soles of your feet: perhaps warmth or firmness or gentle pressure. Let your mind rest as you reside in your body and feel grounded, stable, and secure right where you are in this moment. Now imagine that elevator riding upward to the area around your heart. Begin to notice your breathing here, as if breathing in and out directly through your heart center. Feel how your heart expands on the in breath; feel how your body softens and relaxes on the out breath. Sense the tremendous wisdom of your heart, knowing just what to do without you instructing it. Sense the wisdom of your heart, guiding you with its intuitive sense, opening and expanding when you feel safe, allowing you to connect with others, and allowing you to connect with what you care deeply about.

Take a moment to reflect on these questions:

What was your heart's longing as a child? Were there things that you longed to do, adventures that you longed to have? Were there things you were fascinated to learn about? What brought your heart joy? What excited and energized you when you were younger? Are there any things you may take from this and carry forward into your adult life now?

What is the longing of your heart right now? If your heart could speak to you right now, what would it whisper? What would it say? What would it shout?

Notice what happens as you simply listen to whatever is arising.

Take a few deeper, more intentional breaths in and out of your heart center. Feel your feet on the ground and your body connected with the surface that is supporting you. Take your time, coming back into the room when you are ready.

CHAPTER 6

The Audience View:
Learn to Zoom Out

If you change the way you look at things,
the things you look at change.
—Wayne Dyer

All the vantage points in this book are helping you to be aware from a new place, to shift the place from which you are looking. So far you have been working on becoming aware from the anchor view, which helps stabilize you amidst strong emotional energies and create a felt sense of safety within. You have practiced becoming aware from the child view, learning to bring curiosity to your bodily states, emotions, and patterns of behavior, and reawaken childlike qualities to bring to your everyday experiences. Now you are ready for the next shift in vantage point, learning to take a half step back from your inner experiences of strong emotions and difficult mind states that might otherwise have a powerful grip on you. When you become aware from the audience view perspective, the way you experience inner thoughts and emotions shifts profoundly.

Things Are Not Always as They Appear

I was sitting in a parking lot of a Barnes & Noble bookstore on an early summer morning waiting anxiously for the call. The bright pink case holding my cell phone sat centered on my lap, ready to snatch it up within an instant of hearing my familiar ringtone. I had blocked out this time and intentionally picked this destination, landing halfway between my home and my office, where I wouldn't be interrupted and could give full attention to the call. 8:55 AM. Plenty of time to take a few deep, meditative breaths to settle in and sip on my now lukewarm but still tasty matcha green tea. 9:05. Hmm. Okay, no biggie. 9:10 Huh? Okay, she's just running late. Just a year earlier I would never have imagined I would have written a book, and yet here it is, manuscript and all, sent out into the world, and now I have a phone meeting today with this publisher who is interested in publishing my first book. My excitement began to morph into concern by 9:15. Now this is getting a little strange. 9:25. I call my sister in a panic. What do I do? I'm not even sure if I have her phone number. Maybe she had an emergency. 9:30. The concern turns to worry and self-doubt. Maybe she changed her mind, maybe this is going to fall through. The self-doubt melts into irritation, agitation, even anger. No e-mail, no nothing. Narratives start forming about how unprofessional and discourteous this is to leave me hanging like this. 9:40: Yes, I have her number. Okay, I'm calling. Half expecting her not to answer, I dial shakily.

A voice on the other end says "Hello?" She sounds surprised, confused, a little disoriented.

"Hi, it's Beth Kurland," I say. "I was just checking if we were still having a phone meeting today. I thought I would reach out to you since I hadn't heard from you." I'm not sure what I expected

*her to say but I can tell you that not once did it cross my mind
what was about to come next.*

*"It's 6:40 AM. I thought we were talking at 9:00." Then it hit both
of us. I was in Massachusetts, and she was in California—a
three-hour time difference.*

*Seeing the world through my narrow, habitual way, it had never
occurred to me to even ask what time zone she was in (and apparently it hadn't occurred to her either). We got a good laugh
about it and rescheduled the meeting.*

Our Thoughts Are Not Facts

Without realizing it we are often caught up in our own thinking, entangled in our thoughts that create our version of reality. Our thoughts feel very
real and true, as solid as the table upon which my computer rests as I am
typing right now. But what we don't realize is that our narratives are not only
subjective, but are often distorted, inaccurate, and sometimes untrue. They
are no more solid than this table which in fact is made up of invisible particles moving faster than the naked eye can see.

Until I realized the time zone difference in the story above, I was sure
that my publisher was late and had not reached out to let me know that. That
felt like fact to me. From that narrative, all sorts of emotions evolved. Those
emotions primed me to want to act and react in certain ways (which thankfully I didn't). The lens through which I was looking made me believe that my
thoughts were facts, when in fact they weren't.

How Our Past Conditioning Affects Our
Narratives

In addition to our higher brain structures trying to make sense of messages coming from our nervous system (as we explored in the previous

chapter), our narratives are additionally influenced by our past conditioning and memories, which inform how we interpret present-moment experiences. Those interpretations in turn influence the emotions that we experience.

Our thoughts, interpretations, and inner narratives play a huge role in how we experience the world. This may sound obvious, and yet when we look more closely, we can see the way this is not so obvious in our day-to-day lives. Psychology tells us that many of the thoughts that we have are "automatic" thoughts that fall below the surface of conscious awareness. According to one researcher[73] we have somewhere around 60,000 thoughts per day. Many of these are automatic thoughts. Do you know that incessant inner dialogue that you have going on all day long, the inner mental chatter in your mind? As we go through our day, we often don't pay attention to that voice directly, and yet it has something to say about almost everything we experience. Start to listen and you'll see what I'm talking about. Listen more and you'll realize that much of that inner chatter is quite negative, filled with worries, self-criticisms, exaggerations, and distortions.

Imagine a baby before it has language, exploring a spoon. That baby has no previous experience with this spoon. It can be present with this spoon with all its senses, staying open and curious without judgments or preferences or narratives. Now imagine an adult with that same spoon. There may be a whole story attached to that spoon. If your Aunt Linda gave you that silverware set for your wedding, and you love your Aunt Linda, you may pick up that spoon, think of Aunt Linda, and have warm memories of her love and support, and feel secure inside. But what if you greatly dislike your Aunt Linda? What if she treated you terribly as a child? Now when you pick up that spoon you may start to remember all the ways she mistreated you and made you feel badly about yourself. You may feel insecure and start to wonder what's wrong with you. Or maybe you pick up that spoon and compare it to the fancy silverware set that many of your friends have, friends who have more money to afford such things. If you have grown up believing that material things equal a person's value, you may in turn start questioning your own worth and feel like you are falling short in some way. Now imagine that many of these thoughts and emotional reactions are happening outside of your conscious awareness. Without realizing it, that spoon, and all the memories associated with it, might set in motion a whole cascade of thoughts, emotions, and behaviors to follow.

The spoon is a neutral object; it is not good or bad. And yet we can project an entire narrative onto it based on our past experiences which have shaped the lens through which we see the world. We then think that what we see is true. We do this all day long, and for a lifetime. The spoon is just a silly example, but so many of the situations you encounter in your outer world are experienced through this mostly unconscious interpretive lens. This is why two people can be in the exact same situation and experience very different things, based on their past conditioning and the interpretive lens through which they are inclined to look. One person can experience a setback and think that they are a failure; another person can experience that same setback and see it as an opportunity or a challenge to rise above. The narratives they attach to their experience will greatly influence the ensuing emotions and behaviors.

Our thoughts are so powerful that they feel real, true, and solid even when they may be distorted, inaccurate, or even untrue. These thoughts can often act as dominoes, one setting off the next, so that we are no longer dealing with isolated thoughts but instead trying to manage difficult mind states created by these thoughts. These mind states can be a great source of suffering for us.

The Connection Between Difficult Mind States, Emotions, Sensations, and Behaviors

When we take our thoughts as facts, they can have a direct impact on the emotions we feel. If I think that I'm worthless because I didn't get a good-enough grade on an English essay, because I have underlying beliefs about how my self-worth is tied to my performance, it is easy to see how I might very quickly feel down in the dumps, discouraged, or insecure after getting this poor grade. Likewise, if I go to a party and no one comes up to talk with me and I interpret that as no one liking me, I may feel sad or depressed. Those feelings, in turn, can influence my behaviors. If I'm feeling worthless, maybe I decide not to post this blog I wrote because I imagine it isn't good enough. If I think no one likes me, I may not bother going to the next party I'm invited to. This is how our inner mind states can impact our future behavior choices. In turn, if I choose not to do those things, I may feel increasingly isolated, or reinforce some belief of not being good enough. Do you see the cycle that we can get trapped in? Additionally, these thoughts also may be experienced as threat to my nervous system, causing me to feel increased tension in my body, shifting my heart rhythms, and keeping me stuck in my survival circuitry. From this narrowed place, it is harder for me to see my way to a different perspective.

Our thoughts influencing our emotions and behaviors is not the only direction in which this works. If I am at a party and my nervous system picks up threat cues (for example, no one is talking to me), I may start to experience anxiety in my body. I might interpret this anxiety as something wrong, something that needs to be avoided. I may decide to leave the party because these internal sensations are so strong in my body. After leaving the party, I might tell myself that there's something wrong with me because I left the party, that I'm a loser. Consequently, I might feel discouraged, sad, and alone. So, just as our thoughts can influence our physical and emotional states, so too our physical states can lead to the creation of narratives to explain that physical state. Alternatively, I might feel sad about something that happened. If I then judge myself for this emotional reaction (*What's wrong with me? I'm weak, I shouldn't be feeling this way*), those self-judgments (negative automatic thoughts) can cause constrictions in my body and be experienced as threat by my nervous system, sending me into a protective survival state of collapse or shut-down mode.

Can you see the way in which all of this can create additional suffering?

When we are caught in our mental mind states, automatic thoughts, emotions, and physical sensations without having any distance or perspective, we can suffer. Even when outside situations may be difficult, *the narratives that we attach to those situations and the accompanying emotions which ensue can make things far worse.*

If we shift the vantage point from which we are standing, if we take a half step back from our emotions and thoughts and be the witness *of them instead of being in the middle of them, what we see looks very different.*

If we shift the vantage point from which we are standing, if we take a half step back from our emotions and thoughts and be the *witness* of them instead of being in the middle of them, what we see looks very different. From this new perspective, we are no longer locked in by our old, conditioned view of things. Possibilities open up that weren't there before. Our relationship to our experience changes. The audience view will help you make this shift.

Shifting to the Audience View

When my son was in preschool, the class put on a Dr. Seuss play called "The Sneetches." The basement of the church where the school rented space had a built-in stage. The teachers spent many weeks having the children make paper-bag costumes and painting "sets," rehearse their simple lines, and choreograph the movements back and forth across the stage as these twenty or more small bodies bustled around to tell a story. This was my son's first experience with any kind of performance, and he was excited. Unlike some children who are by temperament naturally shyer, my son loved the spotlight and had no compunctions about performing in front of various audiences of family and friends. Finally, the big day came, and he was excited that his dad and I would be coming to watch the show. At one point in the show, some of the children with stars on their bellies (attached with Velcro) went through a special "machine" that removed their stars. When it was my son's turn, he proudly went through the star-removal machine and then turned directly to me from stage and yelled loudly and proudly, "Look Mom, it's magic!" In response to this adorable and unexpected moment, the audience burst out in affectionate laughter. Microseconds later, my son's joyous delight quickly turned to hysterical crying. He was inconsolable. He couldn't possibly understand why everyone was laughing at him. It was unusual for him to be this upset, and it took quite a while before he calmed down. Even after I tried to explain to him why everyone was laughing, he struggled to understand this and was still visibly upset.

From his vantage point on stage and his limited preschooler point of view, this experience felt devastating and embarrassing. Yet from my view from the audience, I could witness both his excitement and then despair from a half step back. The experience did not swallow me up. I was an observer, yet I was not a dispassionate observer. I felt deep care for my son and wished for his well-being. I could see and feel his pain, and yet I was not his pain. I could be with him in his distress, while remaining as the one witnessing and attending, with caring attention.

The audience view is an important step in learning to hold our experiences in spacious awareness, from the vantage point of the observing self and not the actor on stage. Most of the time we think that who we are is the one on stage, having the experience. *I'm so angry. I'm so anxious. I'm so stupid,* we say to ourselves in the midst of difficulties. But have you ever stopped to question who the "I" is that is having the experience? Our physical body feels sensations that we call anxiety. It also experiences emotional energy, created by a complex interaction of physiological state shifts that we call anger. And our minds generate thoughts all the time, many of which are self-referential and judgmental. But how do you know these things are happening? There is a consciousness, a witnessing Self that knows.

Many wisdom traditions and spiritual teachers (e.g., Michael A. Singer, Loch Kelly, Eckhart Tolle to name a few contemporaries) teach us that who we are is *not* our thoughts or emotions. We are not even the body that is having these experiences. We are the conscious awareness that witnesses these experiences, the impartial observer. We are the one in the audience who sees the internal and external events of our life as they are unfolding.

This is a profound shift in the way we think about reality and how we experience the world.

Similarly, in Internal Family Systems (IFS) therapy,[74] there is thought to be a capital S Self that is separate from all the sub-personalities that make up our psyche. The capital S Self is like the CEO or wise overseeing Self who knows what is best and is supposed to run the show. However, these sub-personalities, as mentioned before, often hold strong beliefs (often inaccurate ones that developed when we were young) and strong emotional energies from past events that can get triggered when current, challenging things happen. When this occurs, the sub-personalities take over and forget the CEO is even there.

I see this time and again with myself and with my patients. For myself, one of these parts or sub-personalities that frequently emerges is a manager who tries desperately to control everything, believing that this will keep me safe. This part developed when I was an adolescent, trying to protect me from the pain of any future loss after my mother died. When something happens that is out of my control, even if minor, this part can get triggered and send me into a panic and tailspin. When this part takes over, when I forget that I am the larger observing Self that has far more wisdom and perspective than this part that got frozen in time, I can feel quite frantic, anxious, and alone.

When we identify with these parts and believe that is who we are, it limits our access to the vast resources of the larger Self, the self that has the wisdom to see things as they are, from our newest operating system.

Don't worry! You don't need to believe or grasp any of this to experience the benefits of the audience view. On a simpler level, you have likely had an experience of being caught in something (perhaps an argument or conflict with someone, or a moment of something stressful occurring), and then later being able to take a step back and see things from a larger perspective. From this step back, you realize you had overreacted or hadn't considered the other person's perspective, or perhaps you recognize a solution or way to cope that you had not seen before. This is the gift of the audience view. Because of our biological wiring and conditioning, it is easy for strong emotions and narrowed thinking to take over and shift us into our old operating system. The audience view will help you find your way to a new vantage point, from which you can better navigate challenges that come your way, no matter large or small. The audience view shifts us out of small self view and engages our newer operating system and its integration with our higher thinking brain (the prefrontal cortex, among other structures). This ability to step back and create some space between our Selves and our inner experiences is an essential part of mindful awareness, our next step on the journey.

Learning to Take the Audience View

It's funny how the memory etches certain odd details into the mind that stick there like gum on a sneaker sole that never quite comes off. I was riding as a passenger with the Subaru repair guy beside me. He had a scruffy beard, wore a black T-shirt and a baseball cap turned backwards as he drove with me to try to hear that odd noise I'd been hearing in my car. You know, the one that magically disappears via Murphy's Law as soon as someone else is listening. We were cruising along on Pleasant Street (how ironic) when the phone call came. I recognized the number immediately: my daughter's school, never a good phone number to see pop up on my cell.

"Hello?" I said with a little anxiety in my voice. "Yes, yes—you found what?! Okay, I'll come right in. Oh, God," I said shakily, hanging up, before going into freak-out mode.

The poor guy next to me didn't realize he was in for this ride, to see the lady who seemed to be so quiet and polite and have it all together come unraveled right next to him, in full four-letter words and all. After a time, I felt like I owed him an explanation, so there it was: my daughter had head lice.

It was the head lice that unraveled me, the ones on my daughter's head, all two hundred nits of them as it turns out, that made me lose my shit, that cracked open my tightly held world of control and spiraled me into a place of familiar anxiety that this time could not be ignored. I, who had my world tightly controlled, or so I thought, suddenly had to contend with these little hideous creatures no bigger than the size of a pen point, secretly and exponentially multiplying in the voluminous, thick, and luscious hair of my twelve-year-old daughter. In a desperate attempt to avoid using toxic chemicals on my daughter's scalp, it was the professional nitpicker (who knew there was such a thing?) that removed the two hundred nits and showed me how to comb daily through my daughter's hair and meticulously remove the nits each night so that they did not survive and take over our home. It was, in the end, the head lice that compelled me to begin this back and forth, forty-five-minute trek to Providence, Rhode Island, each week, to sit in the oversized and well-worn chair, a cup of tea in hand from the welcoming waiting room outside the office door. On my first drive to Providence, I wondered who would greet me, who I would meet within the walls of this office that would become my safe space for quite some time. Would I feel comfortable with this person? What would he be like?

This was not my first experience with therapy, but it had been a while since I had undertaken such a journey, to work on the anxiety that arose for me when triggered by feelings of loss of control. Perhaps I had been wired anxious from birth—I believe I was. But trauma has a way of magnifying the fear of loss of control and creating deep grooves in the nervous system that can make things feel unsafe even when they are no longer. The sudden and traumatic loss I experienced at age fifteen, when my mom died in a car accident, left its imprint in ways that I knew I had to face in order to find peace in this life, especially in the face of so much that cannot be controlled. Sitting in that comfy, oversized chair for my first time, I immediately felt at ease with my new therapist, sensing that this would be a supportive relationship that would allow me to use the head lice incident as an opportunity to explore something much deeper at the core.

My meeting with my therapist was not unlike what I expected and hoped; what was unexpected, however, was who else I would meet and develop a relationship with within those walls over the course of our time together, the unlikely cast of characters, the hidden parts of myself that I had put away for many years. It was my relationship with those parts of myself that I had ignored for so many years, parts that I didn't even know existed, or didn't want to acknowledge, that became transformative in my healing. It wasn't about fixing what was broken, or changing myself to become a new, improved, and better version of myself; instead, it was about learning to relate to and befriend these parts of myself and about learning to make space for the difficult emotions present from a place of healthy distance, acceptance, curiosity, and compassion. In shifting my vantage point, in seeing those parts of myself from the wholeness of who I am, my relationship to my inner experiences shifted, and with it, my world began to change.

**Shift Your Vantage Point:
You Don't Have to Stop Your Inner Experiences;
Just Remember You're in the Audience Watching.**

Part One: Learning to Take a Half Step Back Warm-Up

Practice: I Notice That . . .

Here is a simple but powerful exercise that I find helpful to do with my patients and with audiences to whom I speak, to give an experience of shift in vantage point to the audience view. Think about a typical stressful situation in which you might say the following to yourself, through that inner dialogue that I mentioned earlier. Feel free to change the words around to fit the inner experiences that you most typically have.

I'm SO angry.

I'm SO anxious.

I'm SO stupid.

As you say these statements out loud or silently to yourself in your mind, and as you think about a typical triggering situation, notice physical sensations that arise in your body. Notice the area around your heart. Do you feel increased muscle tension, tightness, constriction? An increase in autonomic nervous system arousal? More contraction and closing in, versus expansion and opening?

Now, repeat these phrases but before each add the phrase, "I notice that . . ." Once again, bring some curiosity to how these phrases feel in your body and heart as you say them out loud to yourself.

I notice that I'm feeling strong sensations of anger in my body right now.

I notice that I'm experiencing a lot of anxious energy in my body in this moment.

I notice that I'm having the thought that I'm so stupid.

What happened? For many people, the second set of phrases has a felt sense of stepping back and creating some space between you (the observing self), and the you that is experiencing the stressful event (the actor on stage). Many people also report a shift in the body toward more ease and less constriction around the heart with the second set of phrases.

After writing this, I came across a variation of this exercise that meditation teacher Loch Kelly[75] offers, where he adds a third step after the first two steps. It involves saying, "I notice that a part of me is feeling . . ." You might try this with the above exercise. After saying "I notice that I'm feeling strong sensations of anger in my body right now," you might try saying, "I notice that a part of me is feeling strong anger in my body right now." What do you notice shifts or changes about your experience as you say that?

This exercise is aimed at helping you experience being the noticer and witness, rather than the one who is caught in the middle of strong inner thoughts and emotions. You might use this exercise throughout your day, whenever you notice strong emotions or negative thoughts arising. Try saying, "I notice that . . ." silently to yourself as emotions, sensations, and negative thoughts arise. Bring curiosity to what happens as you shift your vantage point. Is there perhaps a little bit of space between you and your inner experiences, from which you can be less reactive and can see more clearly what might be helpful?

Questions for Reflection: Point of Possibility

- What choices are available to you when you can *notice and observe* your own thoughts, feelings, and behaviors, that aren't available when you are caught in the middle of them?

This is the point of possibility. When you can bring curiosity and friend-liness to the noticing, this becomes your greatest superpower.

Questions for Reflection: A Half Step Back

- Think about a time when you were caught in a heated or emotional moment but were able to take a half step back. Rather than reacting automatically (and perhaps in a way you might later regret), what did you do instead? As you recall that situation, replay it in your mind and reexperience how it feels in your body to be able to witness what is going on in your inner experience *without getting pulled into habitual patterns of reactivity.* What did you gain from having this perspective?

Notice that you don't have to get rid of any of your thoughts, emotions, or the parts of you that want to react, any more than you would try to get rid of actors on the stage. All parts are welcome—just remember that you are the one in the audience.

Elliot's Story: Elliot came to see me because he had what he referred to as "anger issues" and they were getting him in trouble. While he loved his wife, he described to me that he was easily triggered by things she said to him, or even certain looks that she gave him, and this led to unintended blowups due to his intense reactions that were putting their marriage in jeopardy. He loved his toddler but when his son started misbehaving, Elliot reacted harshly and in ways he later regretted. He was content with his job, but when confronted with certain requests from his co-workers, he snapped easily and overreacted, leading to conflicts that made the workplace uncomfortable.

In our sessions together, I taught Elliot how to take a mindful pause by finding an anchor (slowing his exhalation), and then imagining he could take a half step back from what was happening and observe with curiosity from the au-dience view. We practiced this first with neutral things but eventually Elliot was able to create split-second pauses in more heated moments. A breakthrough came one day when he was with his wife. She was expressing frustration about a chore he hadn't followed through on, and he immediately noticed intense energy coursing through his body. He said to himself, *I notice my nervous system is revving up with fight energy; I can see myself ready to pounce, to fight.* When he was able to notice and name what was happening, this interrupted his habitual reaction. He recognized that his nervous system was feeling threatened, but he was able to remind himself in that instant that he was actually safe, with someone who cared about him, who was simply trying to express her needs. From the audience view he saw a version of himself that was taking things personally, as an attack on his character, but he also recognized another viewpoint that he hadn't seen when he was caught in the drama onstage. Having just a few seconds of space between him and the actor on stage, Elliot saw the possibility that he could respond in a softer, gentler way—which he did. This moment became a turning point upon which he could build, and in doing so, his relationships improved. His anger didn't go away, but he was able to relate to it in a new way that allowed him to soothe himself and choose more helpful responses.

Zooming Out

When my daughter was a new driver, she and I took a several hour defensive-driving course aimed to teach things that you might not learn in a traditional driving school. One of the things that we were taught was where to focus our eyes. We learned that most drivers focus their eyes in the wrong place: looking directly in front of them on the road. Instead, we were encouraged to start focusing our eyes out toward the farthest vantage point, resting them more toward the horizon or the farthest point ahead in the road. In this way, you are taking in not only the patch of road right in front of you but also the car pulling onto the road five streets up, and the little girl chasing after the ball toward the road three houses down. You are able to see these things through your peripheral vision and with a wider lens than you would have otherwise been able to by just staring at the road in front of you.

Interestingly, I later learned in a course taught by Rick Hanson[76] that shifting one's eyes to the horizon activates a different part of our brain than when we are looking directly in front of us. When we are focused on what is right in front of us, we activate a part of our brain that tends to be more egocentric in nature. When we shift our eyes to the horizon, we engage a part of our brain that offers a more allocentric perspective, sensing ourselves as part of a much greater whole.

Practice: Shifting Your Eyes

Experiment with this in various ways to see for yourself how it feels when you rest your eyes in different places.

1. First, right now, just let your eyes rest on an object right in front of you. As you focus on the object, notice how this feels in your body. Next, shift your eyes as far out in front of you as you can. As you do that, try to include the original object in your field of awareness. Notice how this feels in your body. For me, with the first instruction, there is a very focused, single-pointed concentration that arises, and it creates a sense of "me" as a contracted self, converging on this point. When I shift my eyes, I have much more of a sense of an expanded self that includes a much wider frame and sense of inter-connection with things outside of "me."

2. Practice this when you experience slight shifts in mood toward irrita-tion, frustration, stress, or upset. Rest your eyes on the farthest point in your visual field and see if that shifts anything about the emotional experience for you or widens your perspective.

3 . Another way to experiment with taking a half step back from your thoughts and emotions is to close your eyes and think about a mildly stressful or irritating situation. As you hold this situation in mind, imagine relocating your eyes from the front of your forehead to the very back of your head. Imagine looking out at the situation from this new vantage point, with your eyes in the very back of your head. Notice the way that this widens your peripheral vision (even with your eyes closed) and may expand your perspective about what you are seeing.

Questions for Reflection: Your Mindscape

◉ As you go through your day, check in and ask yourself, *What is the inner landscape of my mind in this moment? What is your mindscape?* Is it calm like a lake without ripples; it is tumultuous and uneasy; is it skittery and busy; steady and focused? Don't think too intellectually about this question. Instead, see if you might have a visceral, intuitive, holistic sense of the nature of the inner landscape, from the audience view. What is it like to observe your mind states from this perspective?

◉ In what way do you have a sense, when you notice difficult mind states present, that observing them in this way allows you not to be swallowed up by them and better able to see what might be helpful?

⑨ Meditation: Who Is in There?

Find a comfortable position where you can sit for this meditation. Close your eyes if you are able or bring your eyes to a soft gaze looking downward. Imagine sitting in the audience of a large auditorium, watching actors onstage. This is a performance of your life, and you get to see yourself at all different ages through the life cycle. Imagine seeing yourself as a tiny baby, as a small child, an adolescent, and adult. As you see yourself through the years, notice the ways your body changes, how your mind and intellect change through the years, how your emotions fluctuate from scene to scene, how the scenes and situations constantly change. See yourself through different developmental milestones and life experiences. Be curious about what changes and what stays the same. While your body changes over the years, your mind changes, your life situations and circumstances change, your emotions change, there is one constant. That one constant is *you*, the Self that is in the audience watching all of this unfold. Let this knowing sink in. Let yourself sense the constant presence of the observing Self, the witness. As you are ready, bring your awareness back into the room.

Part Two: Working with Narratives

It was an otherwise ordinary day as I climbed into my vehicle from the tiny parking lot where my car had been waiting patiently during my appointment. I remember that the sun was full in the sky, the way that creates a space, an opening, to see clearly into the transcendent blue, and feel small but held. Opening the car door, I scooted into my usual spot and turned the ignition. Something was different. The sound was louder, clearer. I pulled out onto the road and put on my turn signal. Wait, what—what was that? I heard a distinct clicking, almost clucking coming from the steering wheel area that surprised me. How silly, how funny, that this noise delighted me so much! Before it had been dull, muffled, every day dull and muffled. But this was different, crisp, clear. I heard the jingle and jangle of my keys and smiled— is that what metal clinking sounds like? At home, I headed to my favorite meditation spot: the one behind my house tucked away in the trees as if surrounded by tall gentle friends that are always there for me. In the seeming silence I heard sound traveling through the air like sweet honey, coming closer and delighting me as it arrived in my eardrums, warm and delicious. Ah, the sound of birds, high pitched and beautiful; a symphony that I had nearly missed for much of my life. I had heard birds, yes, of course, but not the nuances, the trills and pitches, the higher frequencies that before had been so inaccessible to me. Tears formed in the corners of my eyes, and I gently stroked the little plastic devices, my new hearing aids, that sat behind my ears, bringing me a world of sound that I had been missing for over twenty years.

The sounds had been there all along but because of my hearing loss I wasn't able to process them and have the noise register as an experience in my mind. My brand-new hearing aids helped me to process sound waves at certain frequencies which had always been there but had previously been inaccessible.

Likewise, when we shift our vantage point, the place from which we are standing, we can experience something that has always been there but was inaccessible to us from our small, narrow, or fixed point of view.

This kind of shift, of experiencing something that we didn't know was present but has been there all along, is not just available through external devices. It is something that is available to all of us. It is available in that figure-ground shift when we change the vantage point from which we are standing. From this fresh vantage point, we see things in a new way even though nothing external has changed.

Practice: Noticing Your Narratives from a Front-Row Seat

When we can bring mindful awareness to our narratives, it is like we hear them in a new way. It is not Beth on the stage hearing her own voice and caught in the drama, but the Self in the audience who notices, the one who has some space and perspective and distance.

Now that you have a little bit of practice taking a half step back and knowing what that feels like, let's practice noticing the narratives and mental constructs that arise in your day-to-day experience. To have a little fun with this you might think of your mind as being the writer of a play. Playwrights have creative license to make things appear however they want. They can create great drama, intense emotion, building tension and high conflict. The bigger the better on stage. Remember too, the playwright of your mind is heavily influenced by evolution and looking through the lens of interpreting events in the service of your survival. Your playwright runs from your old operating system much of the time. There was great evolutionary value to overestimating threat and danger, to anticipating bad things happening, to fear messing up, because not doing so might cost you your life, or ostracism from the tribe.

As you go through your day, notice facts that occur in your day and notice interpretations or narratives that your mind conjures up about those facts. To make a game of this, see how many narratives and mental constructs you can capture in the next twenty-four or forty-eight hours, and keep track of them by writing them down. You might write this out on a piece of paper by making three columns: fact, narrative-interpretation, accompanying emotion(s).

For example:

A fact might be: I shared my thoughts about something in a work meeting today.

The narrative is: Boy, did that sound stupid. People are going to think I don't know what I'm doing and will think very badly about me.

Accompanying emotions: embarrassed, anxious

A fact might be: I am at a party, and no one comes up and initiates a conversation with me.

The narrative is: I'm a loser. I'm unattractive and have nothing to say. No wonder no one wants to talk with me.

Accompanying emotions: sad, hopeless, lonely

A fact might be: I woke up feeling pain in my leg.

The narrative is: Here we go again. Now something else is wrong and this is never going to get better. When will this ever end?

Accompanying emotions: anxious, worried, annoyed

A fact might be: I didn't sleep well last night.

The narrative is: This is going to be a disaster of a day.

Accompanying emotion: irritable

Deepening the Audience View

Heavy, heart-pumping, middle-of-the-night wakings call me from the depths of my slumber into this twilight place of half reality. Here, in the sweat-soaked sheets, here in the tossing onto one side—eye pillow and sound machine by my ears drowning out the gentle snoring of my husband nearby—the unsettled, uneasy place begins to show itself in the shadows. How many nights I have been here now! At first it terrified me—me, who is always in control in my waking life. Not only the worries about not falling back to sleep, which barrel through like a train that has left the station, picking up speed, but the other worries appearing only when darkness descends at dead of night. Now a familiar stop in the middle of the night, these times have become, well, curious.

What at first became the dreaded—and needed to be avoided at all cost place—has now become an opportunity to explore this territory that is my mind.

What I have discovered is that it's all about vantage point. Everything changes based on where I choose to stand. What angle do I choose to look from? When I am swallowed up by my thoughts it is as if I have jumped on that train going 100 mph and I am in some foreign land called WHAT IF SOMETHING TERRIBLE HAPPENS? *What will happen when my parents age and can no longer take care of themselves? What of my own body that is aging quietly in the dead of night? Was Sheila really mad at me when I told her I needed to leave early to go recliner shopping? Oh God, maybe I blew it, and this was my one opportunity to find the friendship I was longing for. Oh boy, my foot is bothering me again and what if this keeps up and I can't run, and am stuck inside all summer unable to take my walks in the sanctuary of nature?*

And then there is the shift. It comes as a tiny aha: a little poke on the back saying, Hey lady, do you see what's going on here? Do you notice these mental constructs parading across as truth?

Isn't that curious that this feels like your reality with a capital R? Isn't it interesting that these thoughts cause your heart to beat faster, and bring you to that familiar anxious spiral that pulls you in?

Then, as I pivot to examine these thoughts from an audience perspective, I am suddenly standing outside of the thoughts, and they are slapping the shore and getting sucked back into the ocean. Here I am on the shore, toes tucked into the warm sand, the earth at my feet: solid ground that cradles me, rocks me, holds me, as I slip back into a gentle sleep.

We can so easily become hooked by our anxious thoughts and accompanying emotions, and, as we've discussed, these fears can create quite a big disturbance for us much of the time. From the worries to the self-critical thoughts to the catastrophic thinking to the mental constructs about ourselves and our self-worth, these mental narratives can be destructive if we give power over to them. When we can practice shifting into the audience view, these inner constructs lose their power. The energy and intensity of these stories and the grip they have on us dissipates. They don't necessarily go away, but they also don't have to trigger and overtake us in the ways they may otherwise.

I spent a year living in Wichita, Kansas, when I was six years old. I never saw a tornado, though I woke up many nights in the basement when my parents carried me down there because of a tornado watch. Instead of fire drills we had tornado drills at our school. In some ways, I imagine our inner mental and emotional life like a tornado, with an intensity and power that can catch anything in its path, with potentially destructive force. If you are standing in the midst of the tornado, surely you will be swept away. But outside of the path of the tornado there is safety. Watching the tornado from afar, I can do nothing to stop it, but I am not caught in it. I can watch it arise and pass while staying out of harm's way. This is the audience view: the vantage point that protects us from the intensity of our inner mental and emotional life when things get stormy inside. This is the mindful view.

Our mental narratives can be particularly destructive or create commotion and turmoil for us when they take one of two forms:

1. Self-critical narratives

2. Narratives about the "what if" future

Go back and notice some of the places my mind took me in the middle of the night story above, and see the ways that my mind was trying—in a misguided way—to protect me:

Worries about aging: Thinking about the future to try and prepare for what is to come (even though there is nothing I can do about it at this time, and it is not part of my immediate reality).

Ruminations about upsetting my friend Sheila: Focused on fear that I had messed up in this social interaction; trying to protect myself from being kicked out of the clan and left to fend for myself.

Worries about my foot: Projecting worse-case scenarios to try and prepare me in case danger befalls me.

Practice: Tracking Narratives

This exercise expands upon the previous exercise.

1. Note any narratives your mind has conjured up in the past few days. (You can use what you came up with in the previous exercise or write down new ones.). After each narrative, add another column and write down any ways that your mind might be trying to protect you (as in the above examples).

2. Make note of any narratives that involve "what if" thinking or projecting into the future. For example, with the narrative from above,
   "This is going to be a disaster of a day" (based on me not sleeping
   well), make note that this is a part of me projecting something into
   the future which may or may not turn out to be true. Most worry
   thoughts have some such narrative attached (from the example above,
   experiencing leg pain and worrying "This will never get better").

3. Make note of any narratives that are self-critical. It is especially
   helpful to write out your thoughts on paper. When they live in our
   heads, they can feel especially real, and we often take our thoughts
   as facts. When we can put them on paper, we create space between
   us and our thoughts, allowing us to see our thoughts as the mental
   constructs (versus facts) that they are.

Working with "What if" and Worry Narratives

*When my phone rang it was one of those moments where I just knew it
wasn't going to be a good phone call. I was sitting on the tan microfiber-covered
chair in my office just about ready to greet my last patient for the day. It was
my son calling. He and my husband had gone skiing for the day, something my
husband hadn't done in years but was so excited about, given the opportunity
to spend time with our son.*

*"Dad's fallen and he can't stand up. The ski patrol is helping him into the car
and I'm going to bring him to the emergency room."*

*When I hung up my mind started spinning. What if he needs surgery?
What if he can't work? What if he can't drive? On and on I went. Until my
sister, whom I called for support, reminded me to use my tools to steady myself.
Taking a few moments to just find my breath and steady my mind, I was able
to take a half step back and see how my mind was like a runaway train, taking
me to parts unknown and far away from the present moment. Coming back to*

what was actually right here (not in some imagined possible future), I reminded myself that my husband didn't hit his head, so whatever injury he had with his leg would be fixable and heal in time. I reminded myself that we are fortunate to have access to good medical care. He would be well taken care of. I spoke to him for a moment, and he sounded okay. It was a lot more manageable to be with what was here in this moment than to try to cope with some imagined future that may or may not happen. Even when this moment is difficult it is usually workable. Remarkably, we find a way to cope. It is when we are trying to cope with what is here plus all the imagined what ifs that we can do nothing about that we greatly increase suffering for ourselves.

Taking the audience view and accessing our newer operating system helps us to recognize what is actually here right now, in front of us.

Thank you, survival brain, for trying to protect me, but most of the time I just need to be with what is actually here.

(Of course, thinking into the future to plan for things is important when doing so will help us take appropriate actions, but most of our worrying amounts to driving up and down a dead-end street.)

Practice: It's Not Actually HERE. and What Is Actually Here Right Now?

Go back to any narratives you have noticed over the past few days that involve "what if" and worry thoughts. Draw a line down the middle of a piece of paper. On one side write, "what is actually here right now," and on the other side write, "all the places my mind wants to bring me." Working with the second column, ask yourself, *Is there anything I can do right now that will be helpful—any action steps I can take today?* (For example, if you are worried about money, perhaps an action step you can take would be sitting down and writing out a budget for the coming weeks.). If there is anything you can do, do it. If not, go back to the first column and ask, "Can I be with what is here right now?" If what is here right now is difficult (e.g., uncertainty about a loved one's health), focus on how you might take care of yourself over the next few hours. Notice how much your difficult emotions are being fed by things that are not actually happening. What happens when you bring awareness to this? In the seeing it for what it is, is there an invitation to loosen its grip?

Practice: Stepping Out of Self-Critical Narratives

1. Collect any of the narratives you have noticed in the past few days in which your inner critic has been present.

2. Give your inner critic an affectionate nickname.

3. Imagine you are sitting in the audience and your inner critic is an actor on stage. Write a letter to your inner critic, thanking them for trying to protect you but letting them know you've got things handled.

For example: "Dear Frieda, thanks for trying to protect me at the party when you told me I was a loser and that I had nothing to say, and no one wanted to talk to me. I know you are trying to spare me future humiliation because you are still mortified about the time in grade school when kids made fun of me. I know that you think that being harsh with me will either force me to retreat and spare me from further humiliation and exile from the clan or push me to change so that this doesn't happen again. The truth is, I know you get quite extreme and carried away and have a hard time seeing the bigger picture that I can see. If you could step back and take a wider view, you would realize that I'm actually shy and don't feel very comfortable striking up conversations with new people. But I do have a lot to say, and once people get to know me, they really respect and appreciate me—I know my close friends do. I'm comfortable in a lot of other settings and parties aren't really my scene. I'm not that little kid in grade school anymore. It just takes me time to get comfortable in situations like this. Be patient. I've got this."

Stepping Out of Narratives from the Past

In a comfortable three-bedroom home on a quiet suburban street, a small infant lay in a bassinet, snuggled in an amethyst blanket handwoven by the loving hands of a relative who lived too far to celebrate this burst of new life in a family of now five. Watching from the door's edge, peering into the room was a small child, four years old, observing as her mother lovingly scooped up the small infant and held her tenderly to her breast. Outside the door, the little girl was told to be quiet, to make sure not to disturb the infant. She was expected, quite suddenly, to share what was most precious to her—her mother's attention— with this little blob of life that did almost nothing and seemed, to her eyes, to get the best of what there was to be had. Assessing the situation, she noted that the infant had darker hair, a darker complexion that was in stark contrast to her golden blonde hair and fair skin. How to make sense of this? This happy home suddenly had an intruder, a thief that stole the one precious thing she longed for most. To her young eyes, the only explanation was that she wasn't enough; wasn't enough for her parents to have just her and her brother. Something was missing, some part of her that couldn't complete this family. Not knowing how to make sense of these emotions, feeling jealous, angry, and confused in ways she didn't understand or have words for, she did what four-year-olds do: she acted out, misbehaved. And when she received disapproval for such behavior, and more than anything longing to please and be loved (and thinking these were interchangeable), she became a quick learner. She put away her feelings. She became skillful at being the good, well-behaved little girl that she thought she needed to be to make her parents happy.

From an early age we learn (sometimes mistakenly) what we think we need to do to gain the love and approval of our caregivers, our teachers, and later on, our peers. These ideas start as messages that are sometimes spoken words, sometimes a subtle look of disapproval, or a firm hand that says do it this way, a nonverbal gesture, or a picture in a magazine with its airbrushed perfection that makes you feel inevitably and profoundly imperfect. Quickly these ideas turn into thoughts about who we should be in order to be loved and accepted. Eventually they turn into beliefs, often ones we carry with us like a heavy backpack that we forget we are even carrying.

And therein lies the problem. We don't realize we are carrying these beliefs around with us, and yet, we take them as absolute truth in a kind of act of blind obedience in which these beliefs (and the parts of us that hold them) can end up directing the scenes on the stage that become our life.

The one who is learning these messages is often too young to fully absorb the context and complexity of what is a much bigger picture than can possibly be understood by a young mind. Yet these messages get downloaded nonetheless, programmed into our wiring, until they become conditioned, automatic responses that get played out repeatedly in unknowing ways.

As much as I grew up in an extremely loving, supportive home, my birth order (being a middle child) and having a sister four years younger than me, and my distorted misinterpretations and limited understanding about the events around me, shaped many of my early beliefs. This, along with events in my adolescence, resulted in me a feeling a deep sense of "not enough," which followed me well into my young adulthood.

These narratives from the past masquerade as if they are current news when in fact, they are often quite outdated and no longer relevant. But we believe them, buy into them, as if they still apply in our current lives.

Meditation and Practice: Backpacks

This exercise can be done as a meditation and/or writing exercise. Picture yourself lugging around a backpack filled with things you no longer need, yet you carry it around with you everywhere you go just the same. This backpack is filled with old narratives that are outdated, that no longer serve you, that haven't been upgraded based on all the new information about your adult life.

Imagine the observing Self, the one in the audience, is seeing the way that this backpack gets carried around and weighs you down. Imagine one by one, that you might take each of the stories from the backpack and lay them out in front of you, for you to see clearly. Self might ask and examine, *Is this an old story I am carrying around with me?* Imagine what it might be like to not put that one back into the backpack. Perhaps that one can be filed away separately. You need not get rid of it. It's part of your story, just not the one you need to carry with you today. You might picture a filing cabinet where there is a folder labelled "old stories." File it away there for safekeeping. You can go back and look at it from time to time if you choose. After you have set aside or filed away any old stories that no longer serve you, pick up the backpack and notice how much lighter it is. Perhaps it is now empty! Imagine yourself going forward into the day with a greater sense of ease.

Take some time to write down all the things you carried around in this backpack that you no longer need, that no longer serve you. What does it feel like to look at these and recognize they are not relevant to your life now? Can you sense some compassion for the younger self, for whom these stories may have been a way to cope with difficult circumstances in the best way you knew?

Here are a few examples of what might be in one's backpack:

I have to remain small because if I'm seen I might be made fun of.

It's not safe to speak my mind because when I did in the past I was shut down by my parents or peers.

I have to take care of everyone around me and make them happy. If someone is upset, it's my fault.

If I rest and take care of myself, I'm being lazy.

I need to look perfect in order to be loved and accepted.

If I don't work hard all the time, I'll amount to nothing.

If I don't have control over a situation, something terrible will happen.

Practice: Two Containers

Here is another variation of the above exercise. It can be especially helpful when you notice that the way you are feeling about something is disproportionate to the current circumstances.

As an example, I have experienced many athletic injuries, especially so during the many years I was training intensely for triathlons. At first when I would get a minor injury, one that would take me out of commission for a few weeks, it would feel devastating, like the end of the world. There was a panic and anxiety present that was disproportionate to the actual circumstances (especially because I was not a paid athlete where this was my livelihood, income, and career). When I would take time to journal and put my thoughts onto paper, I realized that these emotions were coming from somewhere else. Yes, it was upsetting to be derailed, but the deeper fear was about something else. It got stirred up whenever there was uncertainty, injury, and a sense of loss of control. I recognized that these were old feelings that I felt around the time my mom died, but they were showing up in these more present-day moments. There was a narrative about how it was not safe to feel loss of control, that generalized to many areas of my life. Once I could see the old narrative masquerading as a current one, my anxiety diminished and I was able to deal more effectively with what was actually here (instead of what was here now, *plus* all of the emotions that were present from my past).

Try this: From the audience view, notice any situations in which your emotions are disproportionate to the situation at hand. Draw two containers: one labelled "present day," and one labelled "past." Write out everything that is true about the present day and imagine putting it in the present-day container (e.g., My ankle is sprained today, and I won't be able to go for that hike that I wanted; I'm feeling really disappointed). Write down anything that is based on the past and put it into the "past" container (e.g., when things are out of my control, it reminds me of feeling helpless, scared, and devastated, like when I was a teenager after my mom's accident; it can have that end-of-the-world feeling to it). Notice what happens when you dump the contents of both containers out into the middle of the room, and they intermix. Notice how it feels to put the contents of each container appropriately where they belong, keeping them separate. What shifts or changes in your inner experience when you do this?

Putting It All Together

Practice: Change Your Location

The next time you experience some emotional unease, just as an experiment, try shifting where you stand (physically take a step backwards or go to a different part of the room). When you experience some mild frustration, irritability, or anger, notice what is present, and ask who is doing the noticing. What are you feeling in your body, what energy is present, what sensations are arising and passing, what mental chatter is present and what is it saying? Surely it is not the anger itself that notices these things. Certainly, standing in the midst of frustration we cannot see beyond it. But shift your vantage point, stand just a half step back and outside of the frustration, and bring some curiosity and kind attention to it and notice what happens. Sensing into the space between you and it (whatever emotion is arising), be curious about how that shift in vantage point changes what is happening in your body. Is there more space? Is there more ease? Is there a greater capacity to relate to what is occurring, rather than be swallowed up by it? This ability that we all have, this mindful awareness, is like experiencing something that was here all along. It opens up an opportunity for us to see things in a new way, as the observer, not as the one entangled in our own muck. In that new perspective there is a space in which choice blossoms.

Practice: Write It Out

When you find yourself entangled in an inner narrative, write a letter to yourself in the third person about whatever you are observing. I find this really helps to get some distance and take an audience view.

For example, "Dear Beth, I can see that you are getting triggered right now and feeling a lot of stress. I can see how you are putting pressure on yourself to accomplish a lot and how you are scolding yourself, *What's wrong with me that I haven't gotten more done today?* I know that old story about how you are not enough likes to rear its head, even when it is not accurate and doesn't belong. You don't have to hold onto that story so tightly right now; it needn't have so much power over you . . ."

Meditation: Using the First Three Vantage Points

The next time you experience an inner struggle, try the following steps:

1. Drop your anchor.

2. Turn with friendliness and curiosity toward what is going on inside.

3. Take an audience view. Notice the commotion happening on stage with caring attention. You might name it, e.g., "I can see Beth getting triggered and struggling with irritability in this moment."

4. Notice what happens when you relocate your Self in the audience.

Mental Rehearsal: If you are able, follow along with the accompanying audio meditation. Think about a typical event in your week that triggers stress for you. In your mind, see yourself going through the above four steps. Notice the choices that become available to you between steps three and four. See yourself choosing a response to the situation that is best for your well-being and the well-being of others around you.

CHAPTER 7

The Compassionate Parent View: How to Become Your Own Ally

You can sit down with that fearful child inside and be gentle
with him or her. You might say something like this:
"Dear little child, I am your adult self. I would like to tell you
that we are no longer a baby, helpless and vulnerable.
We have strong hands and strong feet; we can very
well defend ourselves. So, there is no reason why
we have to continue to be fearful anymore.[77]

—Thich Nhat Hanh

It was the day before my thirty-sixth birthday, a birthday that
my mother and I shared together for the first fifteen years of
my life before she died, as I was born on her birthday. I was, at
that time, working with a therapist and had come home from a
therapy session where I had touched into some deep pain and
grief that was just under the surface, that hadn't fully shown
itself before. (Especially around a significant anniversary, this is
not unusual.)

I had been adept for many years at keeping my feelings at bay, but in adulthood I had been learning how to deal with these waves of grief, especially as they surfaced for me after becoming a mother myself and missing my own mother. When I got home from therapy, I felt a compelling urge to write a poem, and what came out was saying goodbye to my mother in a way I had never been able to do before. I imagined if I had a year, a month, a week, or just one last day with her, what I would have said and done. It brought forth a deluge of deep, heaving, uncontrollable tears that had been waiting to find their way out. Looking back, it was a pivotal moment in my healing journey, one that released deep grief and allowed me to move with and through feelings I didn't realize I had been pushing away for quite some time.

I have always found writing poetry therapeutic for me, even as a young child. Somehow, in listening to the urge to write, in giving voice to deeply felt emotions, in making the space for them to come out, and in welcoming whatever wanted to show up on the page, it was not just a piece of writing that emerged, but some more vast, expansive part of myself that could be present for the parts of me that most wanted to be seen and heard.

This longing to be seen and heard is, I believe, universal. We need it and long for it from others, but we often don't realize that the one person we most want this from is the one we are most often disconnected from: our Self, the one patiently waiting to be discovered.

So far, we have worked on developing an anchor of stability from which we can watch the passing storms without being swept away. We have worked on cultivating childlike qualities to help us turn toward our inner experiences with curiosity and friendliness. And we have practiced taking a half step back from our inner experiences to remember that who we are is the one sitting in the audience witnessing.

Our next shift in vantage point is one that has been profoundly transformational in my own life and in the lives of so many of my patients. It's the *compassionate parent view*, which brings a deeper compassionate presence to our felt experiences, especially our difficult ones.

Taking the Compassionate Parent View

To give you an idea of the compassionate parent view, consider these three scenarios:

1. A small child is upset having just found out that the activity they had been so looking forward to has been canceled last minute. They are feeling extremely sad and disappointed. Their parent comes over to them and says, "Hey, cut that out! I don't want to see that sad look on your face. There are plenty of other things to do right now. Stop moping around and pick something else to do."

2. Same situation as above. The child is having a difficult time managing their sadness and disappointment and is getting increasingly upset and worked up. Their parent remains in the other room, completely disengaged from the child, leaving the child to fend for themselves and remain overwhelmed in their emotional meltdown.

3. Same situation as above. The parent sees that the child is struggling and goes over and puts an arm around the child, offering these words: "I can see how sad and disappointed you are right now. It's really hard when something you were so looking forward to gets canceled last minute like that. It's okay to feel upset. I'm here with you."

How do you imagine the child might feel in each example? What messages are they internalizing from each interaction? Which child do you imagine will feel most at ease?

Likely, in the first two examples, the child would not feel seen, heard, or understood, and might even internalize a message that something is wrong with them because of how they are feeling. In the first example the parent is giving the child the message to put away their feelings and telling them that they shouldn't feel that way; in the second example the parent is completely removed, and the child is getting swallowed up by their emotions and left all alone to cope. In the third example the parent acknowledges the child's feelings and offers connection and care as a path through the difficulties.

When faced with uncomfortable emotions, many of us treat ourselves like the parent in the first or second example. We react to our emotional distress by either telling ourselves we shouldn't be feeling this way and in turn we suppress our emotions, or we fight against the situation, being taken over by strong emotions in moments of reactivity and overwhelm without anywhere internally to turn. When this becomes a habitual way of being, it can have both negative physical and psychological consequences. As psychologist Elisha Goldstein explains,[78] when we suppress emotions, we send ourselves the message that a part of us isn't worth paying attention to, and this not only can cause us to feel deficient or shameful, but this creates physiological stress in our body. This is a variation of the flight response that we talked about earlier. We can also get pulled more into a fight response and criticize ourselves for what we are feeling, similarly leading to stress, shame, and a sense of something wrong.

There is a third alternative though, and that is to respond to our emotional unease the way that a compassionate parent, loving friend, or benevolent mentor might do. An important note is that while I am using the words "compassionate parent view" to represent the sense of feeling cared for by a loving parent, for many people, the word *parent* might be emotionally loaded, especially if one's childhood involved neglect, abuse, or conflictual relationships with parental figures. Even well-meaning parents can often fall short of meeting our emotional distress in these compassionate ways. The "parent view" is meant to refer to a felt sense of a loving parent (not necessarily thinking of one's actual parent). However, the word parent could be easily substituted with a caring friend, a wise and kind mentor or teacher, a benevolent presence of a spiritual figure, or whatever works for you. When we can view and hold our own suffering through the eyes of a caring other, those parts of us feeling pain or discomfort soften and find ease.

To get a sense of this, you might think about a time you were upset about something and talked to someone (a friend, family member, coworker, mentor) who simply listened with caring attention and presence. Afterwards, you likely felt better, were less emotionally charged, and able to move forward in a more beneficial way. Likewise, if you have comforted a small child or witnessed a small child being comforted and seen them find ease. This is what the parent view offers. It helps us to shift our vantage point and see our own distress through the kind, caring eyes of a Self that can welcome all parts of us and offer a comforting presence.

Why the Parent View Isn't So Easy to Access

Most all of us experience traumas as a kid, whether big T trauma or little t ones, whether the jealousy over a new sibling, or the loss of a pet, or the embarrassment of striking out in the ninth inning with bases loaded, or that kid in second grade who told you you're fat, or the pimples that covered your face for three years, or chronic medical issues, or the bigger traumas that rock us at our core, like abuse or neglect, or when my mom died in a car accident when I was a teenager.

Slowly, and often little by little, we begin to put away these parts of ourselves that have been hurt or have experienced pain. We begin to close off the parts of ourselves that we don't want others to see, or that *we* don't want to see, or *feel*. We close off the shame, embarrassment, anger, sadness, grief—all those normal emotions that we don't know what to do with. So, we take a little trowel, and we begin to bury whatever is uncomfortable.

As we have explored earlier, this tendency to seek what is pleasurable and to push away what is painful is not just culturally and socially conditioned but

it is actually hard-wired into our brain. Avoiding discomfort helped our ancestors survive by avoiding things like sabretooth tigers and poisonous plants.
But that same avoidance survival strategy has manifested in our modern lives
as avoiding our own *internal* experiences, our difficult emotions. This experiential avoidance ends up increasing our suffering and making it harder for
us to heal and live our fullest life.[79]

We have a kind of finger-trap dilemma. Have you ever seen one of these
contraptions where you put your fingers in each end of a straw gag toy and
they get stuck? And the harder you pull to try to get them out, the more stuck
they get. The secret to getting free of this trap is to do something counterintuitive—spoiler alert!—to push your fingers *toward* each other, to turn *in* to
the discomfort in order to release them.

We may unconsciously operate from this mental habit throughout much
of our lives. Without our realizing it, this tendency to avoid discomfort
shows up in many ways. We avoid discomfort by procrastinating, sometimes
at the cost of creating undue stress for ourselves. We numb our discomfort
by constantly being on our electronic devices, or using alcohol or other substances in excessive ways that don't serve us. We might escape our discomfort
through food, even at the expense of our health. Or we avoid doing those
things that we really want to do in our lives because we are too anxious, and
we don't know how to be with and soothe the anxiety in order to go after
what we want. We push away our sadness and grief or anger, only to be left
with anxiety, health, or other problems instead. And, like putting a lid on a
pot of boiling water, when we ignore our inner emotions, when they don't
feel seen and heard, they spill out in unintended and reactive ways.

In addition to this tendency to push away or ignore our inner experiences instead of helping them feel seen and heard, so many of us develop an
internalized voice of a harsh inner critic who feeds us messages about how
it is not okay for us to feel certain ways. This can happen for several reasons.
Some people never had caring experiences as a child from their parents and
may have internalized harsh, judgmental voices of the adults they grew up

with. Even in very loving homes with well-intentioned parents, because of our human imperfections and human tendencies, parents miss the mark at times and inadvertently invalidate certain emotions or give the message that certain emotions aren't acceptable. Additionally, societal racism and systematic oppression of all kinds have given people messages that they are not seen or valued or treated equally, and these damaging and destructive messages can be internalized within populations and across generations.

Furthermore, as mentioned earlier there may be some hard wiring of this inner critic through evolution.[80, 81] It makes sense in one way that there was some survival value in having an inner critic versus an inner nurturer. Having an inner critic may have helped our ancestors survive by putting a high value on not "messing up" and wanting to avoid it at all costs, because doing so may have cost them their lives. Also, to mess up socially may have led to being ostracized from the tribe, so this too may have had a heightened evolutionary value driving our tendencies to be self-critical.

So here we are, with evolutionary wiring and conditioned responses that 1) reinforce the tendency to push away or avoid inner experiences that are unpleasant; 2) prioritize protection over connection, thus making the voice of the inner critic louder than the voice of the inner nurturer; and 3) when under the grips of stress and perceived threat (which often happens in emotionally charged situations), can send our system into overdrive, leaving us overwhelmed and hijacked by our feelings, without the ability to step outside of them.

Additionally, the younger, more vulnerable parts of ourselves often get triggered by things in our present-day lives that remind us of past painful experiences. At these times, the younger parts of ourselves can essentially overreact and take over in an effort to protect us, not realizing that we actually have an adult Self who is right here with us (and that many times, we may not truly be under threat). We forget or don't realize that the childhood responses that may have been adaptive or protective for us at that time (or the only ones available to us as children), no longer serve us. We forget that our adult Self can comfort and soothe us in ways that were not available to us when we were younger.

What we need in these situations, what would be most helpful, is to access our newer operating system, the one that helps us feel safe, supported, and connected. In many ways, this is similar to what a loving, compassionate parent or caring friend would do. How can we learn to look at our own suffering through kind eyes and be that compassionate presence for ourselves?

Eastern spiritual traditions, Internal Family Systems therapy, the field of Mindful Self-Compassion, and my own experiences with hundreds of patients over the past thirty years point me to believe that this compassionate presence is *already here within us*. Shifting our vantage point to the compassionate parent view helps us to find our way home.

Coming Home to Our Self

How do we learn to come home to our Self, to connect to what is already whole within us, from which we can look out and hold all our inner experiences? How do we do this in the midst of our imperfections, foibles, and frailties, in the midst of life's disappointments, self-doubt, challenges, and the background voice that visits so many of us whispering "not good enough"? How can we be there for ourselves the way a loving parent or good friend would be, seeing our suffering, picking us up when we fall, holding us when we need comforting, and encouraging us when we feel unsure? How can we connect with this Self that is already here, already whole, but with whom we can sometimes go for long stretches of time or even lifetimes without ever making contact?

Remember that when we take the audience view, as we learned in the last chapter, we create a bit of distance between our thoughts, feelings, and sensations to realize that there is an observing Self present that can witness what is arising without getting caught in the drama. This is not a passive or dispassionate witnessing, the way we might feel if we come across a piece of cardboard box lying on the ground. It involves a deeply embodied experience of caring attention and wanting what is best for the parts of us that are suffering (whether minor irritations and stress, or deeper sadness and grief). Awakening this capacity in ourselves is our next shift in vantage point: learning to take the parent view.

The school bus ride was long and bumpy as this crowded orange capsule barreled along the highway filled with twenty-six second-graders. We had just spent the day at a natural history museum and my lap was filled with a bag of pink- and purple-colored stones I had excitedly purchased at the museum gift shop. My favorite teacher, Mrs. Pickorelli, was sitting several rows in front of me with two other students on either side of her, laughing and engaging with them as the minutes seemed to endlessly pass by. I had a sinking feeling that I couldn't quite name or understand at that time, but it had something to do with a deep longing to be one of the lucky ones getting special attention from our teacher. Jealousy, yes, for sure. Sadness somewhere deeper inside—yes, that too. After what felt like an eternity with these feelings building, I started to "not feel well." I had enough awareness to know that I was not actually sick. Not at all. But I wobbled down the bus aisle and announced to the teacher that I wasn't feeling well, that I was feeling sick. My voice was weak. My face was weepy. Being the compassionate person that she was, my teacher immediately made room for me to sit beside her. She put her arm around me. She helped the jealous and hurting parts of me to feel seen and heard. I felt a deep, soothing ease through my whole body, sinking into the comfort and care of this adult beside me. This memory has stayed with me, that feeling still vivid after forty-eight years.

Feeling seen and heard is an experience we rarely forget, even if the details might fade from our memory. Looking back, I imagine that my teacher knew that I wasn't actually sick, but she was able to pick up on my need and longing for some care and connection, and she offered this unconditionally. I imagine that another teacher might have ignored me or told me to go back to my seat and tough it out. Mrs. Pickorelli intuitively knew what I needed. As a young child I didn't have the internal resources to comfort and soothe myself at that moment, so I sought it out in the only way my little eight-year-old mind could come up with. It wasn't until later, as an adult, that I learned and realized how to do this for myself.

A New Way to Relate to Our Emotions

One way of thinking about our emotions is that they are not good or bad, they are just energy originating in our nervous system acting either in the service of survival and protection or in the service of connection, safety, and renewal.[82] As we touched upon in earlier chapters, our more difficult emotions such as anger, fear, disgust, and sadness each played important roles in the service of protection and survival. Anger and fear helped us to mobilize, fight, or escape predators and other dangers; disgust helped us to avoid poisonous or other harmful substances; and sadness may have driven us to restore attachment or to signal others for help in the face of loss. Some of our more positive emotions such as joy, serenity, love, interest, and inspiration likely played an important role in survival as well,[83] by moving us toward growth, exploration, connection, and restorative processes (such as digestion and immune functioning, once our bodies were at rest and safe).

Looking at our emotions in this way may help us from judging certain emotions as "good" and others as "bad," from believing certain emotions are okay to feel and others are not okay to feel. They all serve a purpose, and we can learn to listen underneath the surface to what that purpose might be.

Just as we have a fight-or-flight system, we also have a caring system that acts as a kind of counterbalance to our threat response. While our fight-or-flight system is regulated by stress hormones such as cortisol, adrenaline, and norepinephrine, our caring system, when activated, releases the hormone oxytocin and endorphins which help to turn down our stress response and increase feelings of safety, soothing, and connection.[84] Self-compassion is linked to our caring system. Thus, it is accessible to all of us, though it often takes practice to learn how to experience it.

We likely have familiar experiences of offering compassion to others. We also may have memories of others offering us compassion. Calling to mind these experiences can be a helpful starting point in terms of developing the capacity to turn this compassion inward, toward oneself. Importantly, when we sit in the presence of a caring friend, or when a distressed child is held in the arms of a loving caretaker, the distress is not forced away and it is also not ignored. Additionally, it is not indulged and encouraged. It is simply seen, heard, and given space. Sitting side by side with a compassionate other, the distress eases, dissipates, and sometimes disappears entirely. The upsetting situation may not always change, but the internal experience can change quite profoundly.

When we learn to shift to the compassionate parent view, we recognize our emotional distress, and we invite something to sit side by side with it (caring attention). This activation of our "tend and befriend" caring system or social engagement system turns on our ventral vagal pathways and moves our bodies in the direction of growth, connection, renewal, and healing.

Just as our bodies heal and regenerate when we are in a ventral vagal state, so too our inner emotional life can heal when we greet ourselves from a place of connection and care, tend, and befriend. I have seen countless times in the therapy space how, when people learn to accept and greet their emotions with care and attention and be like a loving parent to the hurting parts of themselves, there is deep healing.

This chapter and the following exercises are in no way a substitute for therapy for those who may benefit from deeper work, but they can help you shift your vantage point, so that you begin to relate differently to the difficult emotions that arise within you with more compassion and kindness. Developing the capacity to help the parts of us in distress to feel seen and heard is our next step toward deeper well-being.

Rasha's Story: Rasha grew up in a home where she was largely neglected by well-meaning parents who were severely limited in their capacity to see and respond to Rasha's needs. As a teen she experienced harsh bullying, not just isolated incidents but ongoing cruelty from several peers who harassed her on a continual basis. She began to believe herself as broken, feeling something was wrong with her. Because her caregivers couldn't handle her expression of negative emotions such as anger or sadness and would explode at her when she did show these emotions, she learned at an early age to stuff these away. Additionally, it became adaptive to do so because if the mean girls in her school saw any signs of weakness, they would torment her more cruelly.

What began as adaptive, survival behavior carried over into adult aspects of her life. Rasha ended up in several abusive relationships, had trouble holding down a job, made choices that reinforced the old beliefs she held about herself that she was not enough, and suffered from stress-related health conditions due in part to keeping her negative emotions suppressed and at bay.

When I began working with Rasha in therapy, one of the many things we focused on was helping her learn how to meet, greet, and hold these younger parts of herself, the ones that felt anger, sadness, and shame, with compassion. I tried to provide her with a safe space in which she could allow herself to feel her feelings and know this was okay.

As she began to allow herself to feel previously unwanted emotions and see and hold these hurting parts of herself with compassion (the compassion she never got to experience from her own parents), things began to change. She began feeling a deeper feeling of safety within herself, and this allowed her to connect with other people in deeper ways. She was able to feel less threatened in relationships and began to find nourishing relationships where it was safe to let others in. She developed close friendships for the first time in her adult life, married a loving man, and found a job that was fulfilling for her. This was not a self-improvement journey. These changes came out of a nervous system that found its way back to safety and from helping younger, inner-child parts of herself feel seen and heard for the first time. Over time she learned that allowing herself to feel her feelings was no longer scary, because there was now an adult Self who was reliably there for her. Rather than trying to change herself, she reconnected with parts of herself that she had once abandoned, and with feelings she had not allowed herself to have. From this place of wholeness, all manner of possibilities and choices opened up for Rasha that had not previously been available.

Shift Your Vantage Point:
You Don't Have to Change Your Feelings, but
Help Them be Felt, Seen, and Heard.

Warm-Up

Meditation or Writing Exercise: Feeling Seen and Heard

This can be done as either a writing exercise or as a guided meditation, or both.

Find a place where you can sit comfortably undisturbed for a bit of time and have something to write with. Take a few minutes to find your anchor, whether taking slower, deeper breaths, making gentle movements to help your body settle, connecting with the feeling of your feet on the ground, or anything that helps you to feel safe and relaxed. Write or think about a time that you felt seen and heard. This might be a time when someone was fully present to you without judging you or telling you what to do, just listening and letting you be just as you are. It could be a small moment; it need not be momentous. It could be something recent or something from long ago. It could be as simple as sitting in the presence of an attentive, caring friend having a cup of tea and sharing about your day. It could be a schoolmate in second grade who asked you to play with them at recess. Whatever you call to mind, see if you can allow yourself to experience this moment in as much detail as possible, and if you are writing, capture the details on paper. What do you see, hear, and sense? What are the other person's facial expressions, body language, words? Now notice what you feel in your body, and the area around your heart. What does it feel like to receive this kind of presence and attention from another, to feel seen? Stay with this feeling and let it sink into the deep layers of your being.

Meditation or Writing Exercise: Being a Compassionate Presence for Another

You might do this as a short meditation or writing exercise, similar to the above exercise. Think about a moment when you were a supportive presence for another, as a friend helping a friend, a parent comforting a child, assisting a coworker who was having difficulty, showing kindness to a stranger in need, or whatever comes to mind. As you call this moment up in your memory, focus on the way that you wanted to be there for or help this other person in some way. How did it feel to take on this role? Notice the feelings around your heart. Sense any emotions that are present of care, connection, and compassion. Be aware of this compassion while also having a sense of being separate from this other person, in other words, being there for them without taking on their pain as yours. Notice that you already have this capacity inside of you—you already know how to be a compassionate presence.

As you awaken these caring and compassionate qualities in yourself through practice, they become more accessible. Besides enabling you to be a compassionate person to others, you can turn them inward to care for yourself.

Meditation or Writing Exercise: Being Cared for by Another in a Moment of Difficulty

Similar to the exercise above, but shifting the focus slightly, think about a time when you felt the caring presence and support of another in a moment of difficulty. This could be from a parent, friend, pet, mentor, or even a moment of kindness from an acquaintance or stranger (for example, being lost and someone helping you find your way). Note that for some people this idea of receiving compassion can be much harder than giving it, so be gentle with yourself if you struggle with this. (In this case, see if you might find something very small to focus on for starters.) Also, be mindful to choose something that is not triggering for you and would not feel overwhelming to call to mind. The idea here is to focus on the felt sense of being in the presence of a compassionate other, not on the moment of difficulty itself. Imagine that moment now, or if you prefer, take a few minutes to write about it. What does it feel like to receive the compassion and care of another? Notice how you experience this in your body. Imagine that you could take in this feeling of care, support, and compassion from another and absorb it deeply into your body and being. Let it spread through your body from head to toe or imagine it like a beautiful light surrounding you and soothing you.

As I am writing this, two memories immediately pop into my mind for this exercise. One is pulling into the driveway of our synagogue the day of my mother's funeral. Looking out of the car window I remember seeing two of my close school friends walking with their parents to attend the funeral. For some reason this was quite unexpected for me. They had to miss school to be there. It didn't occur to me that they would come, and yet there they were. I didn't speak to them that day as there were so many people and it was quite overwhelming, but just seeing them present there and willing to sit with me in my pain, showing up for me, has stayed with me after all these years: that feeling cared for in a time of greatest need. Another moment that comes to mind was at the beginning of the head lice incident from Chapter 6. I was literally feeling in over my head that day, having to strip all the linens and wash any stitch of clothing that might be harboring these tiny menaces. I heard an unexpected knock on the door. It was a friend of mine, who showed up unannounced to help me scour my house, do copious loads of laundry, and help do everything I needed to make sure no lice could survive and get back into my daughter's hair. These memories remind me of the power of small moments of compassion. *As we hold these powerful moments in our hearts and let them be felt, we learn to give ourselves nurture and care.*

Questions for Reflection: Dropping into Your Inner Heartscape

- As you go through your day, check in and ask yourself what is the inner landscape of your heart in this moment, in relation to yourself? What is your *heartscape*? Is it harsh and critical there? Is it closed off or guarded? Is it loving and supportive? Expansive and open? Compassionate and kind? Encouraging? Might there be a small movement, gesture, word, or phrase that could move things in the direction of the compassionate parent (for example, placing a hand on your heart, saying "I see you," or giving yourself a gentle hug)?

- In what way do you have a sense, that when you observe difficult mind states from the compassionate space within you, that you might experience greater ease?

Strengthening a Sense of Feeling Cared for in the Midst of Difficult Emotions

Practice: Listening to the Needs of Our Emotions

Keep track of emotions that arise throughout the course of the day. You might use an emotion chart to help you capture the nuances of your emotions and name them (e.g., irritable, frustrated, angry, discouraged, sad, contented, peaceful, joyful). Remember that all emotions serve a purpose and that some are in the service of survival, and some are in the service of growth, renewal, and healing.

For any of the more difficult emotions that you experience, thank them for trying to protect you. Ask them what they want or need from you. Is there a more renewing emotion that might sit side by side with this more difficult emotion? What words might be helpful to hear?

For example, if you are feeling angry there may be a sense of your needs not being met, or not feeling heard by another. Perhaps what this emotion wants from you is for you to validate your own needs. Perhaps you might invite care to sit side by side with anger. Maybe it would like to hear from you: "Your needs, thoughts, and opinions matter, even if they can't be received by the other person right now."

If you are feeling disappointed, perhaps this emotion wants to know that it's okay to feel that way. What might it be like to invite nonjudgmental acceptance to sit side by side with disappointment? Perhaps what it would like to hear is, "It's understandable that you are feeling disappointed right now. It's upsetting that this happened, and I'm sorry you are going through this."

When we can invite more renewing emotions to sit side by side with our more uncomfortable ones, we widen the container in which the difficult emotions are held (shifting from the cup of water holding the teaspoon of salt to the lake holding that same teaspoon of salt).

Renewing emotions sitting side by side don't involve us having to change what is there. We don't get rid of the salt any more than we do the more uncomfortable emotions. They simply act as a vaster and more spacious container. Some such containers include ease, care, compassion, courage, comfort, trust, love, serenity, acceptance, and awareness itself. In the presence of these, notice how the heart moves from a contracted state to one that is more relaxed and expansive.

Deepening Practice: Nurturing the Seeds of Self-Compassion

Last night my husband burst through the door when I was finishing my work notes from the day. He grabbed my hand, pulling me to the sunroom like a kid grabbing their best friend to get

*on line at an amusement park ride. "I have a surprise for you,"
he said, piquing my interest as to what could possibly be so
important as to be needed to be seen at this moment. "Look!"
he pointed, like a proud parent showing off his new baby. And
there it was, his tomato plants, grown from seeds in thirty-six
tiny little black compartments of soil, now standing about seven
inches high. I swear they must have grown several inches in the
past few days, since when I was last in the sunroom, they were
hardly towering over their tiny planters and seemed more what
one would expect poking out from the tiny seeds from which they
began.*

*This growth, so natural, surprises me still. That from this tiny
seed can sprout a shoot that will grow into a plant that will
grow juicy, ripe red, tongue licking all around the mouth, can-
dy-tasting tomatoes that will nourish my palate and my body,
seems somehow astonishing. So simple, this biological blueprint:
plant this seed in soil, feed it water and sun, and out spurts life
itself in its most glorious fashion. A few simple ingredients and
out comes this best expression of itself that Nature intended.*

*And what, dear friend, of our biological blueprints? What in
us is waiting to be nourished, tended to simply and kindly, to
burst forth into its fullest expression? How curious that the one
ingredient so essential for our fullest expression is the one that is
hardest to give: self-kindness, compassion, and the care as if of
a loving parent or dear friend. How often we deprive ourselves,
unknowingly, unwittingly, of this one thing we long for most,
to be cared for by the one who is with us from birth to death,
the one who has an opportunity to offer a kind word, a hand
on heart in the midst of the storms, and a gentle hand on the
back as if to say, "I am here, I am always here." No simple feat
this act of self-care that we hardly learn and so easily forget, as*

the voice of self-criticism, "Not good enough," creeps in like a fungus stealing the best of what is possible in its effort to protect us yet. These tiny plants are a reminder of the magnificence that is possible with some tender care. Just for today I pause and hold my heart, the one that has kept me alive for over five decades. And I wonder what is still to sprout from this body, mind, and heart, growing older but growing nonetheless, as it turns toward the sun, ever eager, ever open to soaking in the nourishment for which it longs.

Practice: Buckets of Well-Being

Think about things that you do to nourish your well-being. Consider different categories that nourish you, such as learning something new, physical movement, being creative, contributing to others, being in nature, connecting with others, etc. Imagine each of these as representing individual buckets. If you'd like, you can draw these buckets or write them out on a piece of paper. Now identify things that you do to fill each of these buckets. These are the drops that go into each bucket. For example, if movement is one of your buckets you might write down doing yoga, going for a walk; for your creative bucket you might list writing poetry, drawing, or cooking new recipes; for connecting with others, you might list seeing a friend, calling family members, gathering at church, and so on.

Consider one thing that you might do each day to put a drop in one of your buckets. This form of self-care can be essential to making time for your well-being and taking care of the parts of you that need nourishment.

This can be especially helpful during difficult times. I know for myself at the beginning of the pandemic when our state was in lockdown and there was high fear and uncertainty, identifying small ways that I could put a drop in one of my buckets each day helped me to offset my heightened stress response and get through that scary time.

Comforting Yourself in Times of Unease

Practice: The Quilt Exercise for Self-Comfort

This exercise was inspired by an exercise from Rick Hanson's course[85] that I took many years ago. Imagine a beautiful patchwork quilt, where each square represents someone or something that is comforting and supportive to you in your life. This could be loved ones or friends, favorite mentors or teachers, pets, special places in nature, images you find soothing, or any creation of your imagination. If you like to draw, take some time to draw a picture of each of the squares of your quilt, or just imagine them in your mind. Imagine that in times of distress or unease, you could wrap yourself in this quilt and feel a sense of comfort from each of the squares and the energy of care that they represent. Take some time to imagine wrapping yourself in that quilt now. Let the caring energy that each square of the quilt represents sink into your body and fill your heart. Sense that you are not alone.

Practice: The Bathtub Exercise

This is a variation of the exercise "Listening to the needs of our emotions" from above. In this exercise, the focus is on inviting a renewing emotion to be present with your discomfort using the following visualization. With difficult or painful emotions that you might be feeling, imagine that you are soaking in a bathtub. Instead of filling the tub with Epsom salts, which helps to ease sore or painful muscles, imagine filling the tub with whatever kind of comfort you are in need of (care, kindness, compassion, acceptance, validation, encouragement, etc.). Imagine that as you soak in the tub, the painful parts of you are being held and soothed. Take some time to stay with this feeling. Even better, treat yourself to a nice warm soak in the real thing, enjoying the hot water and surrounding yourself with thoughts and reminders of compassionate care.

👂 Meditation: Caring and Feeling Cared For

Think of someone or something (e.g., a pet) that you deeply care about. As you call that person or creature to mind, feel your love and caring attention for them as a felt sense in your body. Notice where you are most aware of it, and what sensations are present. Imagine this caring energy as a growing and glowing light from your heart that you can direct outward toward that person. Rest in the warmth of your heart. Now think of someone who cares about you; it could be a family member, coworker, pet, spiritual figure, etc. Let their care surround you like a glowing light, and let it be absorbed and sink into your body and heart area. Now, have a sense of sending out caring energy through your heart and taking in the caring energy of the other through your heart, in a rhythmical back-and-forth fashion. If it feels comfortable, you might on the exhalation imagine sending out care, and on the inhalation imagine taking in care. Now imagine that this care could reach down and into the hurting parts of yourself. Sense that you can direct this care toward yourself, receiving your own caring energy. If this feels too difficult, go back to imagining a caring other sending caring attention to the hurting parts of you.

Getting to Know (and Accept) Our Uncomfortable Parts (It's Okay if You Sit Here with Me)

My first experience with "Miss Fuck You" was sitting on the oversized and worn armchair, cup of Bengal spice tea in hand that I had made in the little waiting room outside the door. It was not my first time in this chair and so I settled in comfortably, quickly, allowing my otherwise rigid posture to soften in the support around me. Before much time had passed, I was in a meditative space, dropped into the awareness of anxiety in my body like a familiar screw wound tightly. "What are you noticing?" my therapist would ask, having me sense into what was present in this moment.

In a short bit of time, I was transported backwards to a painful and earlier part of my life that I would rather have put away and kept neatly locked and shut and bolted. It was a time of deep grief, and though I had done much work with this, it remained charged and difficult to revisit.

I watched with curiosity, wondering who would show up today, who would walk through the metaphorical door. It had been an interesting cast of characters who had paraded through that door, walking through from the depth of something so pushed down, yet clawing through earth and dirt to have a voice in this sacred space.

But I was surprised today at who arrived at the door. It was not the adolescent with the sadness, who bravely mustered on without missing so much as a day of school. It was someone else, someone I hadn't seen before. She had unkempt hair and dark eyes, and she wore a black hooded sweatshirt that she wore tightly around her face, as if telling the world that she didn't want anyone to come unwelcomed into her space; as if saying "Fuck you" in an attempt to protect herself from all that felt too vulnerable and fragile to bear. She was rebellious, angry, even full of rage–everything that I, the perfectly well-behaved girl for so many years of my life, could never be.

She was the one without the voice for so many years. The one who stuffed down her anger when all she wanted was to be seen. There was no space for her anger back then. But here—ah— here she can scream her layers of grief and rage and be met with warm eyes that soften years of silence.

Looking back, perhaps it is no wonder that this young girl, the one whose mother left the world at far too young an age, the one who felt so out of control because her world had been undone and could not be put back together—the one who didn't know when, at any given turn or knock or pause, another accident might come crashing into her world—it was no wonder that she did the only thing she knew how to do with her feelings: in a self-protective act, she stuffed them deep inside where no one could see.

But as I made contact with Miss Fuck You and helped her feel safe through my presence, patience, and curiosity, she began to relax. As I started to show up for her, she realized that there was an adult Self here with her; she was not alone.

Miss Fuck You had a lot to show me. She showed me the places where I felt stifled, the places where I had left parts of myself abandoned like an unwanted toy. I had become the version of myself that I thought others wanted me to be. She showed me the dark corners where I dared not look, and the darkness within myself that I dared not admit could be present in such an outwardly "put together" person.

Mostly, she wanted to be heard and seen: which is what any of us ultimately want, is it not? She wanted me to do the opposite of what I had done for years, the opposite of my instinct to disown her and pretend that I had nothing to do with the likes of her and ignore that she had been waiting in the shadows alone and scared. What she deeply longed for was a chance to be seen for who she was, in all of her messiness, her imperfections, her unacceptable feelings. She wanted to know that she was not alone, that there was some greater part of me that could invite her into my home and not need to change a thing about her. She longed

to be accepted, that was all. A simple ask from someone who had
achieved, succeeded, overcame. A simple ask . . . a simple ask.

Tucked away in the deepest places of our souls, our secrets reveal
the essence of our true nature: the parts of us that have been
abandoned, disowned, told to go underground; the parts we
think we need to make disappear because we fear they will not
be accepted, heard, or understood. But there is a door—there is
always a door—and sometimes all we need to do is put our hand
on the knob and let through a crack of light.

Practice: Finding a Voice

What parts of you are you aware of that you have pushed away, in the service of survival, self-protection, or fear of others judging you? If you have ever seen wooden nesting dolls (wooden dolls of decreasing size where one fits within the next), you might imagine three such dolls: the largest, outer doll represents the parts of you that you show to the world; the middle next-sized doll represents the parts of yourself that you show to only select people in your life (close friends, family, etc.), and the third, smallest doll represents the parts of yourself that you have hidden away from others (sometimes even from yourself).

Whatever parts you might identify that you have kept more hidden or less visible, see if you might invite those parts (only the ones that feel safe enough to do so) to come and sit in the room with you. You need not pick anything too intense; it could for example, be a goofy part of you that only a select few get to see. (I have one of those parts that mostly remains hidden, except in the presence of my immediate family!). Imagine what this part looks like and give it an affectionate nickname. If you are inclined, draw a picture of this part and invite in an element of playfulness and creativity.

What would this part of you like to whisper?

What would it like to say?

What would it like to scream out loud?

⚆ Meditation: I See You, You Are Welcome Here

In the following meditation, we will work with what I consider three fundamental steps to meet and greet the parts of us that we have pushed away, ignored, or neglected, this time with self-kindness and compassion. I encourage you to choose to work with unpleasant emotions that are not too intense and that won't overwhelm you. If you have experienced trauma you may want to do this with a therapist or pick something small and manageable. The three steps are:

1. Acknowledge whatever is here and help your inner experiences feel seen: **"I see you."**

2. Give it space to be as it is versus judging it or shooing it out the door: **"It's okay if you sit here with me; you are welcome here."**

3. Invite large Self to sit side by side with that part, to offer comfort to whatever is there. **"I'm here, you're not alone."**

Importantly, when we can begin with the anchor view and child view, and then combine the audience view (taking a half step back) with the compassionate parent view, this helps to prevent us from being hijacked and swallowed up by difficult emotions. From this more spacious place within us, we can hold the parts of us that are suffering with greater care.

Get into a comfortable position and close your eyes if that feels right for you or bring your eyes to a soft focus. Take a few minutes to find your anchor, whether by focusing on sensations of the soles of your feet resting on the ground, focusing on your breath, sounds around you, or anything else that feels grounding. Be aware from your anchor.

Now bring some awareness into your body and notice what emotions are present. If there are any difficult emotions present, see if you might name them and bring some awareness to them. You might observe, *I see that irritability is present. I see that sadness is present. I see that anger is present. I see that contentment is present.* You can do this with any emotions, but for the purpose of this meditation notice if there are any of the more unpleasant emotions that might want some attention.

When you are ready, imagine opening the door and letting in one of the emotions, for example, irritability. Feel free to do this with more pleasant emotions as well if that is who wants to come in. (Be careful at this stage not to invite in anything that would be too overwhelming or intense, especially if you have experienced trauma.) Invite it to come in and take a seat somewhere in the room. See if you might get a curious look at it. Does it have an image, a color? How much space does it take up? From where you are sitting, consider saying the following phrases to your emotion, taking your time with each one and spending several minutes on each if that feels right. As you do this, notice how this feels for you, the one watching, and for the one who came in the door:

I see you; I am here.

I see you; you are welcome here.

I see you; you are not alone.

Disconnected Parts and the Consequence of Suppressing Our Emotions: Helping Deeper Parts of Ourselves Feel Seen and Heard

If you had come into my childhood room, you would have noticed the wooden toy crib in the corner, filled with all manner of beloved stuffed animals I accumulated over the years. You would have seen the white wooden hutch that held scraps of paper stuffed with ideas, poems, and journal entries pondering life and existential questions that my school-age mind wondered about when I was all alone. And you would have found my Barbie collection: those plastic, blonde- and brown-haired mini mannequins, which I would dress, undress, dress again, with dainty shoes and matching handbag accessories, while imagining all kinds of outings and adventures in which they would engage. There were Barbie campers and Barbie houses and Barbie pools that filled my room and took up space in my mind as I let my imagination take me away for hours on the blue shag carpet upon which I lay.

What you would see is a happy, elementary schoolgirl playing innocently with her dolls, dreaming of her own future as picture perfect as those plastic smiles and perfectly crafted matching outfits. What you wouldn't see is the messages that were getting reinforced underneath the seemingly innocent thing called pretend. The messages about how one's body should look, the messages about what is considered attractive, and sexy and desirable. The messages about being thin, tall, and glamorous. What you wouldn't see is the sneaky way that the disordered eating crept in; the painful, growing wounds of shame and embarrassment about her own body that seemingly failed to develop when other girls were starting to "bloom." What you wouldn't see is the way that she began to restrict her food in an attempt to take control of something—because she couldn't do anything about her short stature and late development, a nagging reminder of feeling less than, less than. What you wouldn't see is the day that she fainted on the threshold of her parents' bedroom, and how her well-meaning doctor read her the riot act about needing to eat more in a way that only made her feel more misunderstood. What you would miss is the evolution of the painful cycles of shameful, secretive binging on anything and everything in the kitchen cabinet until she felt quite sickened, and then the restricting of calories to try and compensate.

It was a secret I kept with myself—the one that followed me through the darkness of the night while others saw the smile in the light of day. It was the one filled with shame, from a place of not enough, that became the familiar ground upon which I returned, starting in my own home, and later in my early years at college.

Not knowing what else to do, I stuffed my emotions, my sadness, my confusion, my pain in a cycle from which I saw no way out.

Our younger selves coped with childhood experiences in the best ways we could, with the limited resources we had at that time. Thanks to our survival brain and nervous system, we unconsciously choose behaviors that are in the service of self-protection. Those self-protective behaviors may have been adaptive at some point in time; sometimes they may have become destructive. But, although usually in our adulthood they no longer serve us, we may unconsciously continue to operate from these old programs. For me as a teen I felt so inadequate about my body that trying to restrict my eating became a very unhealthy coping attempt at trying to fit in and be accepted; if I couldn't control many aspects of my appearance, at least I could be thin. This had a rebound effect of leading to cycles of binging because my body was not getting the nutrients and calories it needed. So, I was caught in a self-protective spiral from a harsh inner critic who was trying to help me fit in but didn't know any better than to use methods of restriction and punishment, self-criticism and loathing, that only led to deeper shame.

As I began to develop a compassionate parent view, as I found ways to accept and befriend the inner parts of myself that were hurting, I naturally began to choose behaviors that were more aligned with a supportive, encouraging Self. The Self that wanted what was best for me became more present in my mind than the misguided, self-critical parts. In college I discovered aerobic exercise and realized how much I loved to move my body in these new ways. It brought me joy to go for a run or take a group exercise class and challenge myself. As I began to take care of my body in ways that felt nurturing and energizing, I naturally began to choose healthier foods because they made me feel better physically and became a way of fueling myself to have the energy to do the things I loved. What was punishment and deprivation as an adolescent and young adult gave way to self-nurture and self-care as I began to listen more deeply to the parts of me that most wanted to be seen and heard. In that deep listening, well-being emerged that became the catalyst for change.

Practice: Letter to Your Younger Self

Part One:

Write a letter to your younger self. Choose whatever age you would like to write to. Perhaps you are aware of a certain point in your childhood that was particularly challenging, or maybe there was a particular event that bothered you and stayed with you. For example, maybe you had difficult middle school years and struggled to fit in, or you have a memory of being picked on in third grade. Be careful to choose something that feels manageable and that will not overwhelm you. If you have experienced trauma as a child, you might want to do this under the guidance of a therapist or choose something less intense to work with.

Write to that younger self from the perspective of your adult self. Write in the third person (e.g., Dear Beth) or whatever name you want to give to this part. Let this younger self know that you see them and understand that they were doing the best they could with whatever circumstances and challenges they were managing at that time. Let them know that you understand what they went through, and that you are sorry that they suffered, but that you are here now to be with them, and that this younger version of you is no longer alone. If it feels right to you, show this younger self what your adult life is like and the wisdom you now have that they couldn't possibly have known at that age. Tell them what you wished someone had told you at that age, something you would have wanted to hear, or that would have felt comforting to you back then.

Part Two:

If you would like, give your younger self a chance to write a letter to you, expressing anything it may want you to know. Consider any ways that this younger self may have wanted to be seen and heard back then and give it an opportunity to express itself to you now.

Part Three (Meditation—Caring for Your Younger Self):

Imagine the younger self that you chose being in the presence of a caring, supportive person in your life. You might refer to the earlier exercise at the beginning of this chapter "Being cared for by another" and think of that person or imagine your younger self in the presence of anyone who comes to mind for you as a comforting presence. Imagine what words, gestures, nonverbal body language, and heartfelt emotions that person might offer to your younger self. What would it feel like for that younger part to be in the presence of this person?

Now call up that compassionate, caring part of you that has offered support and presence to others in your life who have suffered. You might think back to the exercise at the beginning of this chapter "Being a compassionate presence for another." See if you might call up that feeling of compassion in yourself by recalling what it feels like to offer compassion to loved ones in your life. Notice the heartfelt emotions that are present within you. Notice what the area around your heart feels like. Is there openness? Expansiveness? Caring energy?

Finally, imagine yourself giving care and sending compassion to your younger self. You might do this through words, gestures, images, or anything that feels right for you. Let the openness of your heart, and your heartfelt emotions, surround your younger self and be a wider container in which they can feel held.

From Small, Contracted Self to Large, Expansive Self

Yesterday I drove past Bigley Road, a road I haven't passed in nearly twenty years. It was one of those déjà vu moments similar to what I experience when I watch a movie that I haven't seen in ages and have that familiar feeling that I've seen this before but can't quite recall the details.

I remember this road, yes. If I had driven up the hill and stopped at number nine and peered into the two-story apartment house window with its gray boards and faded trim, if I had pressed my face up against the glass, I might have seen a young woman inside, in her mid-twenties, sitting at a small wooden desk with an affectionate, talkative Siamese cat on her lap. The woman would have been intensely focused, typing on a big clunky computer for hours on end. The man she was with would come and go at strange hours, in and out to his residency at the hospital nearby. She, still in graduate school, grinding out the last of her dissertation right on cue—one of the few students to finish this program in four years. She had a clear plan and a life path, and it was illuminated with bright yellow arrows that said, "This way."

Ever since eleventh grade she knew what she wanted, and she went after it with the kind of determination that doesn't need to stop and consider other options or detours or alternate paths. This life's journey took her to a small college in a rural town, and straight from there to get her PhD and have the family she always wanted, and the career she dreamed of. Privileged, yes, for sure; lucky, absolutely. Driven—always.

It seems like another lifetime ago now: the pregnancies and small children, the playdates and make believe, starting my career and finding such delight in the mind-body practices that I increasingly integrated into my work. When I drove past Bigley Road, the first apartment my husband and I lived in together before we were married, it was almost surreal, as if it was another lifetime indeed.

Looking back, that lifetime feels very linear and predictable, and there was much comfort in that. Sure, there were unexpected detours and both welcome and unwelcome surprises along the way, but it was grounded in a resounding sense of clear purpose and a well-defined path. Connect the dots by following the numbered trail and you end up with a picture that comes into sharp focus. Paint by number and your illustration comes alive on the page with all its usual patterns and foreseeable outcomes.

Look a little closer and what emerges is the identity that we begin to define ourselves by: the student, dancer, mother, wife, meditator, psychologist, triathlete, writer. Step even closer and we begin to see the attachments that we cling to like a lifeline in a turbulent sea. Not willing to abandon these plastic rings that have the illusion of keeping us afloat, we carry them with us and even wear them around our necks like medals we can proudly display when we look in the mirror or carry on at a dinner party or when we wake with a startle in the dark of night.

But eventually, the darkness catches us, overtakes us. It creeps in insidiously at first and appears as a quick stumble from which we recover. Over time it becomes more steadfast, picking up strength and tugging at our fingers until we can resist no more and the clasped hand opens against its will. As we come up against the truths of aging, loss, and ultimately death, the identities, the small selves begin to lose their luster and ultimately their form, as they fade into a shapeless night that engulfs them in its gentle grasp.

From this darkness—not the darkness of evil, but the darkness of no form—something else begins to emerge. Nothing linear, no solid lines and straight paths, but something more solid, enduring. It is the Self with a capital S, the one that watches, the one that sees. It is the one that helps us settle when we wake in fear with sweaty brow and thumping heart; the one that offers its light when we cannot make out the road ahead. Resting in its expanse, tight threads loosen, unwind, and re-form in new and unforeseen patterns. Abiding in its vastness, old ways of being fall away like the shedding of dead skin to reveal something unexpected in its place, something of new growth and wise eyes and a heart that holds our suffering as if to say, "I am here, I was always here, you are home."

Questions for Reflection: Your Enduring Self

- What is enduring in you, that transcends your specific roles, accomplishments, achievements?

- What is enduring in you, that transcends across the years and decades, that is the essence of who you are? (These might be qualities in you, a felt sense of aliveness or energy within your body, a certain way that you show up in the world, or a way that you show up for others.). You might capture this in words, images, body sensations, movements, or whatever modality speaks to you.

Meditation: Your Wise Self

In this meditation, I invite you to imagine a wise, future Self visiting you. I added "future" here because for many people picturing a future Self is a bit easier than just imagining a wise Self. However, "future" is simply used to help with the imagination. In essence, the wise Self is always present, but it can sometimes be more easily experienced by imagining it coming to visit you from the future.

Picture yourself in a beautiful, peaceful place. Imagine sitting on a bench, or somewhere of your choosing that is comfortable, inviting, and safe. Now picture that your wise, future Self comes and sits beside you. This Self is loving and kind and knows what you need, knows what is best for you, wants the very best for your well-being, and is always with you. This Self is ageless, though it's okay if you picture it as a certain age. This Self accepts you for who you are, it accepts all parts of you, and in its presence, you are enough just as you are. Sit beside and in the company of this wise Self. Sense into the expansive nature of this wise being that is you. See if there is anything that this wise Self wants to tell you. Perhaps there are words, symbols, gestures, or images that it might share with you.

Possibilities

There is a glimpse into what is possible when we can soothe the parts of ourselves that hold our own suffering, when we can perceive with clarity beyond the self-critical messages and distortions our minds would have us believe. When we weave together disowned parts of ourselves and the stories they hold, we revitalize our life energy and find flow. When we see our own inner strengths and hold our shortcomings with kindness, we begin to act from a place of courage and meaning. When we can learn to hold our emotional suffering with kind eyes and relax into the ways we don't need to change, things begin to change.

CHAPTER 8

The Mirror View: Your Strengths and Imperfections Are Welcome Here

The challenge is not to be perfect;
it is to be whole.

—Jane Fonda

The motor tics started when my son was around seven years old; once in a while at first and then over time and years becoming more noticeable, frequent, and troublesome. It came on as an uncontrollable urge to throw his head and neck into twisted, contorted patterns of movement that looked quite odd and over which he had no control. Sometimes it was exhausting for him. Often it was embarrassing, especially as he got older and more self-conscious among his peers. We tried alternative methods and then exhausted traditional ones to treat his Tourette's, but by fourth grade it had become a persistent and significant problem for him, showing up daily in the classroom and among his friends. This was not something that could be ignored by others, and it often drew strange looks and long glares, becoming quite painful for a ten-year-old, who wanted nothing more than to fit in.

I remember sitting together in the sunlit kitchen one day after school talking with my son when he made the decision. He e-mailed his teacher and asked if he could have a chance to share with the class about what Tourette's was, to explain what he knew about the disorder, and to give his peers an opportunity to ask him questions about it. He wanted to share what it was like for him to experience these uncontrollable movements, he wanted to take the mystery out of it, and most of all, he wanted to be seen as a whole person and not as this disorder. It was a turning point moment. It was boldly courageous. Looking back, I think it was transformative for him. His peers were curious, inquisitive, full of questions but understanding. Removing the mystique, naming it, he was able to go about his business with greater ease, not having to try and suppress this thing that had such force and surely could not be hidden. His classmates began to accept that this was just a small part of who he was and moved on from focusing on it.

As he accepted himself in all his imperfections, without losing sight of his strengths, I watched my son as he shifted his vantage point and moved away from "hole self" toward "whole self." He was able to look in the mirror and see beyond his tics to the exuberant, energetic, athletic, compassionate, curious boy who loved, more than anything, connection with others. Even long after the tics resolved sometime well into middle school, this moment has stuck with him and has since become a catalyst in his adult life for him to see the wholeness not only in himself, but in others with whom he works, who have all kinds of medical conditions and diagnoses.

The Mirror View

When you look in the mirror, what do you see? Often, we see our own imperfections, faults, the things we don't like about ourselves, the labels, the things we worry others will see in us that they won't like, our shortcomings, and what we perceive we are lacking.

This "hole" self view is in part wired in through our survival conditioning, thanks to the negativity bias of our brains. As Rick Hanson says,[86] our brains are like Velcro for negative experiences and Teflon for positive ones. The negative experiences stick right to us, like the sticky surface of Velcro, and the positive experiences can so easily slip away, like the slippery surface of Teflon. This negativity bias—focusing on, learning from, and remembering the negative experiences over the positive ones—was an adaptive strategy for our Stone Age ancestors in a world where day-to-day life revolved around avoiding being eaten by predators. But one of the ways this translates into our modern lives is that we can overfocus on our imperfections and overlook our own strengths. We can home in on the perceived negatives about ourselves and overlook the positives. We can see the hole, and not the whole.

As I mentioned in the introduction, I had the good fortune of working early on in my psychology training with my mentor Dr. Robert Brooks when I was an intern at McLean Hospital in Massachusetts. Bob had discovered through years of experience working with adolescents with challenging behaviors that the way to bring about positive change was not by focusing on their weaknesses and trying to improve them, but by focusing on their strengths and trying to build upon them. He taught me and others how to look for and find "islands of competence"[87] in the patients with whom we worked, and essentially, how to hold up a mirror and help them to see these islands of competence in themselves. He taught me about "working from strength" and how to help patients build and expand their islands of competence. From this place, profound change can happen.

This was a radical concept for me at the time, as so much of the field of psychology was focused on treating psychopathology and starting with what is "wrong," not beginning with what is already working well. At that time the positive psychology movement, spearheaded by Martin Seligman and others, had not yet come onto the scene. This would later become a transformative field of psychology,[88] studying human flourishing and focusing on the strengths that allow human beings to thrive.

The mirror view is about learning to look in the metaphorical mirror and shift your vantage point to see the version of yourself that includes your imperfections but emphasizes and recognizes your strengths. Notice that the word "hole" rests inside and is held in the word "whole." It is not that we have to get rid of seemingly undesirable parts of ourselves that we can't change (we all have shortcomings, we make mistakes, we are human and none of us are perfect). The mirror view is about holding the Whole Self view. Looking in this mirror, you can accept your shortcomings but see your islands of competence, see the things you are already doing that are nourishing your well-being, see the opportunities that come from building upon strengths that are already there, and see the possibilities that emerge when you rest in a more spacious sense of already whole.

How the Mirror Changes Everything

After my training with Dr. Brooks, I began to think of my role as a therapist in some fundamental way as holding up a mirror for my patients and helping them to see their strengths and a version of themselves that they may not see on their own. For the persons who experienced years of trauma and come in feeling "broken," I reflect back their courage and resilience and help them to see the values from which they have chosen to live their lives. For the ones with intense anxiety, I reflect back for them the brave choices they have made, despite their anxiety, and the courage it takes to walk through the therapy door. For those who feel defective or less than, I help them to see the common humanity we all share, and to find areas of their lives or small moments in their day where they felt competent, confident, or brave. Time and again, as people begin to change—not who they are but the way they view themselves—positive changes ensue. It is not that they need to get rid of unwanted parts of themselves or pretend that their human imperfections don't exist. But when they can see their own strengths, they begin to build upon what is already working for them. They start making choices more consistent with the large Self, not the contracted small self. They move from hole self to the Whole Self that is already here.

Why We Need a Mirror View

Many years ago, I wrote a short story that I was proud of and was thinking that I might try and get it published into a children's book. I showed the story to a friend, who offered constructive criticism and seemed a little lukewarm about the whole thing. What I took away, though what I don't believe was intended, was negative feedback and a sense that it wasn't worthy of pursuing. I put that story away and never wrote another thing for years.

Over more recent years I have had the good fortune of participating in Gateless Writing workshops, a specific method of writing developed by Suzanne Kingsbury, in which writing prompts are given and the pieces we write are shared out loud among participants. One of the major "rules" of the Gateless method is that people share only authentic positive feedback, only what worked about the piece, what moved the listener, what strengths they saw in the piece, or anything they liked about it. Interestingly, feedback is shared in the third person (e.g., "I really loved how this writer used metaphor to convey . . .") so as not to have the writer feel put on the spot, but instead allowing the writer to simply listen from the outside and take in all of the things shared by others that worked well about their piece. This method is quite remarkable in the writing that it produces from participants. In this atmosphere, where people feel safe and nurtured, creativity thrives, and amazing pieces of writing evolve.

When we focus on our imperfections or weaknesses, or others call attention to them, this can activate our stress response as well as our own inner critic and can quickly lead to constriction in the body, narrowed and guarded thinking, and a shutdown of creativity. Our fight-or-flight response, quick to jump into action as it perceives threats, tries to protect us through its primitive, adaptive survival pathways. Conversely, when we focus on our strengths or our innate goodness, or others highlight this for us, this activates very different pathways in the brain and nervous system. From this more safe, relaxed, and open-hearted place, creativity thrives. When the nervous system feels safe, we can take actions, think in more expansive ways, and tap into motivation that isn't present when we are under the grips of our primitive survival circuits.

This is not to say that there isn't a place for constructive feedback and honest self-evaluation that invites us to acknowledge areas that could use improvement. That is certainly important. But when we lead from that place and when it becomes the predominant mode of operating, we miss a huge window of opportunity for thriving.

The Brain as a Predicting Machine and Why the Mirror View Helps Us Upgrade to Our Newer Operating System

One of the things the mirror view does is allow you to intentionally search your memory bank, find moments that represent islands of competence and strengths, and then rewrite—or, perhaps more accurately, overwrite—old narratives that no longer serve you. It also encourages you to create new, present-moment experiences that help you notice, acknowledge, and celebrate your strengths. This is a very powerful antidote to some of the default habits of our mind.

You may recall from Chapter 3 that according to Lisa Feldman Barrett, our brain's main purpose is to figure out how to allocate body resources to best survive. In order to do this, the brain became a predicting machine, able to anticipate needs even before they arose, to ensure that appropriate resources were readily available for our ancestors. Essentially, sensory information comes through our brain and nervous system and then the brain predicts whether the incoming information is safe or not safe, based on all our past memories of what is similar to or different from this situation. If that thing I am seeing now moving in the distance looks like that tiger I saw yesterday, I'd better start running now!

But here's where I think this gets really interesting (and challenging). As I talked about above, our brain has a negativity bias, holding onto negative things that happen more strongly than positive experiences. In this way, I have seen time and again with myself and my patients how our memory banks can often steer us astray. "Bad" things that happened in the past that are not relevant to the present moment (e.g., being laughed at as a kid; folding under pressure during a performance in sixth grade) can easily get called up in that memory bank when our brain is assessing current safety or threat of giving that talk or going after the thing I want today.

If we assess threat based on old memories and past conditioning (it's not safe to do this public speaking engagement because as a kid I got laughed at in front of my class) this can greatly affect our brain's decision-making process of allocating resources toward survival, even when that old threat is long past.

The mirror view is a helpful antidote to this. Every time we take the mirror view, we update our memory stores, making our strengths more accessible. Over time, this can help us more accurately discern what is a true threat and what is safe. Instead of falling back into old stories and self-sabotaging patterns of behavior based on old past experiences, we can call up new stories that speak of our strengths, resilience, competence, and inner resources. When we shift our vantage point, we see things in a new way and lay down pathways that help support our growth and wellbeing.

Benita's Story: Benita came to me in her early thirties because she was suffering from anxiety and depression. Underneath this was a chronic sense of "not good enough" and a sense of not belonging or fitting in anywhere. Benita had a difficult and traumatic childhood. She grew up in a chaotic household with a single mother who was narcissistic and unable to meet Benita's needs. In addition, her mother was intermittently violent (verbally and occasionally physically), and Benita recalls often hiding or running away to try and escape her mother's unpredictable moods. Benita was the oldest of two children, and her sister, five years younger, was the golden child in her mother's eyes. In Benita's experience her sister was treated quite differently by their mom and could do no wrong, while Benita was often criticized and blamed for things. While Benita was intelligent, compassionate, and creative, she came to believe that she was defective and unwanted. In her adult life, whenever she found herself in social situations she felt left out and alone and often disappeared before things even got started. At work she doubted herself and worried that others would find out she didn't know what she was doing and fire her. This created a lot of anxiety for her.

One of the things we did in working together was to help Benita understand and appreciate the role of the adaptive, survival responses that she developed early in her life to help her survive some real threats and challenges. Mobilizing and running away or isolating in her room helped her at that time to cope with lack of safety and unpredictability around her. It was understandable that she would continue to be on high alert, continuing to operate from these old adaptive patterns of behavior.

After some time of helping Benita find ways to feel safe in her nervous system (using the anchor view and practicing with breathing and other mind-body modalities), we began to work with the mirror view. I invited Benita to start noticing and tracking very small moments when she felt some glimmer of competence, connection, or belonging. For example, she started to notice how her coworkers would smile at her and say hello in the morning; how her boss asked her to take on an additional project; and how when she asked someone to join her for lunch, they were receptive and enjoyed her company.

I also helped her to rewrite the narrative of her early life. Rather than seeing something as wrong with her, she began to understand her mother's mental illness and the challenging family dynamics in which she grew up. This helped her recognize the impact that had on her view of herself. She began to see the ways she was resilient even in the face of all of this: doing well in school, finding a teacher who became a mentor for her, becoming a caretaker for stray pets, finding her voice in the school paper, and earning a scholarship to college where she could move away from her unhealthy environment.

Over time, as Benita began to take the mirror view, the lens through which she looked began to change. A turning point came when she was at a social gathering and realized that she was not being intentionally left out; she just wasn't making herself visible enough and perhaps was giving off cues to others that she did not want to be approached. Rather than seeing people with their backs turned as a cue of threat, she recalled some of the friendly exchanges she had with her coworkers which helped her to reevaluate threat and feel safer. She found that by moving to a more visible location where she was facing others, she could notice cues of safety in other's faces, and this gave her the courage to initiate interacting with others. This was met more times than not, to her surprise, with warmth and reciprocity.

Little by little, by shifting her vantage point and being able to see her own strength, courage, competence, and resilience, Benita began to make choices that reinforced this new story. What emerged was that she discovered that she was enough just as she was, and that she always had been.

Shift Your Vantage Point:
You Don't Need to Eliminate Your Imperfections,
Just Find Your Strengths.

Part One: Building Strengths
Warm-Up: Discovering What's Already Here

Meditation: Seeds of Inspiration:

Think about someone influential in your life (it could be a fourth-grade teacher, a mentor, someone who inspires you whether or not you have met them personally). What is it about them that you admire? Take some time to identify the qualities and characteristics that you most value in them.

Now find some spark of that quality in yourself. Recognize that you are drawn to that person because there is something in you that already embodies that quality or that deepest value. Maybe it is a seed, or a sprouting shoot, or a bud ready to bloom or it is already in bloom. In whatever stage of growth it is in, honor that it is present in you.

What might you do to notice this and nourish it in yourself? What we put our attention and energy on grows. How might you direct your attention and energy to ignite this spark in yourself and help it thrive?

Practice: Others See Your Strengths

Ask people you trust to name and write down three things they deeply value in you. Give them some time to reflect on this so you don't catch them on the spot. Read over what they wrote and really see if you might take this in and let it land inside of you. Whether or not you see these qualities in yourself, can you appreciate that other people see and celebrate this in you?

Practice: Seeing the Good in Yourself

There is a beautiful, short exercise in Rick Hanson's Positive Neuroplasticity Course workshop[89] where he asks participants to go around the room and say, "One strength in me is X," and then the other person responds genuinely, "I see X in you." This continues, going around from participant to participant, taking in a sense of being seen by others and having others see your strengths.

While it is harder to do with oneself, I invite you to try the following:

Make a list of strengths and qualities that you appreciate about yourself. For example, you might write: "my sense of humor, my warm heart, the way I am willing to help others in need, my artistic abilities, my creative ideas, the way I make others smile, my perseverance, my ability to whip up a delicious meal on leftovers, my kind spirit, etc." If you feel stuck with this you might check out Dr. Martin Seligman's Values in Action Survey of Character Strengths,[90] a 240-item, self-report questionnaire that will help you identify your character strengths.

Now go through whatever you wrote down, slowly saying, "I appreciate X in myself" (e.g., "I appreciate the way that I'm able to make others smile;" "I appreciate that I'm honest and fair"). As you say that, stay with it for at least thirty seconds or more as you recognize this quality in yourself and sense how that feels in your body. See if, without intellectually trying to figure out how, you might invite your large Self to validate and see this quality in you.

🎧 Meditation: Over the Years Through the Mirror

Picture yourself as a newborn infant, pure, innocent, precious, and whole. Imagine coming into the world knowing how to breathe and nurse or suck on a bottle. See the ways that your body knows just how to grow and develop, to connect with others, take in information from the world, and be constantly learning at an exponential rate. Look back at yourself as a toddler. You might marvel at the way that you learned to walk, run, climb, talk, and express your needs.

Picture yourself as a child. From this viewpoint as an adult looking back, see all the things you might appreciate about yourself at that stage in your life. You might imagine telling that child the things that you notice (e.g., "You were really brave to handle that situation when . . .," "Even though school was difficult for you, you worked so hard and persevered . . ." "Look at the ways you expressed yourself so creatively").

Keep going through the years. See yourself as an adolescent. Can you notice and appreciate strengths in yourself now that you may not have seen back then? In what ways were you resilient, courageous, curious, kind, creative, etc.? How about as a young adult, and all the way up to your current age? Were there ways you were a leader, an avid learner, passionate about fighting for something important to you, fiercely loyal, determined, etc.?

Imagine all these qualities and strengths within you now. They are all there. See and feel them as part of you. Imagine them as part of your well of well-being. You can draw upon any one of these strengths whenever you choose just by calling attention to them and honoring how they live in you.

Practice: Turning Up the Volume

Have you ever had the experience of blasting some favorite music and feeling a deep sense of aliveness, energy, motivation, inspiration, or joy? If there is something that is playing in the background that isn't so pleasant, you don't need to get rid of it or make it go away, but you might turn up the volume on what energizes and enlivens you to experience greater well-being.

When I think back to the many years in my adolescence and young adulthood that I struggled with disordered eating, looking back I realize that I didn't need to force out the parts of myself that felt inadequate, but I did need to focus more on what helped me feel good and strong and healthy. As I rediscovered the joy of movement and turned the volume up on joyful movement that brought me in connection with others, something began to shift.

For this exercise, consider what you might want to dial the volume up on, to make it bigger and more present in your life.

Consider these questions:

1. What qualities and values are present in you that, when you experience them, make you feel a deeper sense of well-being? For example, kindness, compassion, self-compassion, perseverance, love of learning, artistic creativity, etc.

2. Write down any possible actions you might take to "dial up the volume" on them. For example, for kindness you might reach out to a friend, volunteer at a shelter, cook a meal for someone in need, or give a family member a warm hug before you leave the house in the morning. For love of learning you might read a book on a topic of interest, listen to an interesting podcast, learn a new hobby, or challenge yourself with a new kind of puzzle.

3. What are things that you already do that bring a feeling of well-being into your life? Identify as many of these as you can, in multiple areas of your life (personal time, work, family, friends, spiritual life, etc.). Some examples might be: going to church or temple, taking initiative with a project at work, going for walks in the woods, meeting friends for lunch, finding time to journal, etc.

4. How might you turn up the volume on any of these? What might you do today, this week, and this month to turn up the volume on any of the things you identified that nourish you?

5. Identify something you are struggling with (impatience with your child, feeling stagnant at work, feeling lonely or disconnected). How might turning up the volume on something from above, or something else you can identify, be helpful in moving you in the direction of greater well-being or ease?

The Messiness and the Muck

The day I fed my kids plastic was not one of my better parenting moments. The morning hadn't started off on the best note. It had been one of those tossing and turning, expelling and then grabbing the covers kind of sleeps, on and off throughout the night. The clock time remaining before needing to get the kids off to the bus stop was tight. Just enough to squeeze in one of mom's healthy, disguise- the-greens smoothies in my attempt to get some nutrition into my kids' growing bodies, while still attempting to make it taste good.

Our new Vitamix blender had become a delight—a transformative tool on the nutrition path for all of us. However, on mornings like this, where my husband was still sleeping, I would have to haul it into the guest bathroom to do the noisy blending, so that my husband didn't feel like there was oil drilling going on underneath our bedroom. On this particular round of smoothie making, I had gotten a bit overzealous on the frozen fruit, so much so that it created an ice dam in the blender, from which even the powerful blades of this amazing machine could not cut through.

No problem, that's where the handy plastic tamper that comes with it comes into play, right? Well-designed to push and prod until the frozen solids begin to blend into a more palatable liquid. I didn't realize the lid was not secure. Something suddenly broke loose and with it green and red smoothie spewed all over the bathroom counters, floor, and even the newly painted wall. Frantic to try to salvage what I could in the little time I had left, I removed the lid completely and pushed that tamper down into the blades, attempting to break up the remaining ice and turn this thing into something my kids could drink. The clean-up of the floor and walls would have to come later.

Back in the kitchen my kids were bustling in with backpacks plopped down, ready to dart out the door at any minute. "Here," I said, pouring the smoothie into two tall, purple plastic glasses to disguise the green color of all the spinach and kale I had jammed in there. Whew.

Sitting at the counter, my son and daughter commented almost in unison: "There's something crunchy and hard in here." "Oh no worries," I responded, just some leftover frozen fruit that didn't blend in. Off they went, moments later, running down the road to catch the bright yellow school bus to carry them onward.

And that's when I discovered it, when I was washing up the whole mess. I picked up the tamper to notice curiously that about

one-third of the plastic top part was missing. Wait, what hap-
pened? Then it all came together, like puzzle pieces connecting in
my brain leading to some yellow light bulb illuminating—why
the instructions stated never to take the top off the blender and
to only stick the tamper through the designated hole—and re-
alizing in a moment of horror where the remaining third of the
plastic tamper ended up.

Despite our best efforts, we mess up. We make mistakes. We do things sometimes with unintended consequences. (Thankfully the little bit of plastic that my kids ingested was non-toxic according to their doctor and the poison control hotline that I called. So much for my healthy smoothie. Thank goodness they spit out more than they swallowed!). This was a silly example, but plenty of times as a parent I messed up in other ways, losing my patience and reacting to my children's misbehaviors and meltdowns in ways that I must admit I am not proud of. I am human. I know that I am not alone. I know for a fact that I am far from perfect, and long ago stopped striving to be.

Welcome to This Human Journey— You Are Not Alone!

I must admit that I, as a psychologist, have a big advantage about something. Having had the privilege of sitting with hundreds of people over three decades, I have learned a lot about the human condition. Being given an intimate window into people's lives and psyches, I have a good sense of the very wide range of "normal" on this human journey. People sitting in my office often come in feeling like there is something wrong with them because of how they are feeling or what they are going through, that somehow, they are different, and often alone in their experience. What they don't realize is the common humanity that we all share; that so many others have walked in their shoes and share the same struggles; that they are not alone. Neither are you!

As I shared in a previous vignette, some of the most memorable talks given by psychologists over the years are ones where people whom I have looked up to and respected shared ways that they were far from perfect parents, where their family vacations were fraught with challenges and fighting and not the picture-perfect postcard you might expect, where they messed up in ways that brought a deep sigh of relief inside me, reminding me that even *they* are quite human, and therefore it's okay that I am too.

Still, how do we look in the mirror and hold our imperfections (and work to improve things where appropriate) while also holding ourselves in a larger frame of "human"? How do we tip the scales so as not to let our negativity bias get the better of us and have us overlook all that we do well?

How do we accept our human imperfections *and* see our strengths clearly?

Practice: Yes, and . . .

There is a fun way I want to suggest working with this, something that I learned from some classes I took in improvisational theater. With improv, you must take whatever the person on stage throws at you and go with it. If the actor across from you turns to you and says, "Hey, Mom, I need my laundry done, can you throw it in?" you don't turn to them and say, "Wait, I'm not your mom, I thought I was so and so." And you don't say, "Yes, but actually we don't have a washing machine." Instead, you embrace whatever was thrown at you with, "Yes, and . . ." You accept what the other actor offers and simply build upon it.

With this exercise, you will practice saying "Yes, and . . ." to your imperfections and the things you may not like about yourself or your inner experiences that you can't necessarily change. Instead of trying to get rid of these imperfections or inner experiences, you allow them to be there with yes, and.

Think about things you may not be able to change about yourself or your inner experiences. Think about your strengths. Put these together in a sentence using Yes, AND. Find things for the "AND" part that are heartfelt, that feel authentic, and that resonate for you. Here are some examples:

Yes, I have an anxious temperament AND I can choose to not let my anxiety stop me from doing those things that most matter in my life.

Yes, I wish my body was shaped differently AND I can choose small ways each day to take care of this body because it is my home here on earth.

Yes, I get impatient and yell sometimes at my kids AND I am working on this, and I intentionally create many loving, caring moments with them each day.

Yes, I am feeling deeply disappointed about this injury AND I know that I have had the courage to get through things like this before and I'll get through this one too.

Yes, I take longer to process information and complete assignments AND I put myself wholeheartedly into my work and turn out a thoughtful end product.

Practice: The "hole" Within Whole

Take a piece of paper and draw a large circle. Within the circle, draw smaller shapes like pieces of a jigsaw puzzle so that the circle is divided up into these smaller pieces that make up the whole. Take a pencil or pen and write down anywhere in the smaller pieces of the circle some of the things that make you human (e.g., lose my patience, terrible sense of direction, often forget people's names, my sadness). In colored markers, also in the puzzle pieces of the circle, write down the strengths and inner qualities/values that you appreciate about yourself. Make sure to come up with at least as many, if not more, strengths and qualities you value as the things that make you human, so there is a balance of both in this circle. Step back and recognize that they are all just part of the whole. The whole is not complete without all the parts, including all those things that make you human.

The Hidden Strengths You May Not See

Kai's Story. He sat with his head slumped down into his chest, arms folded in front of him like a shield saying: stay away, danger, do not enter. His demeanor was sad, as if being here was putting him on trial in some way which would result in him writhing in pain. He was twelve years old, and for anyone that age, therapy can often feel more like punishment than like support. I can feel much more like the enemy at first sight, rather than the ally.

He was here because he had "impulse control problems." Sometimes he got so angry that he punched walls hard enough that he left marks; at times in anger he yelled mean things at his mom that went well beyond your typical "I hate you" or "leave me alone" that preteens are known to exclaim when things don't go their way and when parents come up against the edge of what feels like an invasion on their growing independence. I could see on his face that he was expecting me to scold him, tell him why he needs to shape up, change himself; he was waiting for me to point out all the ways he was bad—and it was going to hurt.

"Do you know why you're here to meet with me?"

"Yah, because I mess up a lot; my parents think there is something wrong with me. I can't control my anger."

"Tell me about that, when does that happen?"

"When my parents tell me to do stuff I don't want to do; when my sports team loses, when life isn't fair."

"Does that ever happen when you're with your friends, at your friends' houses?"

"Nah."

"Really? What happens when you're with your friends?"

"I don't know, I just kind of feel it—and then I let things go. They don't get to me the same way."

"So, what you're telling me is that there are times and places that even when you're feeling angry, upset, or disappointed, you have found ways to manage those feelings so that they don't overtake you? Wow."

"Ya, it's no big deal."

"Ya, well I think it's a big deal. Do you know that that is actually a superpower?"

"What do you mean?"

"You have this superpower, and you may not even realize it, but it's there. In the middle of big storms, when you're with your friends and you get really upset, you have ways to calm yourself. Not everyone can do that. This superpower is like a muscle that can be strengthened. Just like all those practices and drills you do for basketball where you get stronger, faster; you make more shots, you learn how to be a team player and pass the ball. Maybe at first, you're just good at shooting baskets in your own driveway. But then you learn how to play well with your friends at the playground, and then together on the basketball court—and eventually you can get out there even under pressure and play against those really tough teams.

"You see, you can learn to strengthen this superpower and take this superpower into other areas of your life too. What if you could even learn to use this superpower when you're around your parents?"

When we look in the mirror, we can see many things. We often see our own imperfections, our faults, the places we feel we fall short. But there is a different kind of mirror, and it is available to all of us. This mirror helps us to see what is already here: our strengths, the things we do well, what is already inside of us. From this new perspective, everything begins to shift.

Growing Strengths

In light of the negativity bias, you likely are not capitalizing on moments of strength that are already here, that are easily overlooked as your imperfections may hover in the foreground. Here are two exercises to help you capitalize on your strengths.

Practice: Growing Strengths Writing Exercise

Think about something you consider a shortcoming: procrastination, impatience, short temper, etc. Find examples of when you were able to access the opposite of that or some other quality that helped to shift you in the direction of well-being. Perhaps you lose your patience at home but are able to remain remarkably even keeled at work. What helps you do that? What do you think about or focus on that helps you remain even keeled at work, even in the face of challenges? Remember what that felt like. What did you do or think to yourself that helped you? What could you do to strengthen that muscle, to grow more of that? Recognize that quality is likely already here, but may need to be practiced, cultivated, and strengthened in order to apply it to other areas of your life.

Meditation: Growing Strengths

Picture a quality you want to grow or strengthen that you have experienced from time to time (e.g., patience). See it at first like a small seed. Think of a time you felt this way (e.g., a moment of patience you experienced). What were you doing, thinking, and feeling? Try to recall as much detail as possible so that you can re-experience that now. Call this up as a felt sense in your body. Notice the area and energy around your heart. What was rewarding for you about experiencing that? Envision yourself finding opportunities to practice this more throughout the weeks, as you go through the moments of your day. Mentally rehearse this now. How does it feel as you do that? What is rewarding about that? You already know how to do this. See your seed sprouting, growing roots, and flourishing.

Building Momentum: Working Through Fears and Expanding Our Comfort Zones

Our new dishwasher arrived today. Such a simple pleasure, it's shiny stainless steel, and the sleek look blends with the speckled granite that has been waiting for its arrival for oh so long. Our old dishwasher, the one that was here since we moved in, had been falling out of its brackets for perhaps a decade. Every time I rolled it out, I would have to catch it to make sure it didn't spill out onto the floor, dishes and all. Yet I resisted getting a new one, year after year. My husband kept asking repeatedly, "Isn't it time now? How about now?" Each time I resisted—not now, not yet. This one is still working . . . sort of.

Such a simple delight, trying out this new thing! So exciting to load dishes that are actually dirty and have them come out sparkly clean, as if I should be surprised by such a thing. With our old dishwasher you had to scrub and scrub before you put them in, and then inspect them on the way out to make sure that the particles of food had actually been removed.

I have been stuck in a bit of a routine this past year of quarantine, hardly leaving my house except to run through the woods nearby, past pond and stream and all my favorite heart-opening spaces. Afraid to be in public places, trying to follow rules and mandates, I became comfortable in my living space in a way that kept me safe, protected, and yet. . . .

This arrival of the new dishwasher is a simple reminder to me of the ways we can get very comfortable in our small spaces, doing the same things over and over, sometimes in a kind of monotony that feels rhythmical and automatic all at the same time. Over time, our routines and small spaces can become protective,

wrapping us tightly in their invisible webs, keeping us from ven-
turing out to avoid the discomfort of something new.

When I first decided to put my writing out into the world,my
first blog sent out on LinkedIn, it felt like jumping from a plane
with a parachute and not being sure if I could find the strings
to open the chute. I was unsure how or where I would land, but
trusting that something, something deeper, not visible but more
expansive, would help me find my way to a soft landing. There
is a leap of faith, this thing we do when we step out of what feels
safe and comfortable into something unfamiliar, that calls for
us to operate from a very different program than the one lit up
by the well-marked control panel. From a place within that is
wisdom itself, intuition, a guiding voice that knows what is best,
we can begin to listen, to grow beyond our edges, and expand
our bounds, to grow into the fullness of who we are.

Sometimes the results are surprising. Who knew that a new dish-
washer could actually fully and completely clean dishes caked on
with food and grime? Who knows what things are possible when
we try something new? Potential: limitless potential is what we
are. Sometimes all we need to do is jump.

Listening to Your Heart's Calling

Fear plays a big role in trying to protect us, and if we're not mindful, we can let it have a good amount of power in our lives. We often (mistakenly) believe that we need to wait until fear dissipates or goes away before we can do that thing that our heart wants us to do (e.g., ask that person out on a date, say yes to a speaking engagement, try a new activity, share our creative ideas, etc.). But what if we have it wrong? What if we can learn, as the field of Acceptance and Commitment Therapy[91] (ACT) teaches, to accept some amount of discomfort and be willing to tolerate this if it means being able to live a valued life? What if, instead of trying to get rid of fear, we could bring it along for the ride, as well as a host of other "passengers," such as acceptance, courage, and the things that we most value?

Of course, we need to distinguish fears that need our attention, that indicate true danger, from fears that masquerade as that. Most of us know how to do this already. My survival brain may not be able to differentiate a true life-threatening risk (e.g., running into a burning building) from one that is not so dangerous (getting up in front of a hundred people to give a talk), but *I* know the difference.

I love what author Terri Trespicio says in her book *Unfollow Your Passion*.[92] She writes that instead of forcing ourselves to get out of our comfort zone, we can learn to *expand* our comfort zones in ways that feel safer.

One way that we can learn to expand our comfort zone *and* help our nervous system feel safe is by breaking things down into small, manageable steps. I have seen, time and time again both in my life and in the life of my patients, how very powerful this can be. It can create a kind of momentum in which one small step begets the next. For example, for patients who are feeling depressed, just the simple act of making one's bed or going for a five-minute walk can help create the momentum to take other small steps that can help to get out from feeling in a hole. For people who want to do something new but are too afraid, taking small steps can create enough safety and also the momentum to take bigger steps.

Practice and Meditation: Expanding Your Comfort Zone

Part One: Small Steps

What is calling to you from your heart? What is something nourishing or meaningful that you might like to do, but fear, overwhelm, or other uncomfortable emotions get in your way?

Write out any ways your old operating system is trying to protect you.

Write out any ways that your newer operating system might support you toward growth.

Whatever that thing is that you would like to do, how might you take small steps to nurture it and move in the direction that your heart is calling you? For example, if you want to start dating, perhaps you just commit to signing up for some dating apps (without using them yet), creating a personal profile, or asking your friends if they know of anyone who is looking to meet someone. Don't worry about anything more—just focus on that one step, see how it feels, and reassess once you do that where you want to go next.

The idea here is to pick a step small enough that feels safe for your nervous system. Pay attention to how that small step feels in your body when you select it. If you want to change jobs, perhaps sitting down to redo your resume feels too threatening right now. But reaching out to three friends in the industry you are interested in to get further ideas feels more doable. It's okay to have some discomfort (see part two below), but to the extent that you can make a step smaller to find ease, do that.

Keep a log of any small steps that you take and celebrate them! It can be easy to overlook these small steps since the brain wants to focus on what you didn't do, what might go wrong, or come up with narratives about why you can't or shouldn't do this thing.

I have a little confession to make. As much as I teach practical tools for well-being to people, I don't always remember to use these tools myself. I try, but I am quite human. In order to help myself notice and celebrate my successes, I have created a file on my computer called "personal experiences using my tools," where I write down things that I did that I found helpful in moving me toward ease and well-being. I started this several years ago and it is quite helpful to go back and see all the things that have been beneficial for me.

Part Two: Packing Your Car Meditation

What might you be willing to do, if you could accept some emotional discomfort as part of your human journey and take it along with you for the ride? If you are willing to bring some discomfort along in your car (with you as the driver!), who or what else might you bring along for support? What strengths could you call upon, to take along with you for the ride as well? Write out as many things as you can think of.

To help answer this, think about a time when you did something a little scary but got through it? What helped you? What did you say to yourself? What inner qualities did you draw upon to help you cope with this situation (e.g., courage, determination, grit, acceptance, self-compassion, encouragement, etc.)? What might you remind yourself of (e.g., why this thing is meaningful or important to you; that the risks and stakes are not life-threatening or dangerous) that would help your nervous system to feel that this was a risk worth taking?

Imagine that you are getting in your car, driving toward your heart's calling. Picture putting your fear or discomfort in the backseat and buckling it in with care, the way you might do with a small child. Invite in other "passengers" that might feel supportive for you (actual people in your life who encourage you, or emotions such as courage, trust, grit, etc.) to sit beside you. See yourself in the driver's seat, taking fear along for the ride and driving toward what matters, toward that thing that you'd like to do.

Stop Striving for Perfect and Celebrate What Is Here

I had this fantasy as a kid that played out over and over in different variations, like the closing movement of a symphony with a grand, smashing conclusion, before the audience explodes in applause. In this fantasy—whether it be kickball, softball, or football—it is the last inning, or final few minutes of the game. We're down by a few runs, bases loaded, or by several points on the football field, and there I am making the winning move for the team, bringing us to victory. Not a unique fantasy I am sure, but one I imagined frequently throughout my childhood.

The real version of that scenario was never even close. When I was in fourth grade, I remember being at my friend Tracie's house. She was my dear friend with a Samoa dog, a giant white bear of a thing that followed along at her side on our playdates. On this particular day her brother and a bunch of the neighborhood kids came over for a big game of kickball. I wanted to prove myself, show that I could keep up with the best of them. I wanted to get that home run kick. The only impression I made that day was when I farted, praying that no one would notice, since it was outdoors, and I wasn't standing super close to anyone. To my dismay, I was called out and it was humiliating.

Then there was the time in gym class in fifth grade when I was sure I could score some winning points in Wiffle Ball to impress my teammates (especially the boys, who hardly gave me the time of day with my short stature and flat chest). No victory there that day, but it got worse. When I went to pull my red pinny off—the one demarcating which team I was on—not only did the pinny come off, but my shirt with it. Thankfully, and for some unbeknownst reason, my father had encouraged me to wear an undershirt that day (perhaps because of the cold weather), so I was not completely bare-chested. Nonetheless, I was mortified and ran to the girl's bathroom in embarrassment.

Despite those embarrassing moments and never making that game winning home run, some of my best memories are of the extended family or neighborhood football and softball games on those warm summer evenings, on the flat patch of grass in our backyard, just enough of a breeze to smell and even taste the aromas of summer childhood. I quite enjoyed these games, the challenge, camaraderie, and connection. They filled me with a kind of joy that, looking back, I realize held everything I wanted.

And so it is that we go in search of this thing, this thing that

we think will fill us, will bring us happiness, will be that golden
moment when everything changes. And sometimes we wait for
weeks, months, and lifetimes, not realizing that the victories are
here, so easily missed right in front of us, and always have been.

Questions for Reflection: Right Here Now

- What are you grasping for, or waiting for to arrive that you tell your-self will bring you happiness? Fill in the blank: when I accomplish X, or change Y about myself, or get to Z, then I'll be happy.

- What can you identify about where you are right now, just as things are, that brings you a sense of meaning, satisfaction, or contentment in your life? What are the little moments in each day when you find a taste of this?

- What might you celebrate that is right here now? What small daily accomplishments do you overlook or dismiss because you are focused on that big thing that feels unattainable? What might you appreciate that you do on a regular basis that you don't usually see?

- What are the moments of simply being (versus doing/accomplishing) that bring you joy or well-being?

- What if you were whole, right now, just as you are? If you believed this, what might shift or change for you? How would you feel? How would you act? What choices would you make today and this week?

Part Two: When Things Go South

When Challenges Can Become Opportunities

It came from the most unlikely of places. It started the day my
phone crashed, and all my contacts were lost. These were the

connections with people whom I had met and admired, leaned on, and turned to in my professional life, and my dear friends, the ones that I could see regularly, but also the ones who lived forever in my heart and a car or plane ride away. Not knowing what else to do, I started rebuilding, from scratch, from memory, from little scrawled notebooks, from phone calls to people who knew people . . . Funny how such an event can become the catalyst for a dream, a hope materialized, an endeavor brewing within for twenty years . . . a life.

In the panic of losing my contacts, I began thinking about what else I might be devastated to lose. I found it shoved in the back of my bedroom closet, covered in a layer of dust, letting me know it had been quite some time since I had greeted this big old plastic bag, its seams expanded like stretch marks from a pregnant belly. And inside there it was: every poem that I had written since I was six years old, scrawled on little scraps of paper, notepads, torn sheets from notebooks forty years old, some typed on that thing called a typewriter with the little white tape marks to strike out errors. In a surge of energy to protect that which I didn't want to lose, I began scanning poem after poem into my computer and then saving and backing up and printing them out and compiling them. Without an endgame, I proceeded to organize them, putting them in chronological order from age six to age fifty, page by page holding precious moments of life itself. Out of the clutter from a dusty bag, what emerged was a story of a soul, an unfolding of a journey over decades that I put together into a book of yet unpublished poetry. But what evolved from that experience led me to write, to pick up the pen and do that thing that I love. This time however, instead of burying my writing in a dusty bag, I held my breath, then let it go, all of it—the written word like a bag of feathers released into the air—trusting that the wind would scatter it to safe and welcome ground.

I love looking back at my life and seeing, from this glancing back vantage point, how many possibilities cracked open out of challenges. After putting together this first book of poetry that is yet unpublished, I began to have other creative sparks. I put together the curriculum for an eight-week therapeutic group and was excited to get it off the ground. Unexpected obstacles prevented me from doing so in the end. From that disappointment, the idea emerged to take the curriculum I had already created and put it together into a book, which became my first published book.

I remember neuropsychologist Rick Hanson talking about not feeling seen as a child and not fitting in with his peers. As a young adult, these experiences led him to find ways to cope with these "holes" within himself by discovering ways to build inner strengths and resources that he was missing. This inner work became the impetus for him to go on to study, develop, and then teach positive neuroplasticity to people around the world. His work has changed thousands of people's lives. I wonder what would have happened if he had been accepted as one of the "cool" kids as a child? I wonder if his life would have taken a rather different turn, and his current contributions may not have emerged.

Questions for Reflection: Finding Opportunities Within Setbacks

- What was a time when a challenge became an opportunity, when something seemingly bad turned out to have a gift in it? This is not to say that you need to find the silver lining in every challenge or experience some kind of forced positivity amidst difficulties. But it can be helpful to discover or notice the gifts or lessons when they are genuinely there.

⊕ Was there a challenge that you experienced in your life in which a
strength emerged? (For example, my son, who suffered many athletic
injuries which sidelined him from his beloved sports in high school,
developed a great deal of resilience and calm strength to handle
setbacks.)

What to Do When Things Go Sideways: Life's Unexpected Detours

*It is a cloudy July afternoon, with the kind of heaviness and hu-
midity that hangs in the air that makes you want to stay indoors
and wonder where the sun has been after all these weeks of incessant rain. As I am writing this, some hundred or so miles
away, my dad and stepmom are bailing water out of their basement—again. Ironically, it is on the day when they just signed
a non-disclosure with their Realtor to put their house on the
market, excited that all their water issues had been permanently
resolved. This came after months of fighting with the condo as-
sociation, multiple missed attempts by the construction company to solve the problem, waking up repeatedly in the middle of
many nights to sop up water with towels and lug them up three
flights of stairs, waiting long winter months before their frozen
front yard could be dug up to put drains in, and finally having
shrubbery and plantings replace the ripped-up soil and exposed
ground. And now to discover they were back to square one!*

*It has been a difficult few years, one of unexpected challenges
and unanticipated hardships. Despite all the ways my father has
taken such good care of himself and his health for his whole life
he suffered through a diagnosis of lymphoma and subsequent
chemotherapy, two small strokes which left him with ongoing
balance issues, and this past December, a fall and hip fracture*

right in the middle of the pandemic. This last was the worst by far, causing him to spend almost a month in the hospital with not so much as a single visitor (due to COVID restrictions) to offer him emotional support through immense physical pain and complications that would have been fear-inducing and dis-heartening for anyone. Still, through it all, my father came home determined to recover and rehab with rigorous physical therapy and exercises that he has continued on his own, to regain his walking and his independence. Through it all, my stepmom has been by his side, encouraging and supporting him with hardly a complaint despite all the caregiving that has been at many points exhausting. And here they are, with water coming into their basement yet again—plans of moving derailed yet laughing on the phone with me with the kind of genuine, heartfelt humor that serves as a sort of lifeline to stop one from getting pulled under by the turbulent sea. Unable to change their life circum-stances, they do the next best thing: they change their relation-ship to what is happening. Unable to sidestep disappointment and immense frustration, they invite humor and care to sit side by side with it, in order to make it more bearable.

Questions for Reflection: Inner Resources

- What qualities within yourself do you most commonly draw upon to help you through life's difficulties?

- In what ways have you found humor or laughter helpful in an other-wise upsetting or frustrating situation? What other qualities have you found helpful (e.g., self-compassion, trust, acceptance)?

- As you go through the week, pay attention to the qualities and inner resources you draw upon to manage day-to-day challenges, and per-haps bigger ones. What qualities can you continue to strengthen and draw upon to be part of your well of well-being?

◯ When you are able to access your newer operating system, in what ways are you better equipped to handle the challenges that life throws your way?

Life's Unexpected Turns

Three and a half pounds is the weight of this bag of flour, this handful of rocks, this glass bowl. Three and a half pounds can fit into the palm of my hand, as small as a seashell and as precious as life itself. When things go sideways, three and a half pounds can turn your world upside down and can be the greatest blessing of a lifetime.

The pain began around 3:00 AM. I remember checking the digital clock because I knew my husband had gotten to bed late and I didn't want to wake him. Must be my stomach, maybe something I ate. 3:30: this really hurts, not something I've felt before. 4:30: starting to get worried. Pacing now back and forth from kitchen to living room windowsill, though I know I should rest, back to the oversized couch that holds me for a time, starting to double over. 5:30 AM: enough, something's not right. I need to wake my husband.

It was only yesterday we had returned from the ER being told by some doctor that was not my own that everything was fine. Early contractions. Modified bedrest. Great—just how I wanted to spend the last eight weeks of this first pregnancy, laid up on a couch instead of engaging in the busyness of my life where I felt most alive.

By the time we are in the car it's 6:00 AM, rush hour traffic starting early for a Monday morning. We are thirty minutes from the hospital but with traffic and all it feels interminable. The pain is now acute—sharp and aching—surrounded with waves of nausea that for sure make me think I have the stomach flu. By the time we arrive in the circular driveway and pull up to the Emergency Room door (is this déjà vu? feels like I was just here),—I am retching on the pavement and feeling like hell. The wheelchair escorts me quickly inside and before I know it, I am whisked away for tests while I tell my husband, "Please go to work—I'll be fine—it's just a terrible stomach bug. There's nothing you can do for me here."

Not sure how much time passes between the x-rays and ultrasounds and blood tests before my doctor walks into the room and tells me in a steady, firm, straight-out announcement the way a coach might call for a play in the last few minutes of a game with the other team at winning advantage:

"We are going to deliver your baby now. Your body is rejecting this pregnancy. You have pre-eclampsia with HELLP syndrome—your liver is becoming toxic. We need the baby out today."

And just like that, before I could even call my husband, before I could gather my thoughts, I was given Pitocin and an injection to help strengthen the baby's lungs in the hopes that it will be able to breathe on its own and was whisked away to another room where the labor began. Or, at least, tried to.

After a few hours of not progressing—that cervix of mine stubbornly not opening more than a few inches, and my liver functions plummeting, my wishes for a natural birth slipping away and gone. My body had other ideas about how this journey ends. Surrender and trust holding me as what felt like the SWAT team rushing in—masked and covered doctors and nurses rushing me off to the operating room within minutes as my labs start to show signs of serious trouble; not for the baby, but for me. In a carefully orchestrated dance, the epidural is inserted into my back and the knife slices my abdomen open as if a top crust of pie being slit before being put in the oven—my skin being pulled and pushed, tugged and peeled away, then hands reaching in and pulling out the tiny life not quite ready to leave its warm dwelling, but entering the world, nonetheless; all three and a half pounds of this precious life awaiting her next breath, her next journey.

Out of that experience I was blessed with my daughter. The traumatic and unexpected nature of her birth and the abrupt end of my pregnancy catapulted me into some very deep therapy work. Becoming a mother and the sudden and emergency way that my daughter entered the world had a strange resonance for me to the sudden and emergency way that my mom left the world. I was twenty-nine and becoming a mother brought up new layers of grief for me about not having my mom at this time in my life. I also knew I wanted to have another child but had a lot of fears about going through another pregnancy after this experience. The therapy that I embarked on following my daughter's birth was a gift that allowed for deep growth, connection with lost parts of myself, and healing.

Questions for Reflection: Learning from Unexpected Turns

- What was a time life took an unexpected turn or detour for you? What did you learn from that? What came out of that situation, that may not otherwise have? (For example, I know people whose career paths completely changed based on personal challenges they faced, that led them to choose new careers where they could help others going through similar life situations.).

- Have you grown from that experience in unexpected ways? How?

- What qualities or inner resources are more present in you because of that experience (e.g., perhaps greater compassion for others going through something similar, a sense of creative problem-solving, increased flexibility)?

- In what ways did you learn how to be adaptable from that experience? Has that adaptability helped you in any other areas of your life?

- Did it cause you to reevaluate your life or your priorities in any way?

Meditation: From hole self to Whole Self

Find a comfortable position where you can sit or lie uninterrupted for a few minutes. Bring your awareness to the surfaces that are supporting you and notice sensations at the surface of your skin (perhaps softness, firmness, warmth, something else). Notice the sensation of breath coming in and out at your nostrils. Notice the rise and fall of your chest. Become curious about any sensations in your heart center. What is your heartscape like? Are there places that feel tight, contracted, or restricted; open, relaxed, or expansive? You might imagine you could breathe in and out directly through your heart center, feeling the natural rhythm of breath soothing any places of constriction. Let the muscles around your face and eyes relax. Invite softening into the muscles of your neck, shoulders, and back. Notice the expansion and then softening of your belly with each breath. See if you might have a sense of your whole body breathing. Sense that there is an anchor of stability right here in this moment. From that anchor, look out and get curious about what you see. Look through kind, compassionate eyes, remembering you are the one who is observing, from the spacious awareness that is already here. Whatever is here, can you welcome it and let it be just as it is, meeting yourself right where you are? Can you sense the space to let yourself be just as you are: nowhere to go, nothing to do, nothing to fix, nothing to change?

The Japanese art of kintsugi is the art of repairing broken pieces of pottery by putting them back together using material dusted with gold or other precious materials. The idea is not to try and restore it to what it was like before, or hide the flaws, but rather to embrace the imperfections and create something stronger and more beautiful. Imagine that all your imperfections and the things that you might consider your "cracks" are simply a part of your story, a part of your human experience, and part of what makes you human. Imagine that around each crack there is gold that represents your strengths, the ways you have grown from setbacks, the things you have learned along the way, and the heartfelt qualities within you that can hold your suffering and let you know that you are enough and beautiful just as you are. Rest in this sense of imperfectly whole. There is nothing more you need to do.

CHAPTER 9

The Ocean View: We're All in This Together

I am not my thoughts, emotions, sense perceptions, and experiences.
I am not the content of my life. I am life. I am the space in which all
things happen. I am consciousness. I am the now. I am.

—Eckhart Tolle

The moment I began to work on the last chapter of this book
I was standing by the white wooden bar with speckled granite
top overlooking the pool, breathing a deep sigh of warm summer
air as if to take it deep enough into my lungs and being so
that I could hold onto it just a bit longer. The world was quiet,
peaceful, still . . . except, what? Something pulls my attention
to the right. Oh, that's just the black soaker hose that has been
abandoned since last season. No wait, something is moving. Oh
God, it has eyes and a head. My breath quickens. How funny,
this automatic reaction, left over vestiges of my fight-or-flight
response in full motion now, trying to protect me. I keep my dis-
tance but become more curious. Yes, it's a snake, but way bigger
than the little water snake that was recently living in my pool
skimmer. This one is scarier, thicker, slithering and writhing in a

dance of sun and dirt and life that entrains my attention while at the same time I want to pull away, look away. I continue to watch—its little tongue keeps flickering in and out, mouth as if gaping for something that it cannot grasp.

The chapter that I'm working on has to do with connecting with something larger than ourselves—transcendence—the interconnectedness of which we are all a part. Somehow this snake feels important in a way that I cannot quite name but know in my gut the way you know the truth of a thing.

The next day when I come to the same spot to write I cautiously check for the snake, not expecting to see him there, in the same spot no less, but there he is. This time though, he is lifeless, still, without movement. Without knowing it, I had, on the video of my phone from the previous day, perhaps captured his last breaths before he succumbed in the bed of dirt and shade of my hydrangea.

This snake reminds me that everything is connected and interconnected—yes,—the pleasant and unpleasant alike, all part of this dance we call life. That which we push away, would rather turn away from or not feel, is just a part of this human life that calls for us to see it and embrace it yet. And when we do, we realize that we are a part of something much larger; each of us just waves in the ocean, in an interconnected dance of wave and ocean, ocean and wave, indistinguishable, nondual and whole.

The Ocean View

As much as the previous five vantage points help us work toward a sense of inner wholeness and connection with our Self, there is also a wholeness we experience when we connect with and feel a oneness and interconnection with the greater world outside of us. There are many ways one might experience this interconnection: being part of a larger family unit, part of a community of some kind, sensing a connection with the natural world, the global world, the spiritual world, or the universal consciousness.

Regardless of one's religious beliefs or orientation, most of us long for or are curious about some kind of spiritual connection, some sense of being part of something larger than ourselves, whatever our own personal spirituality or spiritual journey looks like. Often there is a search for the sacred, a search for meaning and purpose in this journey. Since the beginnings of time humans have grappled with the mysteries of life and have tried to find a larger meaning in our temporary existence here on earth. This quest to connect with something larger than ourselves can lead us to discover deep sources of well-being. This can be especially true as we grow older and realize the changing nature of things, the impermanence that is the very fabric of this life, and as we come up against the first "arrows" of suffering the Buddha talked about, such as sickness, old age, and death.

One does not need to go to the mountains of Tibet and study with monks to experience a deep connection with one's spirituality. In fact, sometimes we need look no further than our children to see that this connection with spirituality is present from a very early age. As Columbia University professor Lisa Miller explains:

"Biologically, we are hardwired for a spiritual connection. Spiritual development is a biological and psychological imperative from birth. Natural spirituality, the innate spiritual attunement of young children—unlike other lines of development—appears to begin whole and fully expressed. As the child grows, natural spirituality integrates with the capacities of cognitive, social, emotional, and moral development. . . ."[93]

Unfortunately, as Dr. Miller explains, without the support and encouragement to develop these spiritual parts of ourselves, and with outside pressures from our culture towards materialism, competition, productivity, and judgement, we can lose connection with this innate capacity within ourselves to nurture our spirituality. In doing so, we lose an opportunity to cultivate an essential aspect of well-being, one that allows us to thrive and flourish.

In addition to the psychological benefits of connecting with our spirituality, Miller describes that there are measurable differences in the brain and nervous system between those who live their lives attuned to and connected with spirituality, and those for whom spirituality is not a part of their lives. For instance, in the former group, the brain is thicker in the area where it is found to be thin in those who are depressed; the nervous system is better able to regulate levels of the stress hormone cortisol after stressful events; and the brain waves given off at rest by people who are spiritually attuned are similar to the brain waves of monks who are meditating. While spirituality is still a relatively new field of study, in a systematic review of the existing research on spirituality and its effects on health and illness, researchers found that spirituality can influence mental and physical health outcomes and should be a focus of whole person-centered care for both those who are ill and for overall health and well-being.[94]

According to the International Consensus Conference on Spiritual Care in Health Care, spirituality is defined as "the aspect of humanity that refers to the way individuals seek and express meaning and purpose and the way they experience their connectedness to the moment, to self, to others, to nature, and to the significant or sacred."[95]

When we connect with a sense of meaning and purpose beyond ourselves, with the world and the sacred around us, and when we bring actions into the world that are aligned with our deepest values, we access something vaster and more transcendent than the small self view that we can get lost in. This kind of connection allows us access to a deeper well of well-being that can help us through life's most difficult challenges.

Evolutionary Shifts

By now you likely have a sense of "small self" or "hole self" and you have a sense of large Self or "Whole Self." Our final shift in vantage point allows us to connect with the Whole—of which "Whole Self" is a part. This inter-connection is another aspect that becomes available when we have access to our newer operating system.

When we are living from our old operating system, and from hole self, our adaptive survival circuits are activated, leading us to experience greater fear, anxiety, worry, distraction, mental rumination, self-protection, tunnel vision, and isolation/separate self. When we can access our newer social engagement system, we activate our ventral vagal pathways and widen our experience to include greater care and connection with others, compassion and self-compassion, openness, perspective, growth, and joy. We live in the realm of Whole Self.

When we open even further to a sense of the Whole that is all around us, and of which we are part, a further shift in consciousness is available. From here we can experience expansiveness, interconnectedness, deep peace, equanimity, and awe.

This shift in consciousness, to a sense of connection with a greater whole, is often reported in longtime meditators. Interestingly, studies that have looked at the brains of meditators have found that there is a decrease in activity of the default mode network, brain regions thought to be associated, among other things, with self-referential thinking, with a sense of small self me, myself, I as separate.[96] While our default mode network also allows us to imagine, daydream, and think creatively, these brain regions are associated with ruminative thinking, depression, and decreased well-being when the default mode network is overactive (as it is in many people).

In previous chapters, we worked on ways to invite a sense of stability, curiosity, perspective, self-compassion, and inner strength to sit side by side with our difficult emotions, to find greater ease within our challenges. In this chapter, we extend that to find heartfelt qualities that include a sense of the transcendent: that which connects us to something larger than ourselves.

This chapter is about meeting and holding life's deepest challenges (impermanence, change, loss, aging, and death) in the space of something vaster and more expansive, that allows us to nonetheless find meaning, resilience, growth, and possibility that reminds us that we are not alone but part of an interconnected whole that is ever present.

Seeing our lives from this vantage point (regardless of one's religious orientation) brings with it ease, acceptance, equanimity, and a deep peace that is possible at our core to sit alongside life's most difficult challenges. As the viewpoint widens, so too does our experience of life itself. Instead of fighting to change ourselves or trying to resist those life circumstances that we cannot change, we look through the lens of a spacious awareness in which everything is held. From that vantage point, coming from a place of already whole and already interconnected with a larger, expansive Whole, deep well-being emerges—a well-being that is already here.

Understanding the Nature of Awareness as Part of Our Spiritual Journey

Whenever my dad pulled out the card deck, I felt this little pulse of excitement tingling through my chest, the feeling of delight like water washing over rivers of stone and rock and splashing as it lands playfully on dry ground. "Pick a card," my father would say as he fanned out the deck. Then he'd turn his head away as my siblings and I excitedly pulled a card from the deck, looked at it, and, upon his instruction, put it back anywhere in the deck we chose. After a few other instructions and mysterious maneuvers, he would hold the deck behind his back and magically pick the card we chose: every single time. It was nothing short of remarkable! When I finally learned the secret of this trick, the biggest delight was the shift in perspective it brought. How marvelous that what was in front of me all along, right before my very eyes, was yet hidden from view until it was pointed out as if staring at the black lines of a picture for all these years and suddenly realizing that where the picture resides was in the white spaces.

Maybe I've got it all wrong. Maybe this life is nothing more than a figure ground shift and I've been focusing on the wrong spaces, putting my attention in the wrong places. Perhaps it is that simple—and that profound.

I read an impactful story once, of two young fish swimming along in the water and an older fish swims by and asks, "Hey boys, how's the water?" The younger fish look at each other and say, "What the hell is water?" (David Foster Wallace[97])

For so many years of my life I thought I was the wave. Me, the self, my-self, this body and mind that feels distinctly mine, that has the years of history and memory and experience that makes me feel like a separate self. When I am angry, it is me who is angry; when I am overwhelmed by frustration; it is me who is caught in an intense storm of emotion.

But what if I took a half step back? What if, instead of being in the water, thinking I'm the wave, I stood at the shore and realized I am part of the ocean itself? In the vast expanse of water there are the waves that come and go, returning to where they came and rising up again. These are our experiences, our emotions, the sensations that rise up in us, and pass away. Yet they are not the whole of who we are. There is a larger whole of which we are a part. That is, when we step back, we are also the one who watches, who sees how all of the waves are interconnected. We are part of the vast space in which it all passes by and through, the consciousness that sees it all.

From that perspective, everything shifts. My anger that is gripping me, spiraling me into a frenzy is now seen from that half step back. There is a space, there is the observing Self with a capital S who can see the anger rise up and who knows the anger will in its own time collapse and fall away, returning unto itself. This intelligence knows that beneath the anger is fear, and in that knowing, in that holding, the self-protective layers can soften, relax. It is not me, the one who is the mother, the psychologist, the roles I define myself by; it is me, the conscious awareness that sees all these roles, that sees the nature of the mind that tries so hard to define me as this or that because it feels more graspable that way.

In moments of insight, moments of illumination, moments that pull back the curtain to reveal the simple truth of how a card can consistently be discovered among fifty-two possibilities—it is in these moments that our perception shifts. We come to see that the background we thought was just backdrop is actually the foreground in which we are swimming, and the foreground that we lived in is just a temporary backdrop, a changing landscape. We come to see that the only constant is our awareness, and that everything else—everything—changes, is temporary. In this knowing, we can grasp a bit less, struggle a bit less trying to stop the waves, and instead let life's energy flow through us as we watch the magnificent dance of sea and salt and sand and sky. Rising and falling. Just this breath. Just this breath.

One area of spirituality that is largely untapped for so many of us is the nature of conscious awareness itself. As Michael A. Singer says,[98] "Psychology studies what is going on in there. Spirituality studies who is in there noticing what is going on in there."

As we learned earlier, one important aspect of mindful awareness is developing the capacity to be the noticer, the one sitting in the audience watching what is happening on the stage of life, through kind, curious, compassionate eyes. This audience view allows us to see what is here, in this present moment, without being swept away by the small self view. From the perspective of the audience, being aware from the audience, we can notice body sensations, thoughts, and emotions, as if we are the observer of our experience. This is different than our typical way of experiencing things by being caught in thoughts, sensations, and emotions. For example, if I am angry, it is easy to let this anger overtake me. I am caught in it, swept away by the sensations and angry thoughts ("This isn't fair; I can't believe he said that") as if I am in the center of the storm. But from the viewpoint of the audience, I can notice anger arising in my body; I can be aware of thoughts going through my mind that may be distorted and highly charged. There is a bit more space between me and my thoughts and feelings, and from this space more possibilities arise. I have more choices about how I might respond to any given situation.

But we can take this now a step further by asking, *who or what is aware of the one sitting in the audience?* Try this for a moment. Think of a time you were caught up in a strong emotion such as anger or frustration. Think of that situation for a moment and feel what that feels like in your body. Now imagine that you are sitting in the audience, taking the audience view that allows you to notice thoughts and feelings from that slight shift in vantage point. Instead of being caught in them, you can be aware of what is happening from this half step back. Notice how that kind of knowing feels different in your body. What shifts or changes when you are able to observe your own experience (especially when you can do so from a place of curiosity, perspective, and compassion)?

Now ask yourself: *How am I aware of the one who is sitting in the audience? Where does this knowing come from?* Further consider that sometimes you may remember that you are in the audience, but many times you may think that you are the small self actor on the stage, bumping into your inner experiences and getting caught up in them mindlessly. Yet at any moment, you can turn the house lights of the theater on and see your Self sitting in the audience. This Self doesn't disappear just because you have forgotten where you are sitting. So go back to the question of who or what is aware of the one sitting in the audience. Stay with that as an inner experience for a moment and see what arises.

What if there is a larger light than the theater lights, an infinite and expansive light that is always present, that never goes off? What if this light is conscious awareness itself—ever present spacious awareness from which all experiences arise and pass? Like the light that illuminates a theater, this light brings all things more clearly into view, it allows us to see the stage and the sets, the small selves moving about on stage, feeling sad, angry, stubbing their toe, and so on. The light also illuminates the Whole Self that is sitting in the audience watching through kind eyes. But the light is not the stage or the actors or even the person in the audience; and while the light allows you to see emotions that are present, it does not *feel* sadness, anger, or pain. The light is unaffected by the experiences which it illuminates. It is the thing in which all those experiences can be seen and known.

What if who we are is not just the physical sensations, thoughts, memories, behaviors, and emotions that arise within us; it is not even just the one sitting in the audience who can see these experiences arise. What if we are part of this vaster, spacious awareness in a similar way that a wave is forever part of an ocean? There is an interconnectedness of wave and ocean, and an interconnectedness of ocean and every wave that ever arises, crests, and returns into the larger expanse. This ocean is always present, always around us, always there to hold us.

Taking a Deeper Dive into Consciousness

My first glimpses into the nature of awareness of the kind I am describing came from a workshop I took with meditation teacher Loch Kelly many years ago. In it he offered short "glimpse" practices of stepping out of one's usual mode of experiencing things and sensing into the awake, aware presence that is already here. He talked about how we have this kind of problem solver that lives as if in the center of our forehead where we tend to think and see the world from. He guided us in some exercises to let this problem solver relax and asked the question for us to experience, "What is here now when there is no problem to solve?" Through his guided exercises and inquiries many people in the room experienced and described a sense of deep peace, ease, and joy that is already here when we can drop awareness away from this local problem solver in our forehead (part of our survival circuitry) and into our bodies and the space around us.

Around the same time as this workshop, I also discovered psychiatrist and professor Dan Siegel's Wheel of Awareness exercise.[99] This meditation invites one to notice inner experiences from the perspective of and using the image of standing in the center of a wheel and sending "spokes" of awareness from the center of the wheel out to the rim of the wheel. At the rim of the wheel are different aspects of our experience that we can know, that we can become aware of. At the center of the wheel is awareness itself, from which we can look out and know things in our inner and outer world. For example, looking out from the center of the wheel, we can send spokes of awareness to the rim and observe our five senses, we can observe physical sensations in our bodies, and we can observe the mental activities of our mind such as passing thoughts and emotions. The center of the wheel represents the awareness from which we notice and know these things. At the end of this practice Dr. Siegel invites people to "bend the spoke of awareness" back on itself, essentially standing in the center of the wheel and becoming aware of awareness itself. In moments of doing this, in sensing into the awareness of awareness itself, I have experienced a noticeable shift of consciousness that has a profoundly peaceful and expansive, ever-present, benevolent, and time-less quality to it. In Dr. Siegel's accounts of doing this exercise with hundreds of people, he described that the majority of people doing this experience something similar. In his book *Aware*,[100] based on the Wheel of Awareness exercise, he describes how as we develop the ability to expand awareness and distinguish awareness from that which we are aware of, this expansion in consciousness has profound effects on our health, well-being, and sense of inter-connectedness.

Many spiritual and meditation teachers have talked about this *awareness of awareness*. Diana Winston, in her audiobook *Glimpses of Being*,[101] talks about three types of awareness: focused awareness (which focuses on what's in front of us such as awareness of the breath); open awareness, which involves being the observer who notices whatever arises in the field of awareness (a passing thought, now an itch, now a feeling of tightness in the chest, for example); and natural awareness, which is the awareness of awareness itself.

Loch Kelly refers to this as "non-dual awareness" or "effortless mindfulness" and discusses how each of these three types of awareness have different brain patterns associated with them.[102] Interestingly, he describes that when people are in a state of effortless awareness, their brains show a balance between the default mode network and the task positive network (the parts of our brain that are active when we are engaging in a focused task), indicating a synergistic dance between being aware of both what one is doing and one's inner experiences all at the same time. EEG studies showed that those practicing effortless mindfulness had an unusually high frequency of gamma waves (the fastest of our brain waves, representing many parts of the brain lighting up in harmony, representing peak concentration, alertness, and consciousness). Dr. Dan Siegel suggests that practicing a state of awareness of awareness leads to a greater integration of differentiated parts of the brain working together in harmony (that is, the default mode network is no longer isolated but is now communicating with other regions of the brain as an integrated whole).[103] In his book *Effortless Mindfulness Now* Loch Kelly quotes meditation teacher Mingyur Rinpoche, as saying:

"We access the mind of calm abiding through recognition. What do we recognize? Awareness. The ever-present quality of mind from which we are never separated even for an instant. Even though normally we do not recognize awareness, we can no more live without it than we can live without breathing. Discovering our own awareness allows us to access the natural steadiness and clarity of mind."[104]

Buddhist nun and meditation teacher Pema Chödrön has a beautiful quote suggesting that awareness is the backdrop from which all of our experiences emerge: "You are the sky. Everything else—it's just the weather."[105] Rick Hanson talks about how there is greater ease when we can be aware of our pain or upset from a place of spacious awareness, because, "Awareness itself is never troubled by what it represents, it is never stained or damaged by what it represents."[106] Said in another way, meditation teacher Cory Muscara and Mindfulness.com shares that: "Meditation is not about 'powering through' or 'tolerating' our suffering, it's about connecting to the part of us that is bigger and more vast than the experience we feel overwhelmed by. When you are able to identify more with your awareness of difficult experiences than the difficult experiences themselves, you begin the journey of finding inner freedom."[107]

While said in many different ways, all of this points to the expansive nature of something outside of our small-self experience that can help us find ease amidst the emotional discomforts of life.

Whether you have had the direct experience or not of glimpsing into this kind of spacious awareness, this chapter invites you to connect with your natural spirituality that is already here in whatever form it lives in you. The invitation of the ocean view is to help you connect with that which goes beyond yourself and brings you in touch with a larger Whole, an interconnected common humanity and expansive world of which we are all a part. This ocean view is an important source of well-being that is available to us all.

Shift Your Vantage Point:
You Don't Have to Stop the Waves;
Just Remember That You Are the Ocean.

Part One: Connection with Presence and Being Part of Something Larger

Warm-Up

4:00 AM: Alarm goes off in the Motel 6 where I am staying, the closest motel I could find to the triathlon grounds where I needed to be at the crack of dawn. Feet hit the ground, so grateful for the sleep I got, albeit not the usual eight to nine hours my body is used to. By the time I arrive at the driveway of the parking lot there are hundreds upon hundreds of cars; each person unloading their bike, carrying their bag filled with running shoes, water bottles, GU, and other forms of mushy and gushy nutrition that can be digested more easily in the course of intense effort. I grab my bike with the new pink seat and pink tape wrapped around the handlebars, noting how such a silly thing as a bright vibrant color can enliven me. I walk my bike over to the transition area with bag slung over my shoulder in anxious anticipation. The Porta Potty becomes my friend multiple times before the starting bell sounds, final call gathering us all by the water's edge. Then wave by wave of groups enter the water, coded and counted by the colored swim caps we are all given; cocooned in skintight wetsuits which turn out to be not just helpful protection against the icy cold water, but also an advantage of buoyancy for this 1.2-mile-long swim. Once I enter the water my nerves oddly dissipate as I am immersed in the open space of this beautiful lake that makes me feel at home and at ease like a giant hug from an old friend. I have always loved the open water, and today is no different, even despite the electronic chip around my ankle that is recording my time, and the hundreds of people swarming around and past me as they effortfully race on to dry land.

The feeling of the water continues to envelop me like a cool even chilly hug that puts gentle, soothing pressure all the way from my toes to the top of my head, covered in a fluorescent-orange bathing cap. The sun is so reflective off of the water's surface that I can barely see the buoys ahead of me, the buoys that mark the edges of this swim course, the sun almost blinding me to the path that lies before me. Surrounded by bodies covered in leathery tight wetsuits, I feel more like a fish swimming with its school than a competitor amongst others who have trained months and months, as I have, to arrive at this lake in the middle of Lakeville, Massachusetts. In this moment all of the training I have done—the mile swims in the pool and 50-mile bike rides and 13-miles runs, all strung together like a Froot Loops necklace in this order or that—none of it matters. It is just this moment, this glorious moment of being alive, of taking in the trees on the shoreline and the gift of movement through space—propelling me forward into joyful.

As much as I loved doing triathlons back in the day and enjoyed the physical challenge of it, what stands out for me most about this experience is always something much more transcendent— the interconnection of hundreds of others moving separately yet together in this shared space and time; the interconnection with nature surrounding me; and a sense of being in a state of flow and presence.

Other times of experiencing this have occurred in more simple and day-to-day moments—walking with friends in the woods, sharing laughter at a family gathering of three generations, being part of a volunteer group serving food at a homeless shelter and interacting with the residents there, or listening to an orchestra play a piece of music that moves me to tears.

Questions for Reflection: Interconnection

- When have you had an experience of feeling interconnected to others, to the natural world, or to something sacred, expansive, or spiritual?

- When have you felt like you were in a flow state, totally present to something you were doing that engaged all of your attention, with a kind of presence that felt beyond ordinary experience?

- See if you might call up such a time now and hold it vividly in your mind. Now drop your attention down into your body and sense this in your body. What inner sensations do you experience? What do you sense around you? What is the interconnection between the two? Take a few minutes to journal about this experience.

Questions for Reflection: Contribution to the Larger Whole

When I was a teenager, I remember a sermon given by my rabbi in which he shared the following quote by William James, one of the founding fathers in the field of psychology: "The greatest use of a life is to spend it for something that will outlast it." This quote has always stayed with me, and I think about it often. I think that we need not be famous inventors or influencers to make enduring contributions.

- What in your life gives you a feeling of connecting with something more lasting and enduring? In what ways do you contribute that feels meaningful or purposeful to you? This could be as simple and profound as showing kindness to those around you. Don't underestimate the power of what might seem small. I know people's lives who have changed because one person showed them kindness when they needed it most.

- Write down small things you already do and things that you might do in the near future, that give you a feeling of meaning, purpose, or contribution in your life.

Questions for Reflection: Spirituality

- Reflect back as far as you can remember into your childhood. Were there aspects of spirituality that you can recall being connected with

(perhaps moments of wonder in nature, moments of interconnectedness as part of a larger group, curiosity about God or some higher
spirit, or perhaps spiritual experiences that you remember having)?

- Do you recall disconnecting from this at any point in your life,
perhaps feeling that it was not okay to show this side of yourself, or
perhaps abandoning this in the service of higher priorities or obliga-
tions that took precedence?

- How about as an adult? How do you define spirituality for yourself
and what does it mean to you? Think about any times when you have
had a spiritual experience: perhaps when you have sensed something
deeply sacred, felt an interconnectedness with others or the world
around you, or experienced something transcendent. It could be in
nature, with another person, in a moment of solitude, in the midst
of a volunteer experience with a lot of people, a time when you had a
sense of something greater than yourself.

- What are some ways in your life now that you connect with something larger than yourself (a group, family, community, etc.), that
brings you a sense of well-being?

- What small step might you take to bring a greater sense of spirituality
into your life?

Practice: Figure-Ground Shift; What Is *Not* Me?

Have you ever seen one of those figure-ground optical illusions that are
black-and-white images that play tricks on your eyes? (If not, I encourage
you to look up "figure ground shift images" on the Internet to take a look at
one.) Many people's eyes are immediately drawn to the black ink, and they
see a solid image of something there. However, if you look long enough,

something else starts to emerge. An image appears in the white space, and the black ink simply becomes background. This is a figure-ground shift. If you can, take a look at such an image now. Notice how what is figure and what is ground is not solid but can fluctuate depending upon your vantage point and what you are focusing on.

For this short reflection exercise, become familiar with one of these figure-ground images. Call it to mind as you settle in and picture yourself for a moment as the black ink part of the image. Have a sense of yourself as solid, sitting there and looking out with eyes open or closed at the space around you. Now ask yourself, *What is not me?* Expand your awareness to include anything that is not the small self that you identify with. Contemplate everything that is not small-self you, as if that is the white space of the picture. Sense the expansiveness of this white space. Now play with a figure-ground shift. Play with the idea that perhaps what is you is (or includes) all the white space around you. What if you are not the solid black image but the white space that surrounds it? What happens if you look back at your small self through the eyes of the white space? How does that feel different than looking out from, and being aware from, the black ink?

🎧 Meditation: Finding Refuge in Wholeness

Begin by finding a comfortable position. Notice your breath at a single point in your body where you feel it the most, whether at the tip of your nose, the back of your throat, your chest, your belly, or somewhere else. Focus your attention for a few rounds of breath there. Now begin to expand your awareness to your whole-body breathing as one whole unit. Sense how everything in your body, all the systems and cells, work together as a unified whole. Feel your whole-body breathing. Now expand your awareness to include all the space and things in the room in which you are sitting. Notice the interconnection between your body and the space around you. Expand your circle of awareness further to include the outside world, expanding beyond where you are sitting to include your community and all beings that reside there.

Expand your awareness further to include your region, and even further and further out if you would like to include this planet Earth of which we are all a part. Feel the interconnection of all living beings. Sense the spaciousness in which everything is held.

The Labyrinth Versus the Road Map

Many years ago, when my beloved Grandma Mae was alive, I went down to Florida to visit her and took her for an outing this particular summer day. I had rented a car and we set out to find a restaurant for lunch about fifteen minutes from her apartment. We had been driving for quite some time, well beyond the expected fifteen minutes. I was hopelessly lost but didn't have the heart to tell my grandma that I had no idea where we were going. At one point she looked out the window and commented, "Isn't that the mall that we just passed ten minutes ago?" I was found out—how embarrassing! Eventually I had to pull over and call my brother to help me navigate (these were the days before GPS, and he has a great sense of direction). Actually, the truth is, I have a terrible sense of direction and have become lost even with my GPS! This was not the first time that I ended up back where I started, circling around in an endless loop.

I have recently been reflecting on this notion of feeling lost and not having a road map. For the first part of my life, I felt like I had a clear road map. I knew exactly what I wanted to do (become a psychologist, get married, have children, etc.). It was a straight path. As I have gotten older, I am realizing that this road-map approach to life doesn't quite fit me anymore. I think of life now a little more like a labyrinth, a single path always leading back to the center. You don't have to worry about getting lost because you will always find your way back to center, back home, no matter which direction you walk.

Practice: The Labyrinth

Draw a labyrinth (or if you are interested, see if you might find one that you can visit and walk). What for you represents the center of your labyrinth?

What is it that you would like to remind yourself of, whenever you feel lost, that you might "come home" to? (This could be a deep sense of stillness and calm within; a sense of connection with nature or spiritual transcendence; a sense of belonging to your community; a deep connection with your loved ones; a connection with God.). Use words, pictures, symbols, or images to represent your center of this labyrinth. Whenever you feel that you are met-aphorically losing your way, picture walking your labyrinth knowing that no matter which direction you walk you will find your way to center.

Dear Reader,

I know that at times you are feeling filled with discouragement, tears, fears, loss, and uncertainty. I know that at times you are scared, pushing away the strong feelings in you that you would rather not feel. I know that at times you feel alone—deeply alone in the immensity of grief that lies at the heart of the darkness that shrouds you and makes it hard for you to see your way. But I want you to know that you are not alone. That within the depths of what feels like an impenetrable blackness, a hole in which you are at times stuck, there is something that surrounds you. This something is invisible, yet palpable. It is spacious yet containing. It has its own energy, and yet it also is woven into the very energy from which you breathe. It is awareness itself. This awareness sees your pain. This awareness is vast enough to hold your anger, your fear, your grief, and everything that rises up within you. This awareness hears that which you long to share; it holds your stories and your memories and the tight contractions and the heaving. And in this awareness, you are safe, you are held. This awareness is who you are, it is the essence of you: it is from you and of you and when you surrender to it, it will catch you every time.

Petra's Story: I started seeing Petra when her daughter was sixteen years old and had been in and out of several psychiatric hospitals due to depression. Petra had a high-powered position in the banking field and worked long hours, but she was devoted to her daughter and did everything a mother could possibly do to be there for her daughter and get her supportive services that she needed. When her daughter left for college, Petra was optimistic that her daughter would do well. That was before she got into drugs. Over several very rocky years, Petra did what she could to get her daughter help, but in the end an overdose took her daughter's life.

As one might imagine, the grief was unbearable for Petra at first. While she had a strong community of support around her, Petra found the most solace in the woods. There she took long hikes, and described in the solitude that she felt a connection with her daughter's spirit, and with the natural world that surrounded her. On these walks Petra allowed herself to courageously feel her feelings, without trying to fix or change her inner experience. She surrounded herself with people who allowed her to feel and express her grief and profound sadness, and disconnected from people whom she felt needed her to be happy or cheerful around them in order for them to feel okay in her presence. Petra began daily meditation, at first just giving herself space to be, but over time, reconnecting with a spiritual presence that she had long abandoned as a young adult.

As Petra made space day after day for her grief, something began to emerge that surprised her: a voice calling from within for her to make a change. A year after her daughter died, she quit her job, went back to school, and became a counselor where she could help teenagers and young adults who were struggling with drug addiction. She found tremendous meaning and purpose in her life in a way she hadn't felt in her previous profession. In this new role, she found she could honor her daughter's memory and give back in a way that connected her with a sense of being part of a larger whole. Out of tragedy, she found some comfort knowing she could make a difference in the lives of so many others and be part of something much larger than herself. While the grief remains ever present for her, there is, side by side, a deep well-being in her heart, knowing she and her daughter are part of something that transcends them both.

Part Two: Dealing with Life's Inevitable Difficulties

One of our biggest sources of suffering, according to the Buddha's teachings and the second noble truth, is our tendency toward *clinging* and *craving*. We want things to be other than what they are. We want things to be permanent when they are in fact impermanent. We want things to remain unchanging when that is not the nature of things. Craving activates our old operating system of contraction, fear, physical tension, and physiological stress. We exert great mental efforts trying to fight against the currents of life. When we learn to accept the impermanence of things and that which we cannot change from the compassionate parent view (holding kindly the parts of ourselves that suffer), and when we can hold this impermanence within a larger sense of interconnection with something beyond ourselves (the ocean view), deeper peace is possible.

Let's come back one more time to the metaphor of putting a teaspoon of salt into a cup and then imagining drinking that water. It would be hard to swallow. But that same teaspoon of salt in a lake would hardly be noticed. Sometimes we can't change the contents that we have to work with (life's inevitable challenges), but we can widen the container within which the contents are held, so there is a sense of more expansiveness, and the contents are surrounded by something more vast, spacious, and supportive that allows for greater ease. As we connect to the wholeness around us that is already here and look out through the spacious awareness that is already and always here, we can hold our suffering in new ways that change our experience of it.

Aging and Changing Landscapes: Widening the Container

This morning on my walk I caught a flashing glimpse of the bold yellow school bus, masquerading as the camp bus, whizzing by at the bottom of our street. Just a glimpse, a passing yellow whoosh that was gone almost as soon as it came into sight. Yet my heart felt like it skipped a beat, my head sending me back to another time indeed, my body filled with pangs of something I can't quite name. So many days and months and years that yellow bus stopped at the end of the street to pick up my son for camp: the little boy who could not stop moving with excitement, the young boy that I used to toss the Frisbee with while we waited, the older teen who was embarrassed to have to ride the bus and not drive himself, but who nonetheless hopped on, excited to have this bus carry him away to day camp, his second home away from home.

This passage of time, this landscape changing before my very eyes, shows up as a visceral feeling, such a deep tug in my body as if something physically pulling on me and reminding me of the way of things, even when I would rather look elsewhere. This little boy morphed into young man, coming home now and again in between friends and college and wispy summer nights.

Turning and walking up the hill, I think of my father and the hill that he will no longer climb. It is a hill far steeper than this one: the one outside their condo door that as a seventy-something he once bounded up in a jog, to my amazement. Later, after his cancer diagnosis, that hill became his challenge, the one that he proudly walked up again and again in between treatments, a sign of his amazing stamina and determination. Some days he announced that he had walked up and down the hill twice in one day: a victory that was pure celebration and a testament to his healthy lifestyle and the strength of the human body. It wasn't the cancer that stopped him, nor the two strokes, but this last incident: a bad fall, a broken hip, and ongoing balance problems that made this hill impossible to climb after so many years. And yet still and remarkably my father perseveres, focusing on what he can do and not on what his body will no longer allow.

*Funny how on my walk up and down my street I am listening to
a dharma talk on the second noble truth; the way we humans
cling to what we cannot hold, trying to grab the water as it cas-
cades over the waterfall; the changing, impermanent landscape
of life. There is no stopping it, not any more than I could stop the
waves washing over me in the ocean as I swam yesterday in my
favorite open-water spot, fighting the wind-whipped waves. The
water, my refuge in the spacious expanse of sea and sky and salty
air. The water that has its own story, its own life. For a moment
I am one, for a moment I forget, for a moment I remember, in
the letting go, the surrender—unsure where my body ends and
the water begins—carried by the currents, disappearing into the
oneness that I am.*

Practice: Expanding Your Container

Image a container within which you experience your life. How might you
expand that container as wide as possible to include people and things that
are important to you, that extend beyond yourself? This more expansive container could include groups to which you belong, it might include the beauty
of nature, the creativity of great art, the lasting treasures passed on through
the generations, the gift of music of all kinds. What helps you connect to a
transcendent feeling?

Are there words that comfort you in the midst of impermanence and inevitable changes of life? Some words that I find most helpful to connect with
are *acceptance, trust,* and *surrender.*

As much as you have changed over the years of your lifetime, what enduring traits have remained? I recently had the experience of visiting with
a dear friend from high school whom I have spoken to but haven't seen in
years. Her parents and brother were also there, whom I hadn't seen for close
to forty years. And yet, when we were together there was a strange sense of a

time warp—of feeling like it was just yesterday, and still feeling inside like my eighteen-year-old self. I know many people have this experience in one form or another. Our bodies change in profound ways over time, but our spirit remains unchanged. What qualities in you are timeless? How might these qualities provide some comfort for you in times of change and transition?

What gifts have you experienced as you have aged? What wisdom (or something else) is available to you now that was not available to you when you were younger?

Cycles of Life: Impermanence

Sitting outside on my deck, sun warming my back like a gentle caress, soothing the tension from my shoulders I have been holding from a year of being on edge; enjoying the avocado melting in my mouth on this salad grown by workers somewhere far across the world, I exhale slowly. It is the kind of exhale that says so little and releases so much. It is that trying-to-let-go kind of feeling of what has been knocking on my door since this tiny body experienced its first loss; the kind of acknowledging of something so deep inside that its only means of escape is through the slow exhalation.

Across the yard I see the bare tree stumps where my neighbors cut down—no, chopped—about thirty trees between our yard and theirs. It was devastating at first; the kind of devastating that makes you want to run and scream and throw things because you just want what has always been there to be there still. The kind of devastating that makes your eyes widen in surprise because you can't quite process what is actually happening (and if you had, you would have run and grabbed and hugged every tree and begged them to spare just this one). To be fair, many of them had seen their life, had been aging, dying now for some time. To be honest, I had hardly noticed that; I mostly just saw the comfort of their familiar tall bodies and outstretched branches grabbing at the sunlight that nourished their cells. This loss of the trees surprised me, surprised me in its reminder of the familiar loss of other things in my life, and how pain lives as physical sensations in the body. After a few days I could finally walk into my yard and be okay, and after more days still, I was able to look around and see the ways that there is now more light filtering through the remaining trees, and I can appreciate their beauty even more now that they are not crowded out by the others.

I have never been very good with change. This year of the pandemic has been quite the roller coaster of emotions—the fear, terror, uncertainty—and loss for so many. In it I see the impermanence, the tentative nature of all things, the way that the world can change in an instant. At one minute you are surrounded by people at work, in the gym, at gatherings, and at the next instant you are in lockdown, fearing for your loved one's safety and wondering if your husband will survive over these months of caring for his patients in the hospital. On one day, my dear friend is telling us that her daughter of thirty years is dying of breast cancer, that it has metastasized, and it is unclear how much time she has. In the next breath, my other friend shares that her daughter is pregnant, expecting her first child. The irony is not lost on me, that in the next nine months one life may be no more, while another will burst forth into the world with a joy like no other.

In this juxtaposition of life and death, of change, growth, and impermanence, I sigh—a deep, bittersweet, long exhalation—as I take another bite of my avocado and gaze off in the distance,

*wondering what new growth is sprouting in the forest ground
around the barren stumps.*

Questions for Reflection: Growth and Renewal

● As you look back on your life, reflect on the growth and renewal that sits side by side with the impermanence of things. Out of that which has not lasted (a job, a relationship, circumstances which change), in what ways have you been adaptable?

● In what ways has that adaptability led to new growth in some way, or something emerging that perhaps you hadn't expected?

● In what ways have you experienced acceptance (i.e., nonresistance) about these things, or some other expansive quality (e.g., self-compassion), that has allowed for greater ease?

Cycles of Life: Death and Inviting Something More Expansive to Sit Alongside Loss and Grief

*I remember the man in the white coat, though he had no face—
at least not that I can recall these oh-so-many years later. Funny
how time erases certain details of things and magnifies others.
I remember the surprise when I heard the car pull down the
gravel driveway and park in front of the lilac bush, green and
lush on this September morning, though its flowers were long
gone. I recall standing on the stairwell when my father walked in
the doorway, confused as to why he would have come home from
work midday. I remember the eggplant parmesan sandwich that
I ordered at the fast-food restaurant on the way to the hospital.
So odd that I had an appetite at such a time! I can remember
thinking that very thought to myself as my body, giving strong*

cues of hunger, somehow allowed me to digest this thing, when the reality of the situation was far too overwhelming to digest: not then, not now, not for years and even decades.

—After days of waiting, hoping for little movements, twitches, an eye movement here, a finger lifting there; after hope had built up like a wave cresting, and then crashing and breaking and receding, slipping away in a current too powerful to command, the man with the white coat told us that my mom wouldn't make it. He explained that she had sustained too much brain damage from the accident. There was nothing more they could do; only wait for my father to decide when and if to pull the plug.

What a strange phrase—"to pull the plug," as if a vacuum or electronic appliance was being disconnected from the wall, not a human life, a person, this person called mom who I am certain loved me more than anyone else in the world for those fifteen years of my life. And now this man in his white coat, the faceless man, was speaking these words to four pairs of ears hovered together in a little white room on the eighth floor.

I remember my father in those moments to follow, maybe not his words exactly, but pretty close. He told us that we would all need to go on, to live our lives and become the people that Mom would want us to be, the people that would make her proud. I remember his courage, especially now looking back, seeing the courage it took to take care of three children, get up for work every day, in the blackest of darkness that life knows, to still go on.

I said goodbye that day, with that last image of my mom, who had never regained consciousness, being the rising and falling of her chest in rhythm with the ventilator, this artificial support of life that could no longer sustain itself. I said goodbye in some blurred reality that didn't feel real, or final, though I knew both were true.

The meaning of life is in the little moments that are right here; that is all. There is no past or future that truly exists, though we like to find solace in those thoughts. It is all right here: in this breath, in this footstep, in this smile, in this tear.

The last memory I have before we left the hospital that September day was going into the small window-filled waiting room, the one that we had come back to again and again over the course of that week. That same woman was there—the one whose son had been injured in a water-skiing accident. I knew I would not be back to that waiting room, or to this hospital, so I went over to her, mustered up some courage of a voice, and whispered, "I hope your son is okay, I hope your son makes it." Then I turned around and walked out the door, toward a very different life than I could possibly fathom.

Looking back on this experience, I remember that, even in those darkest moments, there was something else present, sitting alongside the immense grief that was there. My fifteen-year-old self had some sense in that moment, perhaps from my father's words, that this grief would not destroy me; that out of it I would connect with something meaningful about living my life, wanting to help others in some way. Despite the deepest of pain, I experienced at the same time a compassion in myself and courage in my father that expanded well beyond the pain and offered me some comfort that life would go on.

Practice: Connecting with Values

Health psychologist Kelly McGonigal shared that in the face of great uncertainty and very difficult circumstances, especially where there is much we can't control, we can always ask ourselves one powerful question: *What can I choose in this situation?*[108] One of the things that is always available for us to choose is to connect with heartfelt qualities such as courage, compassion, self-compassion, acceptance, care, or other qualities that speak to our deepest values or who we want to be. When these heartfelt qualities sit side by side with our darkest emotions, although it doesn't take away the suffering, there is greater ease to bear whatever is present.

Identify what are some of your deepest values (e.g., acceptance, authenticity, contribution, compassion, creativity, fairness, friendliness, generosity, gratitude, connection, kindness, patience, respect, supportiveness, spirituality, etc.).[109]

How does connecting with these values give you a sense of being connected to a larger whole, to something more expansive that extends beyond small self?

How might connecting with and keeping these values in view be helpful during difficult times? Even when we can't change the circumstances, we can widen the container in which our suffering is held. How might connecting to these heartfelt qualities and values you have identified help to widen your container to hold your own suffering?

Practice: The Quilt Expanded

Here is a variation of the quilt exercise from the previous chapter that helps us to expand to the ocean view. I recently saw the most magnificent quilt that was a project of a town where many hands worked together to create quite an artistic masterpiece. It was a representation of the beautiful lake in that town. But it not only represented this precious body of water and the aliveness all around it, but the interconnection and interdependence as displayed in the very essence of this patchwork quilt.

Think about a patchwork quilt where each patch represents important aspects of your world. Patches might represent family members, friends, pets or loved ones in your life, both present and past. They might include ancestors you've never met but whose legacy you are a part of. They might represent activities or communities of which you are a part. They might represent favorite places you've visited, or parts of the natural world that you feel most connected to. They might represent religious figures, spiritual figures, spirit guides, or symbols that connect you with a sense of your personal spirituality. You might also include quotes from great thinkers from whom you draw inspiration. Imagine this quilt in as much detail as you can. If you enjoy drawing, take some time to create each patch of your quilt on pieces of paper. Now imagine that in times of difficulty, you could wrap yourself up in this quilt and be held by it and all that it represents. It could be a source of comfort to you, and a reminder that you are not alone.

Practice: Finding Meaning and Purpose in the Midst of Loss

I know many people who have experienced profound losses who have somehow gone on to find deeper meaning and purpose in their lives in ways that hadn't been there before. While many people are familiar with the term *post-traumatic stress*, fewer people are familiar with the term *post-traumatic growth*, which is when someone emerges from a traumatic experience with personal or spiritual growth, a new appreciation of life, an ability to see new possibilities for their life, and a greater awareness of their personal strengths.

Is there a loss in your life in which you have gone on to find meaning and purpose beyond this loss, or perhaps even because of this loss?

If you lost someone close to you in your life, how might their essence or spirit live on in you in some way? What legacy have they left behind that continues to bring life and love to you and others?

Practice: No Regrets

In the book *Reflections on Mortality: Insights into Meaningful Living,*[110] author Robert Brooks writes about his own experiences and reflections on death and dying and shares how connecting with a sense of purpose and meaning and living a life without regrets can help lessen the fears of dying. He describes that he looks in the mirror every day and asks himself, *If today were the last day of my life, would I want to do what I am about to do today?*

Think about some of the things that most give your life meaning (time spent with friends or loved ones, being part of something, contributing in small ways, doing what you love, etc.). How might you connect with these deeper values in small ways on a daily or weekly basis? Are there things that you might regret if you were to die tomorrow? If so, are there actions you can take to realign with that which is most important to you?

Bittersweet Cycles of Life

My daughter forgot to call us back last night. There's a lump in my throat and a tangible feeling of something in my heart that I can't quite name, but it makes me want to sigh deeply, slowly, intentionally.

It's been a bumpy, jolting ride these past fourteen months of the pandemic, the kind of bumpy that makes your stomach drop at points as you're getting jerked along. You wish you could get off because you never signed up for this ride, and worse, it's completely dark so you can't know at any point whether you are at the top of a very large peak, ready to career downward, or coming to a long straightaway, or approaching the end of this nightmarish, surreal experience. So, all you can do is surrender, again and again, with each dip and valley, holding your heart and your stomach simultaneously, instinctually to comfort this frightened organism.

My daughter described it as whiplash, this place, this feeling where we all are right now. Yes, yes! my body says. It's like we came to a sudden and unexpected halt here in the Northeast as we come out of a year of lockdowns and restrictions from this global pandemic, then suddenly we are told we can go maskless and virtually resume business as usual, as if there could be such a thing. (My brain is a slow processor; it always has been.)

This past year has been for me a year of deep isolation from so many loved ones and friends and friendly faces and sources of daily social nourishment. One doesn't even realize how vital this personal connection is until it's missing: the smile of the cashier clerk, the warm greeting from Marilyn at the cleaners where I drop my husband's shirts every so often, the "Hello, Beth!" of Greg at the gym who learned my name early on and made me feel so welcomed by this simple greeting and acknowledgment. Then there is the indescribable feeling of hugging family members once again after endless months that is surely worth any effects of whiplash indeed.

One of the unexpected gifts that came out of this year for me (and I use these words with a heavy heart as I hold the unbearable loss that so many have endured) is time with my daughter that I never thought I would have. Plucked from her normal developmental trajectory and path forward that she had forged for herself—moving to New York City, working and then starting graduate school, venturing out and making new friends while staying close with old ones, even joining a singing group that she had longed to do and finally got up the courage and motivation to join—all of these things came to a crashing halt as she hopped on a train, abandoning all that could not fit into a small suitcase and backpack she had on hand, to land back in the suburbs of our small, quiet town and wooded home. Uprooted from the natural way of things as a mid-twenties something, she, and so many her age, and so many at all ages and stages of development, ended up frozen in time during this unprecedented year.

From behind a small computer screen set up on a makeshift TV tray, my therapy work suddenly gone virtual, I became welcomed (or thrust) into people's homes, even their bedrooms or cars (wherever they could get privacy), as we processed this collective unnerving of this global pandemic and the ways it was impacting their lives. Through the anxiety and uncertainty and fear and loss that they (my patients) and I were both grappling with simultaneously (something that usually doesn't happen in therapy, to be going through the same thing as your patients), I watched as patients young and old faced unimaginable circumstances with courage and resilience that rose up from places they didn't even realize existed.

And so it was for my daughter. I watched her resigned face as she came home just as her trip to London had to be called off, the one she had planned and looked forward to going on with my husband for over a year. It was going to be their special getaway, father and daughter, a chance to take advantage of the low airfares and a late celebration of her college graduation, before starting graduate school. It was to be an exploration of favorite areas of London she had lived in for a semester during college, and a sampling of the best of what theater has to offer, for a girl who had been so in love with theater her whole life. She came home to her purple carpet and lavender walls and love-stained doll of twenty-four years whose stuffing was too far gone to plump her up and whose body couldn't be washed because the fabric would surely disintegrate. She came home to grapple with a pandemic that knocked the wind out of all of us.

And like my patients, I watched as she faced the unfolding uncertainties with all the courage and resilience one could ever hope for as a parent, watching her adjust to the isolation from her friends and beloved activities, watching her adjust to online classes and "Zooming" with her friends to keep some semblance of connection in a world that felt so very foreign and out of control.

It was an unexpected gift, to have her around all the time, whereas for so many years it was just a few smatterings of days to savor here and there. It was the little things that you appreciate as a parent: the conversations in the kitchen as we would both be preparing lunch, the smashingly delicious and healthy desserts she made for us, whose smell would be wafting to the room above where I was "seeing" patients, and whose warm melted chocolate delights would be waiting after a long day. It was those deeper conversations about where she saw her life path headed, her sharing her passion about matters of social justice, and the being there to hold her when unexpected heartbreak sent her reeling. It was the day to day watching this young woman before my eyes as a person with deep compassion and values and conviction, changing the world from her small corner of a bedroom, helping the students she was counseling from behind her own tiny screen some hundreds of miles away, giving these high school girls some sense of feeling seen and heard, often for the first time given the trauma many had experienced.

This gift of having her around all the time didn't come without its challenges. Being up close and personal, you see the day-to-day struggles, the anxious pacing back and forth, the intense fears she faced trying to figure out what it would look like to rebuild her life, and in many ways, have to start over, as many of her closest friends decided they would not return to the city. For the last few months leading up to her returning to New York there was anxiety of the kind that is hard to hold as a parent, because you just want to be able to fix it and you know that you can't.

In the end, we drove her back last week, ironically just days be-
fore everything was opening back up, maskless and all, on the
rainiest weekend in months. We drove her back into a city which
was starting to come back to life after a horror of death had
changed it in ways so extreme that we wondered if it would ever
be the same. We settled her into her apartment and drove home
in the quiet settling-in of another transition come and gone, an
unexpected detour that started as a week or two and turned into
fourteen months.

And then last night she forgot to call us back. So funny that there
are deep heaving tears in this small act of forgetfulness. It is ev-
erything I wished for, for her—that in this moment of being busy
with friends and meet-ups, that she would no longer need us,
could take it from here where she had left off, could find her joy
once again. I check my phone one more time thinking perhaps I
missed the call, then let out another slow, intentional exhalation,
wipe a tear and feel my shoulders drop all at the same time,
knowing that she is launched once again.

Meditation: Finding the Sweet in Bittersweet

Life is often filled with bittersweet moments, joy juxtaposed with sadness,
loss juxtaposed with love, pain juxtaposed with comfort.

Think of something that is bittersweet in your life. As you call that to
mind, notice how that feels around your heart center. Focus for a moment on
the parts of this that feel sweet, tender. As you do, what renewing emotions
are present (perhaps gratitude, appreciation, love, care)? Turn the volume up
on the sweetness, let it grow big in your mind and as a felt sense in your body.
Let it be like a warm light around your heart. Imagine that the sweetness
could surround the parts that feel bitterness, sadness, or pain. Now zoom out
a bit and see that whatever you are experiencing is likely being experienced

in some way by many others who too are struggling with impermanence, change, transition. See if you might sense the common humanity that is present here, that you are not alone in your struggles but are surrounded by so many others who understand your struggles. Zoom out further and see the cycles of nature: of the seasons, of life, death, birth, and growth. See the rhythms of the earth: of the sun setting each night and rising in the morning; of new growth springing up in areas where decay has fertilized the ground; of the tides that come in and go out with the cycles of the moon. Come back to your heart center. Put a hand on your heart and notice the rhythms of your own breath, coming in and going out like the waves at the ocean. When you are ready, come back into the room.

In Sickness and in Health

Sometimes we are touched by the things which surprise us most, the little sprig of parsley on the well-fashioned restaurant plate that reminds me of the Passover seders at my grandparents' house in a small apartment in Parkchester, New York; the empty bird's nest on the ground under the bush, leaving an emptiness in my heart as year after year it was a home and nurturing space to the eggs that burst forth with tiny beaks pecking, and now is no more. And today, the doll, discovered on the side of my daughter's bed, fallen over, losing more than its stuffing now, some twenty-five years past her entry into our home when my daughter was just one. Her stained face and ripped stitching— loved and loved until she could barely sit up in the bed—now slumping over with not enough insides to support her; too worn to be fixed or sewn but loved still and again.

My husband's stitches are surprisingly healing over quickly now, the ones made by the orthopedic surgeon last week when he went in with likely not more than a needle and thread and sewed my husband's bicep and rotator cuff tendon back in place. I gently touch the spots that have turned a strange yellow color under the stress of the surgery, offering my own made-up version of reiki as I try to soothe my husband back to sleep in the middle of night.

The vows that we make in younger days resonate in my ear—"in sickness and in health"—like a reminder of something I had almost forgotten, a whisper of a promise that feels so visceral, pulling at my heart. I am feeling grateful, grateful that I can be there for my husband in concrete ways that let him know I am here for him. Almost like having a young child again, I help him shower, put on his socks, prepare his food, even feed him at first. Driving him to work is its own gift, reminding me of those precious moments driving my kids here and there in circles and loops of frenzied time, savoring the conversations, hanging on the words that linger in the air far after they have left the car, all the while knowing this too shall pass. What unfolds in these moments is, well, everything. It is not what I expected, taking care of my husband in this way, but it is the unexpected that reveals the spaces in which joy arises. Unlike the so worn cloth of my daughter's doll, his tears can be fixed, mended, put back together in time. But there is a fragility beneath it all, a sense of something vulnerable, haunting, taunting, and calling. . . . My father is aging. At eighty-six his body is a reminder of the changes that come, the changes that we cannot stop. Welcome or unwelcome, life moves on and through. And, if we let it, we move through it, dancing and all. I breathe a sigh, sucking in the air, savoring this breath, salt trickling into my mouth. I lift the doll, prop her back on my daughter's bed, resting her flopping head against the pillow, glance back for just a moment, then make my way toward the open door.

Questions for Reflection: Holding the Changing Landscape

- Reflect on some ways that being sick, injured, or ill has perhaps put things into a clearer perspective, helped you see things differently than you may have otherwise, or allowed you to experience a deeper appreciation of that which you might normally take for granted.

- What are some of the current changes you are experiencing in your life?

- What are changes that at first were difficult, but that within which you discovered something unexpected?

- What might happen if you invite heartfelt qualities of *acceptance, trust, spacious awareness*, and *surrender* to sit side by side some change that is happening that you can't stop or control? Holding the changing landscape within this larger container, what do you experience?

Full Circle

Last night my son was asked to watch someone die. Not a usual request for anyone, much less a twenty-four-year-old who had never experienced death firsthand. It was a gruesome death, the kind that no one should ever have to witness or experience, and yet here he was, a medical technician in a community hospital working the twelve-hour night shift and being called upon to sit with this dying man. He had spent time with Richard on other occasions over the past month, assisting him with basic medical needs and getting to know him as a person beyond his medical diagnosis. He had learned that this man was alone, abandoned by his family for reasons one could only speculate, and, with no family present in these final moments, he was asked to bear witness to his final breaths. My son told me that he spoke to Richard, not knowing if this man could hear him, yet speaking to him nonetheless, intuitively, from his heart, telling him he is not alone, offering him comfort as he took his last breath, and passed away not so quietly into the dark night.

While death is part of my life experience, I have never witnessed anyone die. I remember so vividly the night we found the baby mouse in our garage, too small and vulnerable and helpless to survive on its own, unable to reunite it with its mother and knowing that it was only a matter of time. Feeling so helpless and unable to think of anything else to do, I built a little home of grass and twigs for this tiny creature, stuffing a shoebox the way I used to make dioramas in grade school, and placing the baby mouse in there to make her as comfortable as possible, so saddened that she would never leave this cardboard box.

Yet I am reminded each spring how the passage of time brings new and unexpected life and surprises with the changing seasons. The bird's nest that appeared year after year in our lamp post on our front door stoop was a reminder of that. Each year I would excitedly watch as new baby birds hatched from the nest. One year it appeared that a baby had fallen out of the nest onto the ground, but somehow it survived and was able to make its way out into the world. Last year however, some force of nature, whether storm or vulture, knocked the nest to the ground where I discovered it under the bushes, quite heartbroken for the bird's efforts and for the fact that this was the end of a long legacy of birds hatching on our doorstep. And yet, when I opened the door one windy day this March, to my surprise I saw the familiar flutter of my feathered friend and a few twigs in the lamppost. I marveled at her perseverance and innate courage to come back once again, after all was lost, to carry on this biological blueprint of nature.

Isn't it the way for all of us, in one sense or another—rebuilding after our losses, moving forward after our challenges, our suffering—knowing that something deep inside calls us to keep going, this innate courage to keep coming back even in the face of great difficulty and adversity.

After we left the hospital on the day that I saw my mom for the last time in September of tenth grade, we did go on to live our lives in a way that would have made my mom proud. On the same week that my son sat and watched this patient die, my daughter sat for her social work licensing exam. I saw her grapple with deep fear of failure, anxiety, and overwhelm on the weeks leading up to this momentous exam. Then I watched as she courageously found her way, steadied herself, put in the needed effort and aced the thing, surpassing her own expecta-tions. I had a flashback to the day she was devastated when she failed her driver's test, but then mustered up the courage to re-take it weeks later and pass. The legacy of life that my mom left continues in me and in my children. I think that surely some-where she is smiling down, feeling proud of the people we have become, feeling peace in the continuity of life that is ever present.

As much as I fear death, the opposite doesn't sound much better. I sometimes wonder if I would want to remain immortal, eternal in this physical body to the ends of time, and I think that I rather would not. What at first sounds so appealing may not be what I really want after all. I think it is not so much that we fear death, in the end, but that we fear whether we lived fully, deeply,

completely. This one greatest fear that is at the core and the cause
of so much of our suffering; the thought that we try to avoid,
stuff away; the one that quietly wakes us in the dead of night;
the first noble truth that rests at the center of all our suffering;
this fear that drives so much of our behavior—is it perhaps, after
all, an illusion?

I once heard a story about a wave that thought it was all alone
and feared that once it washed up against the shore that it would
be forever gone, until one day it realizes as it crashes and crests
and falls against the shore and is pulled back into the sea that
it was never really alone, never separated after all. It discovers
that it is simply part of the ocean after all, and it has found its
way back home.

Final Practice: Putting It All Together:

Step-by-Step Guide for Working with Difficult Emotions Using the Six Vantage Points

1. Be aware from the anchor view to help regulate the strong energies in your body-heart-mind.

2. Be aware from the child view and bring curiosity and friendliness to what you are experiencing.

3. Be aware from the audience view, and from a half step back notice what is happening onstage as the witnessing Self.

4. Be aware from the compassionate parent view and bring kindness, care, and other heartfelt emotions to whatever you are feeling.

5. Be aware from the mirror view, noticing inner strengths that are here to support you, and a sense of being already whole.

6. Be aware from the ocean view, sensing your interconnection to something more vast, spacious, and transcendent, and the presence of awareness itself from which everything is held.

Final Meditation: From Anchor to Ocean

You might use this meditation anytime, including when you are experiencing difficult emotions.

Find a comfortable position, sitting upright if you are able, with eyes gently closed or in a soft gaze looking downward. Allow your body to settle right where it is. Meet yourself right where you are: there is nothing to change, nothing to do, just show up and give yourself this time to be present with yourself. Bring some awareness to the soles of your feet, gently pushing your feet into the ground and sensing the solid ground beneath you. Bring awareness to the surfaces underneath your body that you are resting upon, that are supporting you. Notice sensations of support, whether firmness, softness, warmth, gentle pressure, or something else. You might imagine that through the soles of your feet are roots, like roots of a tree, spreading far and wide, deep into the earth, keeping your tree—your body—safe, stable, and grounded. Notice your breath coming in and going out, letting yourself settle into whatever pace and rhythm feels comfortable in your body. You might listen to what feels best in your body in this moment. Perhaps your breath may deepen, slow down a bit, or perhaps you may find soothing in slowing down your exhalation. Feel your body anchored, at rest.

If it feels right for you, you might begin to get curious about what is here, looking out through the eyes of a child, bringing interest and friendliness to whatever is showing up. You might bring curiosity to physical sensations and emotions in your body, noticing how your nervous system is doing right now. Is it in a state of protection? Is there fear, anxiety, worry, irritability, anger, despair, sadness? Is it feeling safe and connected, calm, playful, peaceful, content, or something else? What is your heartscape like in there? Can you simply notice? Perhaps there is some combination of mobilized energy and safety, or stillness and safety all at the same time. Can you meet yourself wherever you are, welcoming whatever is here, knowing there is no right or wrong, good or bad, nothing to fix? Your body is just giving you information, that is all. Thank your nervous system for doing its job, wherever it is.

From the audience view you might take a half step back, imagine looking out through eyes as if they are located in the far back of your head and seeing the widest possible perspective in front of and around you, like looking out onto a horizon. You might notice the stories your mind wants to attach to whatever is here. Know that these are only thoughts, mental constructs, not absolute truth. You might notice judgments, narratives, mental ruminations or mental chatter, busyness, or perhaps quiet. What is your mindscape like right now? If it were weather, what kind of weather would it be? If it were water at the surface of the ocean, would it be calm and tranquil, would there be turbulence, crashing waves coming and going, something else? Continue to be aware from the audience view, looking out through friendly eyes at the comings and goings of your mind, body, and heart.

Now bring the compassionate parent view to mind. As you become aware through the eyes of the compassionate parent (or compassionate friend or being), how might you meet, greet, and be with whatever is here? How might it feel for whatever parts of you are here, whatever emotions are here, to be met with the compassionate presence of a Self that simply shows up like a good friend, helping you feel seen and heard? If it is too difficult to sense this in yourself, you might imagine a good friend or compassionate presence or spiritual being sitting beside you, acknowledging and accepting whatever you are feeling. If there are any scared or hurt or upset parts of you, see if you can let them simply be in the presence of this compassionate, caring energy.

If it feels right for you, you might think of what inner resource you might like to draw upon in this moment (calm, equanimity, patience, acceptance, courage, etc.). Call to mind a time when you felt this way and let yourself connect with a felt sense of this in your body right now. If that feels difficult, you might think of someone you admire who exhibits this quality and imagine that you are sitting in their presence, absorbing this quality into yourself. Imagine this quality being mirrored back to you, tapping into your own natural capacities. From the mirror view, invite this quality to sit side by side with whatever you are experiencing. You are already whole. Sense the true nature of who you are.

Finally, you might picture that you are standing on the shores of a vast and expansive ocean. Feel the awe of being in the presence of this endless stretch of sea and sky. Feel the ways you are interconnected: to others, to the natural world around you, to spirit, to the infinite, to all possibilities. You are not alone. If it feels right for you, you might sense that your feelings and experiences are like the waves of the ocean, coming and going, arising and passing, held in the vast, spacious expanse of awareness itself. Rest there for as long as you like.

As you are ready, begin to bring awareness back into your body. Feel your body supported by the surface underneath you, feel the solid ground beneath your feet. Take several intentional slow inhalations, and nice slow exhalations. Appreciate that you made this time for yourself. Taking your time, return your attention to the room as you are ready.

In Conclusion

Reminder to small self: As much as we are wired for survival, and these survival programs can run in the background or foreground of our lives unknowingly, we are also wired to thrive and flourish. When we get stuck in reactive, survival mode without ways of coming back to balance, we tend toward fight, flight, or freeze. We feel fear, worry, anxiety, and anger; we push away ourselves and others in an attempt at self-protection, we experience tunnel vision, and we deplete our bodily resources. In a more responsive mode, from our newer operating system, we experience greater connection and interconnection. We have access to compassion and self-compassion, curiosity and creativity, we experience things from a more spacious, mindful awareness, our bodies can renew and restore, and we are able to use an array of resources to help us meet and cope with our challenges. When we run up against difficult emotions and mind states, this newer operating system helps us connect with our large Self, take in the support of others around us, and open to the gifts of interconnection. We are able to draw from our well of well-being and nourish ourselves, even in the midst of life's difficulties. Possibilities open up.

Each of the six vantage points is a portal to this newer operating system. Instead of struggling to change ourselves, we change the viewing point. Instead of changing our inner experiences, we change the container in which they are held. It is from here that wholeness and healing are possible, and this is where true change lives.

Now let's go back to that island we looked at in the Introduction . . .

> *What if you were living alone on an island and you had been so used to living there by yourself that it just became the way things were? On this island you struggled with all the normal human emotional experiences and challenges such as stress, overwhelm, frustration, anxiety, worry, sadness, loss, anger . . . and you did so alone. Some days these emotions were like a slow drip in the background of your day; other days you were swallowed up by these emotions, or you spent effort trying to push them away, muster on, or question what's wrong with you that you were feeling this way. But now you realize that there is a whole vast land not far from where you reside, and it's connected to your island by bridges that you discover. You come across a map, and it guides you to not one, but six possible bridges that show you how your island is connected with this vast, expansive, and beautiful*

land. Stopping to stand in the middle of each of the bridges you gain a different vantage point of the island that allows you to see things there in a new way. When you follow each bridge, it leads you to discover resources that you didn't realize you had access to, which bring greater ease to your struggles, and richness to your life. Once you cross any of the bridges you realize that you are no longer alone, left to struggle by yourself in your emotional distress. There is a greater sense of wholeness as you recognize the interconnectedness of your island with the land that surrounds it. You feel more connected to others around you, to the common humanity we all share. And perhaps most importantly, you feel more connected with the one you were most separated from: your Self, the true essence of who you are.

Notes

Introduction

1 Hanson, R. (2020). *Resilient: How to Grow an Unshakable Core of Calm, Strength, and Happiness*. New York: Harmony Books.

Chapter 1

2 Brach, Tara. "The Wisdom of It's Not My Fault. Finding Freedom When We are Caught in Self Blame." 9 August 2017. http://blog.tarabrach.com/2017/08/the-wisdom-of-its-not-my-fault-finding.html.

3 Retrieved from: https://dictionary.apa.org/psychopathology.

4 Kabat-Zinn, J. (1994). *Wherever You Go, There You Are: Mindfulness Meditation in Everyday Life*. New York, NY: Hyperion.

5 Susan Morgan (2021). In "The Self View and the Mindful View," an unpublished document shared as part of a sangha led by Bill and Susan Morgan.

Chapter 2

6 "Wenner Moyer, Melinda. "Lean into Negative Emotions. It's the Healthy Thing to Do." *New York Times*, 21 April 2023, https://www.nytimes.com/2023/04/21/well/mind/negative-emotions-mental-health.html?unlocked_article_code=1.90w.cadv.gMzI1C-K27Xp&smid=url-share.

7 Dana, D. (2018). *The Polyvagal Theory in Therapy*. New York, NY: W.W. Norton and Company.

8 Retrieved from: https://blogs.scientificamerican.com/observations/what-neuroimaging-can-tell-us-about-our-unconscious-biases/

9 Stephen W. Porges, PhD. *Cleveland Clinic Journal of Medicine*, February 2009, 76 (4 suppl 2) S86-S90; DOI: https://doi.org/10.3949/ccjm.76.s2.17.

10 Feldman Barrett, Lisa (2020). *Seven and a Half Lessons About the Brain*. Boston, MA: Houghton Mifflin Harcourt.

11 Siegel, R.D. (2010). *The Mindfulness Solution: Everyday Practices for Everyday Problems*. New York: Guilford Press.

12 Hayes, Steven C. (2005). *Get Out of Your Mind and into Your Life: The New Acceptance and Commitment Therapy*. Oakland, CA: New Harbinger.

13 Siegel, R.D. (2010). *The Mindfulness Solution: Everyday Practices for Everyday Problems.* New York: Guilford Press.

14 Killingsworth, M., and Gilbert, D. (2010). A Wandering Mind Is an Unhappy Mind. *Science,* 330 (6006), 932.

15 Germer, C. Interview with Tami Simon. "Chris Germer: The Power of Self-Compassion." 1 August 2017. https://www.resources.soundstrue.com/podcast/chris -germer-the-power-of-self-compassion//.

16 Hanson, R. (2013). *Hardwiring Happiness.* New York, NY: Penguin Random House.

17 Retrieved from: https://www.mindful.org/the-transformative-effects-of-mindful -self-compassion/.

18 Stephen W. Porges, The Polyvagal Perspective, *Biological Psychology,* Volume 74, Issue 2, 2007, pages 116-143, ISSN 0301-0511, https://doi.org/10.1016/j .biopsycho.2006.06.009.

19 Retrieved from: https://www.mindful.org/the-transformative-effects-of-mindful -self-compassion/.

20 Allison, M. (2022). Play Zone Pro: Polyvagal-informed Certificate for Coaches [online program]. Retrieved from: https://pvi.thinkific.com/collections ?q=play+zone+pro

Chapter 3

21 Porges, S. (2022). Polyvagal Theory: A Science of Safety. *Front. Integr. Neurosci.,* 10 May 2022 Volume 16-2022 | https://doi.org/10.3389/fnint.2022.871227.

22 Dana, D. (2018). *The Polyvagal Theory in Action: Engaging the Rhythm of Regulation,* p. 26. New York, NY: W.W. Norton and Company.

23 Neff, Kristen. Interview by Tami Simon. "Kristen Neff: The Liberating Power of Self-Compassion." 6 Nov. 2018. https://www.resources.soundstrue.com/podcast/ kristin-neff-the-liberating-power-of-self-compassion/(2019).

24 Retrieved from: https://self-compassion.org/the-chemicals-of-care-how-self -compassion-manifests-in-our-bodies/.

25 Stephen W. Porges, The Polyvagal Perspective, *Biological Psychology,* Volume 74, Issue 2, 2007, pages 116-143.

26 Gilbert, Paul (2009). *The Compassionate Mind: A New Approach to Life's Challenges.* Constable, London: Constable & Robinson, Ltd.

27 Tirsch, D. (2019). Class taught by Dennis Tirsch for Mindfulness and Psychotherapy Certificate Course through the Institute of Mindfulness and Psychotherapy.

28 Fredrickson, B. (2009). *Positivity.* New York, NY: Harmony.

29 Feldman Barrett, Lisa (2020). *Seven and a Half Lessons About the Brain.* Boston, MA: Houghton Mifflin Harcourt.

30 https://www.heartmath.org/.

31 Retrieved from course manual 2019: Retrieved from: HeartMath Clinical Certification for Stress, Anxiety, and Self-Regulation, p. 3.

32 Alshami, A. (2019). Pain: Is It All in the Brain or the Heart? 2019 Nov 14; 23(12):88. doi: 10.1007/s11916-019-0827-4.

33 Retrieved from https://help.heartmath.com/v1/en/asmts_hrv.html.

34 McCraty, R. (2015). *Science of the Heart: Exploring the Role of the Heart in Human Performance* (Volume 2). Boulder Creek, CO: HeartMath Institute.

35 Killingsworth, M., and Gilbert, D. (2010). A Wandering Mind Is an Unhappy Mind. *Science,* 330 (6006), 932.

36 Retrieved from: https://www.mindful.org/jon-kabat-zinn-defining-mindfulness/.

37 Morgan, Bill (2016). *The Meditator's Dilemma: An Innovative Approach to Overcoming Obstacles and Revitalizing Your Practice,* p. 38. Boston, MA: Shambhala Publications.

38 Fredrickson, B. L., Cohn, M. A., Coffey, K. A., Pek, J., & Finkel, S. M. (2008). Open hearts build lives: Positive emotions, induced through loving-kindness meditation, build consequential personal resources. *Journal of Personality and Social Psychology,* 95(5), 1045–1062. https://doi.org/10.1037/a0013262.

39 Susan Morgan (2021). In "The Self View and the Mindful View," an unpublished document shared as part of a sangha led by Bill and Susan Morgan.

40 Forbes, B. (2011). *Yoga for Emotional Balance: Simple Practices to Help Relieve Anxiety and Depression.* Boston, MA: Shambhala Publications.

41 Schwartz, R. (2021). *No Bad Parts: Healing Trauma and Restoring Wholeness with the Internal Family Systems Model.* Boulder CO: Sounds True.

42 Morgan, Bill (2016). *The Meditator's Dilemma: An Innovative Approach to Overcoming Obstacles and Revitalizing Your Practice,* p. 47. Boston, MA: Shambhala Publications.

Chapter 4

43 Porges, S. The polyvagal theory: new insights into adaptive reactions of the autonomic nervous system. *Cleve Clin J Med.* 2009 Apr;76 Suppl 2(Suppl 2):S86-90. doi: 10.3949/ccjm.76.s2.17. PMID: 19376991; PMCID: PMC3108032.

44 Porges, S. (2021) Retrieved from: https://www.psychologytoday.com/us/articles /202109/sigh-relief.

45 Dana, D. (2018). *Polyvagal Theory in Therapy.* New York: W.W. Norton & Company.

46 Dana, D. (2018). *Polyvagal Theory in Therapy.* New York: W.W. Norton & Company.

47 Porges, S. (2021) Retrieved from: https://www.psychologytoday.com/us/ articles/202109/sigh-relief.

48 Dana, D. (2021). *Anchored: How to Befriend Your Nervous System Using Polyvagal Theory.* Boulder CO: Sounds True.

49 Dana, D. (2021). *Anchored: How to Befriend Your Nervous System Using Polyvagal Theory.* Boulder CO: Sounds True.

50 Porges, S. (2021) Retrieved from: https://www.psychologytoday.com/us /articles/202109/sigh-relief.

51 Clinical Applications of Compassion (2021). Course offered through NICABM. https://www.nicabm.com/program/compassion/?itl=store.

52 Dana, D. (2020). *Befriending Your Nervous System: Looking Through the Lens of Polyvagal Theory.* Boulder, CO: Sounds True audio book, session 2.

53 From Susan Morgan's dharma teachings retrieved from Daily Sit Meditation Series 2020: https://www.billandsusan.org/daily-sit-archives-2020.

54 Dana, D. (2020). *Befriending Your Nervous System: Looking Through the Lens of Polyvagal Theory.* Boulder, CO: Sounds True audiobook.

55 Greenland, Susan K. (2019). Class taught as part of Mindfulness and Psychotherapy Certificate Program.

56 Rankin, L. (2013). *Mind Over Medicine: Scientific Proof That You Can Heal Yourself.* New York, NY: Hay House.

57 Hanson, R. "Just One Thing: Leave the Red Zone." Greater Good Magazine. 4 April 2012, https://greatergood.berkeley.edu/article/item/just_one_thing _leave_the_red_zone

58 University of Colorado at Boulder. (2018, December 10). Your brain on imagi-
    nation: It's a lot like reality, study shows. *ScienceDaily*. Retrieved March 31, 2023
    from www.sciencedaily.com/releases/2018 /12/181210144943.htm.

59 Dana, D. (2020). *Befriending Your Nervous System: Looking Through the Lens of
    Polyvagal Theory*. Boulder, CO: Sounds True audiobook, session 9.

60 Hanson, R. "Hug the Monkey." Psychology Today, 20 December 2011, https://
    www.psychologytoday.com/us/blog/your-wise-brain/201112/hug-the-monkey.

61 Retrieved from: https://www.youtube.com/watch?v=axK-ieZp1vo.

62 Neff, K., and Germer, C. (2018). The Mindful Self-Compassion Workbook: A
    Proven Way to Accept Yourself, Build Inner Strength, and Thrive. New York, NY:
    Guilford Press.

63 Graham, L. (2018). Resilience: Powerful Practices for Bouncing Back from Dis-
    appointment, Difficulty, and Even Disaster. Novato, CA: New World Library.

64 The Science of HeartMath. Retrieved from: https://www.heartmath.com/science/.

65 McGonigal, K. Retrieved from YouTube: https://youtube/9Iqsq1rjlGQ.

66 The   Science   Behind   HeartMath.   Retrieved   from: https://www.
    heartmathbenelux.com/index.php?lang=en&sec=0&id=152.

67 Alison, M. (2022). Shared Through Play Zone Pro: A Polyvagal In-
    formed   Certificate   for   Wellness   and   Performance.   https://www.
    polyvagalinstitute.org/items/play-zone-pro%3A-a-polyvagal-informed
    -certificate-for-wellness-%26-performance-coaches.

68 Toussaint L, Nguyen QA, Roettger C, Dixon K, Offenbächer M, Kohls N, Hirsch
    J, Sirois F. Effectiveness of Progressive Muscle Relaxation, Deep Breathing, and
    Guided Imagery in Promoting Psychological and Physiological States of Re-
    laxation. Evid Based Complement Alternat Med. 2021 Jul 2;2021:5924040. doi:
    10.1155/2021/5924040. PMID: 34306146; PMCID: PMC8272667.

69 Nair, S., Sagar, M., Sollers, J. III, Consedine, N., & Broadbent, E. (2015). Do
    slumped and upright postures affect stress responses? A randomized trial. *Health
    Psychology*, 34(6), 632–641. https://doi.org/10.1037/hea0000146.

70 Alison, M. (2022). Shared through Play Zone Pro: A Polyvagal-Informed Cer-
    tificate for Wellness and Performance. https://www.polyvagalinstitute.org/items/
    play-zone-pro%3A-a-polyvagal-informed-certificate-for-wellness-%26-perfor-
    mance-coaches.

Chapter 5

71 Brewer, J. (2017). *The Craving Mind: From Cigarettes to Smartphones to Love— Why We Get Hooked and How We Can Break Bad Habits.* New Haven, CT: Yale University Press.

72 Dana, D. (2020). *Befriending Your Nervous System: Looking Through the Lens of Polyvagal Theory.* Boulder, CO: Sounds True audiobook.

Chapter 6

73 Comaford, Christine. "Got Inner Peace? 5 Ways to Get it Now." Forbes, 4 April 2012.   https://www.forbes.com/sites/christinecomaford/2012/04/04/got-inner -peace-5-ways-to-get-it-now/?sh=294effec6672.

74 Schwartz, R. (2021). *No Bad Parts: Healing Trauma and Restoring Wholeness with the Internal Family Systems Model.* Boulder, CO: Sounds True.

75 Meditation from website: https://learn.effortlessmindfulness.com/start.

76 Rick Hanson's course Neurodharma. Retrieved from website: https://www .rickhanson.net/online-courses/neurodharma-online-program/.

Chapter 7

77 Thich Nhat Hanh (2014). Fear: Essential Wisdom for Getting Through the Storm. New York, NY: HarperOne.

78 Retrieved from: https://www.youtube.com/watch?v=cS5BppgPTfA.

79 Harris, R. (2019). ACT Made Simple, Second Edition. Oakland, CA: New Harbinger Publications.

80 Gilbert, P. and Woodyatt, L. (2017). An Evolutionary Approach to Shame-Based Self-Criticism, Self-Forgiveness, and Compassion. 10.1007/978-3-319-60573-9_3.

81 From Shame to Self-Worth: Evolutionary Neurobiology of Shame. Retrieved from https://www.rickhanson.net/from-shame-to-self-worth-evolutionary-neu-robiology -of-shame/

82 Hunter, J. (2022). From webinar by Jeremy Hunter offered through Sounds True June 2022 as preview of Your Inner MBA program.

83 Fredrickson B. L. (2001). The role of positive emotions in positive psychology. The broaden-and-build theory of positive emotions. *The American Psychologist,* 56(3), 218–226. https://doi.org/10.1037//0003-066x.56.3.218

84 Gilbert, P. (2012). Compassion-Focused Therapy. In W. Dryden (ed). *Cognitive Behaviour Therapy.* (p.140-165). London: SAGE Publications.

85 Rick Hanson's course: The Foundations of Well-Being. Retrieved from: https://ggsc.berkeley.edu/what_we_do/event/foundations_of_well_being _with_rick_hanson_ph.d.

Chapter 8

86 Hanson, R. (2018). *Resilient: How to Grow an Unshakable Core of Calm, Strength, and Happiness.* New York, NY: Harmony Books.

87 Brooks, R., and Goldstein, S. (2001). *Raising Resilient Children: Fostering Strength, Hope, and Optimism in Your Child.* Chicago, IL: Contemporary Books.

88 Seligman, M. (2004). *Authentic Happiness: Using the New Positive Psychology to Realize Your Potential for Lasting Fulfillment.* New York, NY: Atria.

89 Hanson, R. Positive Neuroplasticity Training: The Science of Changing Your Brain for the Better. https://courses.rickhanson.net/courses/the-positive -neuroplasticity-training.

90 The VIA Character Strengths Survey. Retrieved from: https://www.viacharacter .org/Account/Register.

91 Hayes, S. (2005). *Get Out of Your Mind and into Your Life: The New Acceptance and Commitment Therapy.* Oakland, CA: New Harbinger Publications.

92 Trespicio, T. (2023). *Unfollow Your Passion: How to Create a Life That Matters.* New York, NY: Atria Books.

Chapter 9

93 Miller, Lisa (2016). *The Spiritual Child* (p. 29). St. Martin's Press. Kindle Edition.

94 Balboni, T., VanderWeele, T., Doan-Soares, S., et al. Spirituality in Serious Illness and Health. JAMA 2022;328(2):184–197. doi:10.1001/jama.2022.11086.

95 Consensus Conference Definition of Spirituality retrieved from: https://as-copost.com/issues/december-10-2015/consensus-conference-definition-of -spirituality/.

96 Garrison, K., Zeffiro, T., Scheinost, D., et al. Meditation leads to reduced default mode network activity beyond an active task. *Cogn Affect Behav Neurosci.* 2015 Sep;15(3):712-20. doi: 10.3758/s13415-015-0358-3. PMID: 25904238; PMCID: PMC4529365.

97 Retrieved from: The New Yorker (2008) "This Is Water." https://www.newyorker.com/books/page-turner/this-is-water.

98 From Michael Singer podcast, S1, E4: Spirituality: The Exploration of Consciousness.

99 Wheel of Awareness, retrieved from: https://drdansiegel.com/wheel-of-awareness/.

100 Siegel, D. (2018). Aware: The Science and Practice of Presence. New York, NY: TarcherPerigee.

101 Winston, D. (2021). *Glimpses of Being: A Training Course in Expanding Mindful Awareness.* Boulder, CO: Sounds True.

102 Kelly, L. (2017). *Effortless Mindfulness Now: Awakening Our Natural Capacity for Focus, Freedom, and Joy.* Boulder, CO: Sounds True.

103 Siegel, D. (2018). *Aware: The Science and Practice of Presence.* New York, NY: TarcherPerigee.

104 Kelly, L. (2017). *Effortless Mindfulness Now: Awakening Our Natural Capacity for Focus, Freedom, and Joy.* Chapter 21. Boulder, CO: Sounds True.

105 Retrieved from: https://www.goodreads.com/quotes/506874-you-are-the-sky-everything-else-it-s-just-the.

106 From Positive Neuroplasticity Course, Part 6, "A Taste of Taking in the Good." https://courses.rickhanson.net/courses/the-positive -neuroplasticity-training.

107 E-mail from Mindfulness.com June 2, 2021 retrieved from: https://mail.google.com/mail/u/0/#inbox/FMfcgzGkXdBKGCsrWrdqQkxrQQRPFGCM. Also, Cory Muscara on YouTube, The Relationship Between a Mindfulness Meditation Practice and Suffering https://youtu.be/V_FDFpC4Qqs.

108 Retrieved from: https://www.nicabm.com/3-step-approach-for-managing -uncertainty/.

109 A Full List of Values for Acceptance and Commitment Therapy (ACT). Retrieved from: https://loving.health/en/act-list-of-values/.

110 Brooks, R., and Wilkerson, G. (2017). Reflections on Mortality: Insights into Meaningful Living. iUniverse.

About the Author

©Alan Kurland

Beth Kurland, PhD, is a clinical psychologist with three decades of experience. She is also a TEDx and public speaker, a mind-body coach, and an author of three award-winning books: *Dancing on the Tightrope: Transcending the Habits of Your Mind and Awakening to Your Fullest Life; The Transformative Power of Ten Minutes: An Eight Week Guide to Reducing Stress and Cultivating Well-Being;* and *Gifts of the Rain Puddle: Poems, Meditations and Reflections for the Mindful Soul.* Inspired by her personal experiences and the work with her patients, Beth is passionate about teaching mindfulness-informed practices and mind-body strategies. She loves helping people cultivate deep well-being, access their inner toolkit, and realize they don't need to fix or change themselves to awaken the power of inner transformation and find wholeness. Beth is a regular blog writer for *Psychology Today* and creator of the Well-Being Toolkit online program. Her meditations and audio courses can be found on her website and on Insight Timer. In her spare time, she can be found running through the woods, standing on her head on her yoga mat, and spending time with her two adult children, her husband, and her family. For more, visit BethKurland.com.